THE ETHICS OF
LEVITICUS

RABBI DR. ABBA ENGELBERG

KODESH PRESS

The Ethics of Leviticus

© Abba Engelberg

ISBN: 978-1-947857-12-4

Published & Distributed by

Kodesh Press L.L.C.
New York, NY
www.KodeshPress.com
kodeshpress@gmail.com

TABLE OF
CONTENTS

Transitions

The View of Ramban

The Hebrew names of the books which compose the Pentateuch, as opposed to the English names, do not relate to the contents of each book, but rather to one of the first words in the text of each book. Ramban, in his introduction to Exodus, suggests a more descriptive name for the book of Genesis. It is termed *Sefer ha-Yezirah*, "The Book of Creation," since it describes the creation of the most important elements which compose the world. The reference is not only to the physical elements of the world, from the galaxies to human beings, but to the spiritual elements as well. The Midrash (*Gen. Rabbah* 1:4) speaks of six items that were created, or planned, before the creation of the world. Among them are the Torah, Israel, the patriarchs, and the name of the Messiah. In the book of Genesis, the story is told of the patriarchs and matriarchs, and the division of their descendants into the twelve tribes which composed the Israelite nation. The Jewish *Weltanschauung* is that the world was created in order for the Jews to serve God, adopt the ways of the Torah, and positively influence the nations of the world (whose origins are also related in the book of Genesis) to behave morally, until the eventual arrival of the Messiah. According to another Midrash (*Avot* 5:6), the potential for the occurrence of the miracles which accompanied the Children of Israel during their sojourning in the desert was also part of creation, while Ramban even sees in the deeds of the patriarchs predictions of the future experiences of their children and all of mankind until the coming of the Messiah, and he terms this phenomenon: *ma'aseh avot siman la-banim.*

Ramban, in his introduction to Leviticus, designates the book of Exodus as "The Book of Exile and Redemption," (*Sefer ha-Galut ve-ha-Geula*) where "exile" refers to the slavery and persecution which Israel endured in Egypt, and "redemption" refers in part to the nation's exodus from Egypt, but mainly to the receipt of the Torah on Mt. Sinai. There is a transition from creation and preparation in the book of Genesis to implementation of the program in the book of Exodus. The transition is facilitated by repeating in the portion of *Shemot* (Exod. 1:1-6) the names of the children of Jacob, which first appeared at the end of Genesis in the portion of *Vayigash* (Gen. 46:8-27). According to Ramban's approach, the transition is natural, since the events which affected the Children of Israel in the book of Exodus were intimated by the activities of the patriarchs in the book of Genesis.

Ramban looks upon the book of Leviticus as part of the realization of the redemption included in his title for the book of Exodus. It comprises a book of its own because it is entirely devoted to one subject, namely—in the nomenclature of Ramban— the Laws of the Priests and Levites (*Torat ha-Kohanim ve-ha-Levi'im*). As will be explained further on, Ramban looks upon sacrifices, as well as the Tabernacle and Temple where they were brought, as means of coming close to the Almighty and preserving that closeness through atonement and the erasure of sins against God. The sobriquet was not originated by Ramban, but rather adopted from the alternative name of the halachic Midrash on the book of Leviticus—the *Sifra*.

The transition from the book of Exodus to the book of Leviticus is smooth because the last part of Exodus is dedicated to describing the structure of the Tabernacle, the clothes of the priests, and their inauguration, while in Leviticus the details of their work in the Tabernacle is described. However, Ramban encounters a difficulty, since the basic laws pertaining to sacrifices appear in the first two portions of the book of Leviticus (*Vayikra* and *Tzav*), while the remainder of the book deals with other topics, such as forbidden foods (*Shemini*), purity and impurity (*Tazria* and *Metzora*), incest-oriented prohibitions (*Acharei Mot*), ethical behavior (*Kedoshim*), Jewish holidays (*Emor*), social laws (*Behar*) and admonitions (*Bechukkotai*). Ramban explains most of the supposed digressions from the main subject by noting that some of the situations which lead to impurity—such as child-birth (Lev. 12:1-8), leprosy (chs. 13-14), and physical secretions (ch. 15)—require a sacrifice as part of the purification process, just as the holidays require sacrifices as part of the celebratory process (ch. 23). In addition, one who enters the Temple area in a state of impurity—including that caused by eating forbidden foods (ch. 11)—is required to bring a variable-valued sacrifice if he did so accidentally (Lev. 5:6-14), and a more serious penance if he did so intentionally (Lev. 15:31).

Ramban's explanation weakens with regard to the portions of *Kedoshim*, *Behar*, and *Bechukkotai*, which deal with personal and communal behavior. Additionally, although holiday observance does involve the bringing of sacrifices, the focus in Leviticus is mainly on ritual aspects, while sacrificial requirements are detailed in Numbers 28-29. Perhaps one may suggest that since the majority of Leviticus is devoted to the activities of the priests for the purpose of atoning for the Children of Israel and the priests' permission to approach the holiest places in conjunction with their active presence and involvement in the workings of the Tabernacle, the simple Jew might deduce that on the one hand he is not required to aspire to holiness of his own volition, and on the other hand he is not even capable of doing so. Therefore, it was important for the Torah to openly and publicly declare "You should be holy" (Lev. 19:2)—it is incumbent upon every Jew to sanctify himself by displaying loving behavior in dealing with his fellow man, and also to draw close to God by observing His "appointed festivals which you should proclaim as convocations of holiness" (Lev. 23:2).

Ramban sees a parallel between revelation at Mt. Sinai, as described in the book of Exodus, and the service in the Tabernacle (*Mishkan*), as described in the book of Leviticus, and so he writes at the beginning of the portion of *Terumah*: "The secret of the *Mishkan* is that the glory which rested on Mt. Sinai will rest on it in a concealed manner" (Exodus 25, Introduction).

Based on this approach, Ramban found continuity in Leviticus regarding a number of themes which were raised initially in connection with Mt. Sinai. For example, before the giving of the Torah, the nation, as well as the *kohanim* (i.e., the first-borns who at that stage still served as the priests),[1] were requested to purify themselves, as it says:

And the Lord said to Moses: Go to the people, and sanctify them today and tomorrow... And also, the priests who come near to the Lord should sanctify themselves (Exod. 19:10-22).

In the portion of *Vayikra* the following admonition is found concerning the Tabernacle:

1.Rashi, Exod. 19:22.

If any one touches any unclean thing… and he is unaware
that he is unclean [Rashi: and after becoming unclean he
eats holy things or enters the sanctuary], then he incurs
guilt (Lev. 5:2).

Similarly, the nation was warned at Mt. Sinai not to ascend the
mountain of the Lord (Exod. 19:12), and in a parallel fashion the
high priest was admonished in the book of Leviticus: "He should
not come at all times into the holy place… so that he not die"
(Lev. 16:2).

THE VIEW OF R. DOVID ZVI HOFFMAN

R. Dovid Zvi Hoffman (1843-1921), director of the Rabbinical
Seminary of Berlin (*Sefer Vayikra*, pp. 10-11), suggests a different
subdivision than that offered by Ramban. He opposes relating the
activities described in Leviticus solely to the priests. For example,
although examination of a leper and offering the special holiday
sacrifices are performed by the *kohen*, these rituals obviously
pertain to the entire nation. The priest is no more than the emissary
of the common man for performing the Temple service. This
idea is already reflected in God's commandment to Moses at the
beginning of the second verse in the book of Leviticus: "Speak to
the Children of Israel and say to them…" (Lev. 1:2). The dialogue
which follows that verse relates to the *kohanim*, but is said to the
Children of Israel.

Accordingly, R. Hoffman splits the book of Leviticus in two.
The first section (chs. 1-17) refers to the realization of the verse in
the portion of *Terumah*: "And they will make Me a sanctuary, so
that I may dwell among them" (Exod. 25:8), turning the Tabernacle
into a place capable of hosting the Divine Presence. In tandem, just

as the human body must be capable of hosting a God-given soul, so the Children of Israel must be turned into a nation of priests, i.e., vessels capable of containing holiness, based on the words: "and you will be for Me a kingdom of priests" (Exod. 19:6), and that is the content of the second section. R. Hoffman states:

> This is a goal on its own, and together with this, a means of turning us into a holy nation [as the verse ends "and a holy nation"] by elevating us to the level of Godly holiness and moral perfection, [i.e. it indicates] that in our private and public lives we should aspire to be good and righteous, and to find favor in the eyes of God.

If the nation of Israel is able to achieve the second goal (i.e., becoming a holy nation), it will be able to reach a level of prophecy and to serve as a guide to all of mankind as messengers of God. R. Hoffman thus designates the first section of the book of Leviticus as "The Book of Priesthood," and the second as "The Book of Holiness." In the first section, the ground must be sufficiently cultivated for God to descend upon the nation; in the second, the nation attempts to ascend to the level of God. Unlike Ramban, R. Hoffman's "Book of Priesthood" relates to the entire nation, and not a particular sect within the nation.

The detailed subdivision of the book of Leviticus, according to R. Hoffman, appears below:

First Section - The Book of Priesthood			
Ch.	**Portion**	**Subject**	**Content**
1-7	*Vayikra*, beginning of *Tzav*	Sacrifices	Atonement from sin by bringing sacrifices.
8-10	End of *Tzav*, beginning of *Shmini*	Eight days of consecration	Festive inauguration of Aaron and his sons, who performed the sacrificial service.
11-15	End of *Shmini*, *Tazria*, *Metzora*	Purity and impurity	Preventing defilement of (a) the body, by eating permitted foods and observing the laws of purity, and (b) the Tabernacle by entering in an impure state.
16	Beginning of *Acharei-Mot*	Service of the High Priest on Yom Kippur	The High Priest prays for forgiveness for his own, his family's, and Israel's sins.
17	End of *Acharei-Mot*	Sacrifices and purity of foods	More laws relating to sacrifices, impurity, and forbidden foods (including blood).

Second Section - The Book of Holiness			
Ch.	**Portion**	**Subject**	**Content**
18-20	End of *Acharei-Mot*, *Kedoshim*	Living a life of holiness	Family life and social life must be conducted on the basis of morality and Torah principles, leading to Godly holiness.
21-22	Beginning of *Emor*	Holiness laws for priests	Priestly holiness endows them with additional requirements, and the holiness of their work demands perfection of the sacrifices they offer.
23-25	End of *Emor*, most of *Behar*	Holiness of time	Laws of the Sabbath, holidays, and Sabbatical and Jubilee years.
26	End of *Behar*, beginning of *Bechukkotai*	Holy covenant between God and Israel	The blessings if Israel fulfills the commandments, and the curses if they do not.
27	End of *Bechukkotai*	Sanctification and redemption	Laws pertaining to sanctifying the value of a person or animal; sanctification of houses and fields; sanctity of firstborns, tithes, and devoted objects.

VAYIKRA

The portion of *Vayikra* may be divided into two sections. Chs. 1-3 discuss voluntary offerings, namely the burnt offering (*olah*), meal offering (*mincha*), and peace offering (*shelamim*), while chs. 4–5 deal with obligatory offerings, namely sin offerings and guilt offerings. A voluntary offering is a sacrifice which is brought of a person's free will, while an obligatory offering is one which the law requires him to bring. Another distinction is made between sacrifices brought by individuals, and communal sacrifices which the priests offer in the Temple as representatives of the entire congregation on weekdays, Sabbaths, holidays, and certain other occasions. A more detailed presentation of the various sacrifices appears in APPENDIX I - THE DIFFERENT TYPES OF SACRIFICES.

There is a well-known difference of opinion between Rambam (1135-1204) and Ramban (1194-1270) with respect to sacrifices. According to Rambam (*Guide for the Perplexed* 3:32),[2] the main purpose of biblical sacrifices was to wean Israel from the custom of sacrificing animals, which was common in the heathen Temples of ancient times. Ramban (Lev. 1:9), on the other hand, believes that sacrifices manifest a supreme recognition that one has sinned,

2. The translations of the *Guide for the Perplexed* are based on that of M. Friedlander, with emendations where unclear, based on the translation of R. Yosef Kapach (Mosad ha-Rav Kook).

and represent an effort to achieve atonement, even if self-sacrifice is metaphorically called for.

The View of Rambam

Rambam states the following with regard to Israel's adoption of the sacrificial customs of the Gentiles:

> It was in accordance with the wisdom and plan of God, as displayed in the whole Creation, that He did not command us to give up and discontinue all these manners of service, for to obey such a commandment would have been contrary to the nature of man, who generally cleaves to that to which he is used. It would in those days have made the same impression as a prophet would make at present if he called us to the service of God and told us in His name that we should not pray to Him, not fast, not seek His help in time of trouble; that we should serve Him in thought, and not by any action (*Guide for the Perplexed* 3:32).

Just as a baby nurses from its mother's breast because it does not yet have teeth and a fully functioning digestive system, similarly God purged the sacrificial service of pagan elements, and specifically required all sacrifices to be of sheep, goats, or cows—the very animals that were deified by Gentiles in those days. Rambam explains at length the reason that these animals exclusively were chosen:

> Scripture tells us, according to the version of Onkelos, that the Egyptians worshipped Aries, and therefore abstained

from killing sheep, and held shepherds in contempt, as it says: "Behold we will sacrifice the abomination of the Egyptians" (Exod. 8:22); "For every shepherd is an abomination to the Egyptians" (Gen. 46:34). Some sects among the Sabeans worshipped demons, and imagined that these assumed the form of goats, and called them therefore *se'irim*. This worship was widespread in the time of Moses, as it says: "And they may no more offer their sacrifices unto *se'irim*" (Lev. 17:7). For this reason, those sects abstained from eating goats' flesh. Most idolaters objected to killing cattle, holding this species of animals in great estimation. Therefore, the people of Hodu [India] to this day do not slaughter cattle, even though other animals are slaughtered.

In order to eradicate these false principles, the Law commands us to offer sacrifices only of these three kinds: "You may bring your offering of the cattle, of the herd and of the flock" (Lev. 1:2). Thus, the very act which is considered by the heathen as the greatest crime is the means of approaching God and obtaining His pardon for our sins… To the above reason for the exclusive selection of the three kinds of animals for sacrifices we may add the following, namely, that these species are animals which can be got very easily, contrary to the practice of idolaters that sacrifice lions, bears, and wild beasts, as is stated in the book *Tonitom* (*Guide for the Perplexed* 3:46).

Rambam holds that God's primary intention was to accustom the nation to have faith in the Lord and pray to Him, while His secondary intention was to accompany the prayers with sacrifices. He writes:

As the sacrificial service is not the primary object [of the commandments about sacrifice], while supplications, prayers, and similar kinds of worship are nearer to the primary object, and indispensable for obtaining it, a great difference was made in the Law between these two kinds of service. The one kind, which consists in offering sacrifices, although the sacrifices are offered to the name of God, has not been made obligatory for us to the same extent as it had been before. We were not commanded to sacrifice in every place, and in every time, or to build a Temple in every place, or to permit any one who desires to become a priest and to sacrifice [as Jeroboam did, 1 Kings 13:33]. On the contrary, all this is prohibited to us. Only one Temple has been appointed "at the place which the Lord will choose" (Deut. 12:26). In no other place is it allowed to sacrifice, as it says: "Take heed that you do not offer your burnt offerings in every place that you see" (Deut. 12:13); and only the members of a particular family were allowed to officiate as priests. All these restrictions served to limit this kind of worship, and keep it in those bounds within which God did not think it necessary to abolish sacrificial service altogether. But prayer and supplication can be offered everywhere and by every person. The same is the case with the commandment of *tzitzit* (Num. 15:38), *mezuzah* (Deut. 6:9; 11:20), *tefillin* (Exod. 13:9; 13:16), and similar kinds of Divine service (*Guide for the Perplexed* 3:32).

On the basis of this approach to sacrificial rites in Judaism, it is possible to understand how it happens that a number of the prophets expressed themselves quite caustically in their condemnation of sacrifices, which compose a significant subset of Torah laws. In Rambam's own words:

> Because of this principle which I explained to you, the prophets in their books are frequently found to rebuke their fellow-men for being over-zealous and exerting themselves too much in bringing sacrifices. The prophets thus distinctly declared that the object of the sacrifices is not very essential, and that God does not require them. Samuel therefore said: "Has the Lord as great delight in burnt offerings and sacrifices as in obeying the voice of the Lord" (1 Sam. 15:22)? Isaiah exclaimed: "To what purpose is the multitude of your sacrifices unto me says the Lord" (Isa. 1:11). Jeremiah declared: "For I did not speak to your fathers, nor command them on the day that I brought them out of the land of Egypt concerning burnt offering or sacrifices. But this thing I commanded them saying: 'Obey my voice, and I will be your God, and you will be my people'" (Jer. 7: 22-23).
>
> This passage has been found difficult in the opinion of all those whose words I read or heard. They ask: "How can Jeremiah say that God did not command us about burnt offerings and sacrifices, seeing that so many precepts refer to sacrifices?" The sense of the passage agrees with what I have explained to you. Jeremiah says [in the name of God] that the primary object of the precepts is this: Know me, and serve no other being. "I will be your God, and you will be my people" (Lev. 26:12). But the commandment that sacrifices should be brought and that the Temple should be visited has for its object the success of that principle among you, and for its sake I have transferred these

modes of worship to my name; idolatry will thereby be utterly destroyed, and Jewish faith firmly established. You, however, have ignored this object and taken hold of that which is only the means of obtaining it; you have doubted my existence, "you have denied the Lord, and said he is not" (Jer. 5:12); you served idols, "burnt incense to Baal, and walked after other gods whom you did not know. And you came and stood before me in this house" (Jer. 7:9-10); i.e., you do not go beyond attending the Temple of the Lord and offering sacrifices, but this is not the chief object" (*Guide for the Perplexed* 3:32).

RAMBAM'S VIEW IN HIS CODE OF LAW

Since Rambam looks upon the bringing of sacrifices as a means of distancing Jews from idolatry, one might think that in later generations—when the evil inclination to worship idols no longer exists and the Temple will be rebuilt—sacrifices would be discontinued. But Rambam does not actually take that approach. In his code of law, which is devoted to practical observance of *halachah*, the eighth book (Laws of the Temple Service) and ninth book (Laws of Sacrifices) present sacrificial law in great detail, where the assumption is that when the Third Temple will be built, hopefully in our time soon, the sacrificial rites will once more become functional. How does one explain this phenomenon?

Some say that since Rambam completed his code of law before he was forty, while the *Guide for the Perplexed* was written when he was over fifty, maybe he changed his mind in the interim. However, one who is familiar with Rambam's thoroughness realizes that if he viewed things differently in his later years, he would have updated his earlier works. Therefore, it is more reasonable to assume that Rambam believes that in an ideal world populated by superior human beings, perhaps sacrifices would be unnecessary. However, in the present world, just as one cannot imagine Jewish life without synagogues and prayer, and additional devotion-encouraging devices such as *shofar* and *lulav*, so in the future when the holy Temple will be restored, and even in the days of the Messiah, for the typical Israelite, sacrificial rites will still play an important role. On the other hand, it is possible that even in Rambam's view sacrifices will always be necessary, and what he said in the *Guide* is one, but not the only, reason for sacrifices, since as Nachmanides (Ramban) points out, Cain and Abel brought sacrifices long before the advent of paganism.

Sacrifices as One
of the Biblical Statutes

Rambam, in *Hilchot Me'ilah* (8:8) stresses the importance of observing arbitrary statutes of the Torah no less than comprehensible morality-based ordinances. He states:

> See how severely the Torah rules concerning misusing holy property. Now, if wood, stones, earth, and ash become holy because the name of the Lord of the world was called upon them through speech alone, and anyone who treats them as ordinary articles violates the prohibition against *me'ilah*, and even if he acted unknowingly, he is required to secure atonement, how much more so with regard to the *mitzvot* ordained for us should a person not treat them derisively [just] because he does not understand

their rationale... For it says in the Torah: "And you should observe all My statutes and all My ordinances and do them: I am the Lord" (Lev. 19:37; 20:22), and our Sages commented: "[This adjures us] to observe and do the statutes like the ordinances." The "doing" is well known, i.e., that one should obey the statutes. "Observing" means to treat them with caution and not think that they are less [important] than the ordinances.

The ordinances are those *mitzvot* whose motivating rationale is openly revealed, and the benefit of their observance in this world is known, e.g. the prohibitions against robbery and bloodshed, and honoring one's father and mother. The statutes are the *mitzvot* whose motivating rationale is not known. Our Sages said: "I ordained statutes and you have no license to question them" (BT *Yoma* 67b). A person's natural inclination confronts him concerning them and the nations of the world challenge them, e.g. the prohibition of [eating] the meat of a pig, milk and meat, the calf whose neck is broken, the red heifer, and the goat sent to Azazel.

At the end of his treatment, Rambam surprises the reader by including sacrifices as one of the statutes, in spite of his extensive explanation (in the *Guide for the Perplexed*) of their historical motivation and necessity. He states:

All the sacrifices are in the category of statutes. Our Sages said: "The world exists for the sake of the service of the sacrifices.[3] For through the performance of the statutes and the ordinances, the righteous merit the life of the

___
3. Perhaps based on *Avot* 1:2 or BT *Megillah* 31b.

world to come [and between the two of them] the Torah gave precedence to the command for the statutes, for it says: "You must keep My statutes and My ordinances, which if a man does, he will live by them" (Lev. 18:5).

Why does Rambam, in *Hilchot Me'ilah*, write that the sacrificial service is considered to be a statute, a law with no basis in reason? Why not retain the explanation that it represents a gradual withdrawal from pagan rituals necessitated by the primitive state of the Jews at the time the Torah was given?

Actually, it is hard to understand why Rambam designates any command as a statute, as if it has no reason, when he writes explicitly in his *Guide*:

Every one of the six hundred and thirteen precepts serves to inculcate some truth, to remove some erroneous opinion, to establish proper relations in society, to diminish evil, to train in good manners or to warn against bad habits (*Guide for the Perplexed* 3:31).

Apparently, Rambam means to say that ordinances refer to those laws whose justification is quite clear, while laws whose reasons are not immediately obvious he terms statutes.

Rambam also cites the Midrash (*Ecc. Rabbah* 7) which says that Solomon knew the rationale of every command other than the requirement to bring a red heifer for purification purposes, just that "God concealed the reasons for commandments, lest people make light of them, as Solomon did in respect to three commandments, the reasons for which are clearly stated" (*Guide for the Perplexed* 3:26, based on BT *Sanhedrin* 21b). A number of answers will be proposed:

1. Perhaps there is a difference between interpersonal laws (*mitzvot bein adam le-chaveiro*), where the rationale is important and binding even if not written, and God-oriented laws (*mitzvot bein adam la-Makom*), which must be related to as statutes so that people will not derive leniencies based on the various explanations proffered for the given command. Concerning the case in question, perhaps Rambam realized that when the Third Temple is built, sacrifices will once more form part of the ritual, and he didn't want his reasoning to be used as an excuse to ignore that aspect of the Divine service. In fact, Rambam says in his introduction to the *Guide* that he prepared the work expressly for scholars like his most brilliant student, Yosef ben Yehuda Ibn Shimon. He wanted such philosophically sophisticated intellectuals to realize that the custom of bringing sacrifices did not emerge arbitrarily. Rambam had no doubt that people of that ilk would observe the law in spite of their awareness of its true origin. He did fear the effect of such knowledge on simpler people, who might dispense with the entire procedure once they knew that the motivation for its perfomance was no longer relevant.

   Regarding moral laws, Rambam says (*Guide for the Perplexed* 3:17) that it is necessary to understand the motivation behind interpersonal Torah laws in order for it to be possible to fullfill logical *mitzvot* even when they are not explicitly written. Clearly there is no parallel necessity when dealing with God-oriented laws, and it was previously explained that the attempt to do so may even be detrimental.

   The view of Rambam is that every command has a reason, just that explicaton of the reason is important mainly for ethical *mitzvot*, and so he says:

All of us, the common people as well as the scholars, believe that there is a reason for every precept, although there are commandments the reason of which is unknown to us, and in which the ways of God's wisdom are incomprehensible. This view is distinctly expressed in Scripture, as it says: "righteous statutes and judgments" (Deut. 4:8) and "the judgments of the Lord are true, and righteous altogether" (Ps. 19:10). There are commandments which are called *chukim* (statutes), like the prohibition of wearing garments of wool and linen (*shaatnez*), boiling meat and milk together, and the sending of the goat [into the wilderness on the Day of Atonement]. Our Sages use in reference to them phrases like the following: "These are things which I have fully ordained for you and you dare not criticize them"; "your evil inclination is turned against them"; and "non-Jews find them strange." But our Sages generally do not think that such precepts have no cause whatever and serve no purpose, for this would lead us to assume that God's actions are purposeless. On the contrary, they hold that even these statutes have a cause, and are certainly intended for some use, although it is not known to us, owing either to the deficiency of our knowledge or the weakness of our intellect. Consequently, there is a cause for every commandment; every positive or negative precept serves a useful object. In some cases the usefulness is evident, e.g. the prohibition of murder and theft; in others, the usefulness is not so evident, e.g. the prohibition of enjoying the fruit of a tree in the first three years (Lev. 19:23) or of a vineyard in which other seeds have been growing (Deut. 22:9). Those commandments whose object is generally evident are called *mishpatim* (judgments); those whose object is not generally clear are called *chukim* (*Guide for the Perplexed* 3:26).

2. It is also possible to say that although every command has a reason, what Rambam terms statutes are the hundreds of minor details regarding the various types of sacrifices and how many to bring on each holiday, the details of the requirements concerning disqualifying blemishes and slaughtering, etc. Accordingly, in *Hilchot Me'ilah*, Rambam is not referring to the overall concept of bringing sacrifices, for he explained their motivation in his *Guide*, but rather to the myriad technicalities which cannot be explained logically. Rambam discusses this subject as well in his *Guide*, where he states:

> The law that sacrifices should be brought is evidently of great use, as will be shown by us; but we cannot say why one offering should be a lamb, whilst another is a ram, and why a fixed number of them should be brought. Those who trouble themselves to find a cause for any of these detailed rules are in my eyes void of sense: they do not remove any difficulties, but rather increase them. Those who believe that these detailed rules originate in a certain cause are as far from the truth as those who assume that the whole law is useless.... You ask why must a lamb be sacrificed and not a ram? But the same question would be asked, why a ram had been commanded instead of a lamb, so long as one particular kind is required. The same is to be said as to the question why were seven lambs sacrificed and not eight; the same question might have been asked if there were eight, ten, or twenty lambs, so long as some definite number of lambs were sacrificed.... The repeated assertion

of our Sages that there are reasons for all commandments, and the tradition that Solomon knew them, refer to the general purpose of the commandments, and not to the object of every detail (*Guide for the Perplexed* 3:26).

THE VIEW OF RAMBAN

Ramban (Lev. 1:9) argues stridently against the view of Rambam in the *Guide for the Perplexed*, according to which bringing sacrifices is not seen as service to God having intrinsic value, but rather as a remedy for a historically-rooted malady. According to Ramban, a sacrifice is a sublime expression of recognition of sin, which manifests a willingness to achieve atonement to the point of self-sacrifice. The Torah describes the sacrifices as "a pleasing fragrance to the Lord,"[4] which would imply that they do in fact have intrinsic, and not merely historical, value, and were not designed only "to remove false beliefs from the hearts of the wicked and fools of the world" (Ramban's summary of Rambam's approach). If the purpose were, so to say, to wean Israel from Gentile behavior, it would have been preferable to eat those animals to satiation rather than to perform religious rituals such as sprinkling blood. The ceremony actually grants an aura of holiness to those animals. In his words:

> The intention of the previously-mentioned evil-doers was to worship the sheep and ox constellations, which according to their opinion possess certain powers, and which is why they abstain from eating them in deference

4. Lev. 1:9, 1:13, 2:2, 2:9, 3:5, 23:18; Num. 15:10, 15:13, 28:8, 28:24, 29:13, 29:36.

to their power and strength, but if these species are slaughtered [in homage] to the Revered Name, it is [a sign of] respect and honor of them, and they themselves were in the habit of so doing, as it says: "And they may no more sacrifice their sacrifices to the demons" (Lev. 17:7), and those who made the [golden] calf sacrificed to it... The disease of idolatry would surely have been far better cured if we were to eat them [these animal-deities] to satiation, which would be considered by them forbidden and repugnant in their eyes, and they would never do such a thing!

In addition, if sacrifices were designed to enable Israel to withdraw from the corrupt practices of idolators, why did Abel and Noah bring them before idol-worship made its appearance? Ramban continues:

When Noah came out of the ark with his three sons, there were no Chaldeans or Egyptians in the world, [yet] he brought an offering, and it pleased God, and it says about it: "And the Lord smelled the pleasing odor" (Gen. 8:21), and on account of it [the verse continues]: "The Lord said in His heart 'I will not curse the ground anymore for man's sake.'" [Regarding Abel, Scripture states]: "Abel likewise brought of the first-born of his flock and of the fattened ones. And the Eternal accepted Abel and his offering" (Gen. 4:4). But there was not yet even a trace of idol-worship in the world!... And the [Scriptural] expression concerning the offerings is: "My food which is presented to Me by means of offerings made by fire, for a pleasing odor to Me" (Num. 28:2). And Heaven forbid that they should have no other purpose and intention than the elimination of idolatry from the minds of fools!

Ramban did not invent his approach to sacrifices. He simply expanded upon the view of Judah Halevi, who wrote that the sacrifices were designed to show God's good will toward the nation by accepting their gifts as a means of honoring them and showing His approval. The *Kuzari* had asked:

Now I would like to ask you to explain to me all that I have read about the sacrifices, things which it is difficult for reason to accept. For example, that which it says: "My food which is presented to Me by means of offerings made by fire, for a pleasing odor to Me" (Num. 28:2). Is not the interpretation of these words that sacrifices are sacrifices to the Lord, and they are God's bread and incense (*Kuzari* 2:25)?

Whereupon the rabbi answers:

That which the text says "by means of offerings made by fire" (Num. 28:2) answers every question. It is as if it says: "that offering, and the bread and sweet savor which are ascribed to Me, in reality belong only to My fires," i.e. to the fire which was kindled at God's behest and fed by the offerings. The intention of this command is the arrangement of a well-ordered abode for the King, which allows Him to rest in the Temple—not a physical resting place but a spiritual resting place. Everything that was stated with regard to the sacrificial service was said only metaphorically, to indicate that God is satisfied by good order in the life of the nation and its priests, and receives their gifts, so to say, and dwells in their midst to honor them. However, He himself is sanctified and too exalted to derive pleasure from their food and drink, and their bread is only for their soul. Whenever God favored the nation, fire descended by His will, and this was a sign that their offering and gift was accepted (*Kuzari* 2:26).

To summarize, a sacrifice, according to Ramban and Judah Halevi, provides a means for human beings to come close to God, as Ramban said regarding the reason that Balaam brought his sacrifice: "in order to approach God so that he would receive His communication" (Lev. 1:9). On the other hand, according to Rambam, sacrifices are merely a reactive tool intended to strengthen man in his struggle against false beliefs that might take root and to help him grasp cerebral truths. The command is directed at man's intellect.

There is, however, one more facet to sacrifices that is not just incidental—as Rambam holds, nor intrinsic—as Ramban believes, but rather a means to atone for the nation's sins. The Talmud (BT *Menachot* 110a) states: "You do not sacrifice for My sake, but for your own sake, as it is written, you should sacrifice it to appease [Rashi: to atone for] you" (Lev. 19:5).

Ramban (Lev. 1:9) adopts this facet as well, and so he says:

It is far more fitting to accept the reason which they say for them [sacrifices], that since man's deeds are accomplished through thought, speech, and action, [therefore] God commanded that when he sins and brings an offering, he should lay his hands upon it corresponding to the deed, and he should confess his sin verbally corresponding to his speech, and he should burn in fire the innards and

31

the kidneys which are the instruments of thought and desire, and [he should burn] the legs corresponding to the hands and feet of a person, which do all his work, and he should sprinkle the blood on the altar corresponding to the blood in his soul, so that a person should think when he performs all these acts that he has sinned against his God with his body and his soul, and that his blood should really be spilled and his body burned, were it not for the loving-kindness of the Creator, Who took from him a substitute and a ransom—this offering—so that its blood should be in place of his blood, its life in place of his life, and that the chief limbs of the offering should be in place of the chief parts of his body, and the portions [given from the sin offering to the priests] are in order to support the teachers of the Torah, so that they can pray on his behalf. And [the reason for] the daily [public] offering is that the public cannot avoid continually sinning.

By means of bringing sacrifices, then, the Jew becomes aware of the severity of his sin, and also commences the process of confession (*viddui*), regret (*charatah*) to the extent of willingness to sacrifice one's self, and rehabilitation.

HISTORICAL REPERCUSSIONS OF THE DISPUTE BETWEEN RAMBAM AND RAMBAN

Because Rambam understood that his viewpoint was revolutionary, he cited the views of his opponents in the *Guide for the Perplexed* and justified his approach to the subject step by step, in a deferential and nonaggressive manner. He explained that God also behaved in this manner when He brought the Children of Israel to Canaan on a circuitous route, in order to allow them enough time to become sufficiently strong and courageous to defeat the powerful enemies that lay ahead. In his own words:

> I know that you will, at first thought, reject this idea and find it strange; you will put the following question to me in your heart: "How can we suppose that Divine commandments, prohibitions, and important acts, which are fully explained and for which certain seasons are fixed, should not have been commanded for their own sake, but only for the sake of some other thing, as if they were only the means which He employed for His primary object? What prevented Him from making His primary object a direct commandment to us and from giving us the capacity of obeying it?" Those precepts which in your opinion are only the means and not the object would then have been unnecessary. Hear my answer, which will cure your heart of this disease and will show you the truth of that which I have pointed out to you. There occurs in the Law a passage which contains exactly the same idea; it is the following: "God led them not through the way of the land of the Philistines, although that was near; for God said: 'Lest the people repent when they see war, and return to Egypt;' and God led the people on a circuitous route, by way of the wilderness by the Red Sea" (Exod. 13:17-18). Here God led the people about, away from the direct road which He originally intended, because He feared they might meet on that way with hardships too great for their ordinary strength; He took them by another road in order to obtain thereby His original object. In the same manner,

God refrained from prescribing what the people by their natural disposition would be incapable of obeying, and gave the above-mentioned commandments as a means of securing His chief object, namely to spread knowledge of Him [among the people], and to cause them to reject idolatry. It is contrary to man's nature that he should suddenly abandon all the different kinds of Divine service and the different customs in which he has been brought up, and which have been so general, that they were considered as a matter of course; it would be just as if a person trained to work as a slave with mortar and bricks, or similar things, should interrupt his work, clean his hands, and at once fight with real giants. It was the result of God's wisdom that the Israelites were led about in the wilderness till they acquired courage. For it is a well-known fact that travelling in the wilderness and the privation of bodily enjoyments, such as bathing, produce courage, while the reverse is the source of faint-heartedness. Besides, another generation rose during the wanderings that had not been accustomed to degradation and slavery.... In the same way, the portion of the Law under discussion is the result of Divine wisdom, according to which people are allowed to continue the kind of worship to which they have been accustomed, in order that they might acquire the true faith, which is the chief object [of God's commandments] (*Guide for the Perplexed* 3:32).

In spite of Rambam's temperance, the views expressed in the *Guide* with regard to sacrifices—and other subjects as well—generated much controversy. In the city of Montpellier in southern France in 1232, about thirty years after the passing of Rambam and about forty years after the *Guide for the Perplexed* was first publicized, R. Shlomo Min Hahar and two of his students—R. Yonah Gerundi (known as Rabbeinu Yonah, 1180-1263), a cousin of Ramban, and R. Dovid b. Shaul—sent a letter denouncing Rambam's philosophical writings to various French scholars, some of whom were among the *Ba'alei Tosafot* in northern France. As a result, a ban—which was promulgated in the Jewish communities of France and Spain, was placed on Rambam's writings. In the meantime, in Montpellier a ban was placed on R. Shlomo Min Hahar himself. In the ensuing dispute, additional outstanding scholars participated, such as R. David Kimchi (Radak, 1160-1235), who sided with Rambam and acted on his behalf, even though Radak was over seventy at the time. R. Shlomo Min Hahar and Rabbeinu Yonah wrote concerning Rambam that even if it is true that he observed all of the commandments, there was a greater person than he who served as high priest for eighty years and in the end became a *tziduki* (denier of the oral law). The reference is to Yochanan Kohen Gadol (see BT *Berachot* 29a).[5] According to Rambam's son Abraham, R. Shlomo Min Hahar and Rabbeinu Yonah even contacted the leaders of the Inquisition, asking them to burn Rambam (who was already dead at this stage) and his works. Heinrich Graetz quotes their plea as follows:

> You burn your heretics, persecute ours also. The majority of the Jews of Provence are perverted by the heretical writings of Maimuni. If you cause these writings to be publicly and solemnly burnt, your action will have the effect of frightening the Jews away from them.[6]

---

5. Heinrich Graetz, *History of the Jews*, Vol. 3, p. 529.
6. Ibid., p. 542.

Needless to say, the Inquisition's leaders complied with their request.

In 1238, Ramban—responding to a request by R. Shlomo Min Hahar—sent in the latter's name a letter of rebuke to those Spanish communities which had objected to the excommunication decree, but because of his great veneration for Rambam (even if he disagreed with his approach) and the gentleness of his own personality, he refrained from personally taking sides, instead offering himself as a mediator. Turning to the French rabbis, he pointed out that in his code of law (*Mishneh Torah* or *Yad ha-Chazakah*), Rambam did not issue lenient verdicts, while the *Guide for the Perplexed* was in principle directed at Jews who had left the fold and adopted the approach of Aristotle, Galen, and the Greek philosophers. As a compromise, he suggested cancellation of the ban against Rambam's *Book of Knowledge* (*Sefer ha-Madda*) and retaining it only on the *Guide*. This compromise might have ended the contretemps, but unfortunately it was not accepted.

Consequential to the burning of the books of Rambam, Rabbeinu Yonah regretted his actions, and even feared that the burning of the Talmud in Paris shortly afterwards, in 1242, served as a heavenly punishment for the burning of the works of Rambam. He decided to travel from city to city and publicly atone for his defamation of Rambam. He would then proceed to the Land of Israel, where he would prostrate himself on the grave of Rambam and beg forgiveness.[7] When he arrived in Toledo as he travelled south, after hearing his brilliant talmudic lectures, the local community pleaded with him to remain as their rabbi and *rosh yeshiva*, and he acquiesced. Instead of asking forgiveness on Rambam's grave, he dedicated his books—*Sha'arei Teshuvah*, *Sefer ha-Yir'ah*, and *Igeret ha-Teshuvah*—to this purpose. When he

7. Ibid., p. 580.

passed away from a rare disease in 1263, his opponents related his abnormal demise to his activites against Rambam.[8]

If Rambam was excoriated in the Middle Ages because he supposedly belittled the sacrificial service, in recent centuries one who actually wanted to re-institute sacrifices was attacked. R. Akiva Yosef Schlesinger (1837-1922) was a student of *Ketav Sofer* (son of *Chatam Sofer*) and a son-in-law of R. Hillel Lichtenstein (Kolomiya), a student of *Chatam Sofer*. In Europe, he fought aggressively against the Reform and *Haskalah* (Enlightenment) movements, and in 1870 was successful in realizing his dream to settle in the Land of Israel, against the advice of the Yitav Lev (the reigning Satmar Rebbe). R. Schlesinger had a messianic vision, and accordingly made a point of wearing *techelet* (a blue strand) in his *tzitzit* (ritual fringes), a custom based on a biblical command (Num. 15:38) but not enforced due to the assumption that the formula for manufacturing the appropriate blue dye had been lost through the ages. Another deviation from accepted practice which he made was to blow the *shofar* (ram's horn) in Jerusalem on Rosh Hashanah even if it fell on Shabbat. A third innovation, which he attempted but did not manage to accomplish, was sacrificing the Paschal lamb on Passover. All of these actions were anathema to the ultra-Orthodox Jews of his day, who viewed such behavior as an attempt to preempt activities best left for the Messiah. As a result, zealots assaulted him on a street in Jerusalem and cut his *tallit* with its strings of *techelet* into small pieces. Their rabbis posited that a number of books written by R. Schlesinger were to be treated as heretical works, which according to Jewish law must be burned. In a strange parallel, R. Schlesinger's books met the same fate as those of Rambam. In spite of these incidents, upon his demise, he was greatly honored in a eulogy delivered by R. Chaim Yosef Sonnenfeld.

8. Kalman Shulman, *Toldot Chachmei Yisrael*, Vol. 2, pp. 164-165.

Apparently, both one who detracted from the relevance of sacrifices and one who wished to reinstitute sacrifices in modern times stimulated defenders of the faith to react forcefully and even violently. The question which arises is how vigorously should one stand up for his cherished beliefs? Where does one draw the line? Perhaps the answer may be derived from the following saying of the Sages:

> Great is peace, for even if Israel worships idols, but peace prevails among them, the Lord, so to speak, says: I cannot rule over them and punish them, for peace reigns among them (*Gen. Rabbah* 38:6).

TZAV

INTRODUCTION TO SACRIFICES

THE PURPOSE OF SACRIFICES

As explained in the chapter on *Vayikra*, according to some views, Rambam looked upon sacrifices as a means of weaning the nation from pagan practices, although they will only be abandoned when the Jews reach a very high, and as yet undetermined, level, and others believe that Rambam considered them to be a permanent feature of Judaism., Ramban looked upon them as a means of enhancing one's prayers, moving closer to God, and repenting for sins which were committed.

CLASSIFICATION OF SACRIFICES

Sacrifices may be divided into those which are voluntary and those which the law requires. A second distinction is between those brought by individuals versus those brought by the priests for the entire community. A third categorization distinguishes between the most holy sacrifices (*kodshei kodashim*) and the less holy ones (*kodshim kalim*). Although the meat of most sacrifices, other than burnt offerings, may be eaten, the holier ones may be eaten only by male priests (Exod. 23:20; BT *Pesachim* 59b; *Sefer ha-Chinuch*

102) on the Temple grounds within a one-day and one-night period (Mishnah *Zevachim* 5:3; 5:5), while those of a lesser degree of holiness may be eaten anywhere in Jerusalem by any Jew, for two days and the intervening night, with certain exceptions (Mishnah *Zevachim* 5:6-8).

THE VARIOUS TYPES OF OFFERINGS:

Sacrifices are brought from animals or grain. The latter are called *menachot* (meal sacrifices). Rambam provides the following general introduction to animal sacrifices in *Hilchot Ma'aseh ha-Korbanot*, ch. 1, where he states:

- All of the sacrifices of living animals come from only five species: cattle, sheep, goats, turtle doves, and small doves.

- And all of the [animal] sacrifices—whether those brought by the community or by individuals—are of four types: burnt offerings, sin offerings, guilt offerings, and peace (or well-being) offerings.

- There are also three other types of individual sacrifices: the Paschal lamb, the sacrifice of the first-born, and the tithe sacrifice.

- All of the communal offerings are burnt offerings or sin offerings. There are no communal peace offerings except the two sheep offered with the bread that is waved on Shavuot. They are called "the sacrifices of communal peace offerings." The community never offers a guilt offering.

- The communal offerings are the two *temidim* offered every day; the additional offerings of the Sabbath, New Moons, and festivals; and the sin offering of the goat brought on Yom Kippur.

As far as meal offerings are concerned, they are brought from wheat flour exclusively, with the exception of the meal offering of a woman suspected of adultery (*sotah*) and of the sheaf offering (*minchat ha-omer*) on the second day of Passover (*Hilchot Ma'aseh ha-Korbanot* 12:2). Meal offerings may also be of the individual or communal variety (ibid. 12:3-4).

A short review of the aforementioned information is presented in the following table:

Type of Offering	Hebrew Name	Brought by	Holiness
Burnt	*olah*	community or individual	*kodshei kodashim*
Sin	*chatat*	community or individual	*kodshei kodashim*
Guilt	*asham*	Individual	*kodshei kodashim*
Peace or Well-being	*shelamim*	Individual (mainly)	*kodshim kalim*
Paschal lamb, first born, tithe	*Pesach, Bechor, ma'aser behemah*	Individual	*kodshim kalim*
Meal	*minchah*	community or individual	*kodshei kodashim*

These sacrifices will now be examined in greater detail.

BURNT OFFERINGS

The burnt offering is called an *olah* in Hebrew, which means "rises." It is given this name because its meat is burnt in its entirety and thus "rises" to the Lord, and is consequently shared neither with the priests nor with its donor.

In general, individual burnt offerings are voluntary, and communal ones are obligatory. However, although not incumbent, the contributor may intend it to serve as a means of atonement. This possibility is based on the words "it will be accepted on his account to atone for him" (Lev. 1:4). The Talmud states: "R. Akiva said: A burnt offering is offered exclusively for transgression of a positive command or of a prohibition which may be remedied by a positive command" (BT *Yoma* 36a). Rashi *in situ* (and on Lev. 1:4) cites the Tosefta (Zukermandel *Menachot* 10:12),[9] which explicates the view of R. Akiva:

> For what does it atone? If you say it brings forgiveness for sins punishable by excision or execution by the court— their punishment is stated [i.e. excision or execution], if for prohibitions—their punishment is stated [i.e. lashes]. Consequently, it can only propitiate for [failure to fulfill] a positive commandment [where no other punishment is stated] and for a prohibition which may be rectified by a positive commandment.

Punishment for not performing positive commands is recorded only regarding circumcision (Gen. 17:14) and the sacrifice of the Paschal lamb (Num. 9:13). Examples of prohibitions which may be remedied by fulfilling a positive command are: theft (Lev. 19:13), which is remedied by returning the object (Lev. 5:23); not consuming sacrificial meat within the allotted time period (Lev. 7:15), which is remedied by burning the remaining meat (Lev. 7:17); and capturing a mother bird with its offspring (Deut. 22:6), which is remedied by freeing the mother (Deut. 22:7). Punishment is a form of expiation. But since one does not receive lashes for

9. See also *Sifra Vayikra: Dibbura de-Nedava* 4:8.

transgressing remediable prohibitions (BT *Makkot* 15a), if not for the possibility of bringing a burnt offering, there would be no means of atonement.

Ramban (Lev. 1:4) explains that there are some sins for which one is liable to excision if he transgresses them deliberately, and is required to bring a sin offering if he transgresses them inadvertently. There are other sins for which one is liable to death at the hands of Heaven[10] (e.g. a prophet who suppresses his prophecy [BT *Sanhedrin* 89a]) or lashes if done purposely, and apparently exempt from any punishment if done unintentionally. But for most positive commandments, and for repairable prohibitions, no punishment at all is defined.

Rabbeinu Yonah (*Shaʾarei Teshuvah* 4:6) explains that in the case of not performing a positive commandment, a sacrifice completes one's exoneration after he has verbally repented. In the case of violating a repairable negative commandment, performing the associated positive commandment removes the punishment by lashes, but does not cleanse one of his transgression. For that, one needs the atonement effected by a burnt offering.

R. Yosi ha-Gelili argues with R. Akiva in *Yoma* (36a) and says that the burnt offering atones for "transgressions in connection with gleanings (Lev. 19:9), forgotten sheaves (Deut. 24:19), the corner of the field (Lev. 19:9), and the tithe for the poor" (Deut. 14:29; 26:12).[11] These laws concern contributions to the destitute from the

---

10. According to Rashi (BT *Shabbat* 25b), excision involves shortening of one's life and also not having children, while death at the hands of heaven only involves the former. According to Rambam (*Peirush ha-Mishnayot, Sanhedrin* 9:6), excision implies shortening of one's life in this world and the next, while death at the hands of heaven only affects life in this world. Both punishments are inflicted by God.

11. According to Rashi, the last item is not included. But Tosafot and Tosafot Yeshanim, *in situ*, disagree. It is also not clear if R. Yosi is referring to inadvertent or purposeful transgression.

yield of field owners. R. Yosi's definition is more restrictive than R. Akiva's, since the first three commands which R. Yosi cites are all repairable prohibitions,[12] and the last is a positive command.[13] Hence, they form a subset of those which R. Akiva defines.

According to R. Shimon b. Yochai (*Lev. Rabbah* 7:3; JT *Yoma* 8:7), the burnt offering expiates for improper thoughts. In the Midrash, various Sages attempt to base this claim on biblical verses. R. Levi cites a verse from Ezekiel (20:32) which criticizes the Israelites for having worshipped idols: "and that which arises in your mind will not come to be, when you say: 'We will be like the nations, like the families of the countries, to serve wood and stone.'" The Hebrew word for "arises" is *olah*, the very word used for the burnt offering. Midrashically, the verse can be understood to mean that the burnt offering atones for evil thoughts and erases them, so it is as if they had never occurred. R. Yuden finds a more direct source in the book of Job, which describes how Job reacted to the frequent parties which his children made:

> When the days of their feasting were completed, Job sent and invited them to be sanctified, and rose up early in the morning and offered burnt offerings according to the number of them all, for Job said: "It may be that my sons have sinned and blasphemed God in their hearts" (Job 1:5).

The text makes it quite clear that the burnt offering is meant to atone for evil thoughts.

The Slonimer Rebbe (*Netivot Shalom, Tzav*) believes that the transgressions which the burnt offering expiates, namely improper

---

12. See *Sefer ha-Chinnuch* 217, 219, 593.
13. See *Sefer ha-Chinnuch* 474.

thoughts, are more serious than those expiated by the sin offering, since the former relate to the origin of evil—the mental decision to sin, while the latter relate merely to the inevitable result of that process. One may be thoroughly cleansed only by rooting out depravity from the source. This idea fits in with the commentary of R. Moshe Botschko on the verse: "You must not hate your brother in your heart" (Lev. 19:17):

> Had the Torah only prohibited beating, cursing, and killing, the defendant could excuse himself and explain that I was stimulated to do it by the overpowering force of my hatred, and not of my own volition. But take note at this point that the Torah addresses each person and commands him while still at an early stage—at the emergence of the first element that could degenerate to the terrible sin. Already at this time, one is commanded to refrain from the first cause—from hatred—before things evolve into a situation where he is, in reality, deprived of his freedom of choice (*Hegyonei Moshe*, pp. 94-95).

In addition, after performing an iniquitious act, one naturally feels remorse, as the verse says: "The sacrifices of God are a broken spirit; a broken and a contrite heart, O God, You will not despise" (Ps. 51:19). In contrast, corrupt thoughts do not generate the same degree of regret, as the perpetrator does not intuitively feel that he has sinned.

The Talmud summarizes these ideas in a single statement: "Unchaste imagination is more injurious than the sin itself" (*Yoma* 29a).

SIN OFFERINGS

It has been noted that the burnt offering may be used to expiate for certain sins. However, it is essentially a voluntary offering, and the decision to use it as a means of atonement is personal and not required by *halachah*. Not so with respect to the sin offering, which is legislated specifically for dealing with misconduct. There exist thirty-six sins which, if committed deliberately, are punishable by excision (Mishnah *Kereitot* 1:1), for twenty-one of which the sinner is also flogged if he had been warned in advance (Mishnah *Makkot* 3:1). However, if performed inadvertently (Bartenura: with the exception of the positive commands to circumcise and offer the Paschal lamb), one must bring a sin offering (Mishnah *Kereitot* 1:2), or a guilt offering for some of the more serious sins (such as benefiting from holy objects (Lev. 5:14-16) or swearing falsely concerning a financial claim (Lev. 5:20-26), both performed unintentionally).

Sin offerings are classified as being either external or internal. The former refers to those whose blood is placed on the corners of the copper altar located in the courtyard of the Tabernacle or Temple, while the latter relates to those whose blood is placed on the corners of the golden altar located inside, or sprinkled on the partition or even inside the Holy of Holies. External sin offerings are eaten by the priests on duty, while internal sin offerings are totally burnt (*Hilchot Ma'aseh Korbanot* 1:16). For more details, see APPENDIX I: THE DIFFERENT TYPES OF SACRIFICES.

GUILT OFFERINGS

Sin offerings are brought individually or communally to atone for a wide range of transgressions performed inadvertently, which would be punishable by excision if they were performed deliberately. Guilt offerings, on the other hand, are brought exclusively by individuals to atone for specific sins, possibly done deliberately, which the Torah has designated as being serious. There are five types of guilt offerings; for details, see APPENDIX I: THE DIFFERENT TYPES OF SACRIFICES.

PEACE OR WELL-BEING OFFERINGS

The sacrifices described up to this point serve in principal as means of atonement, both those which are obligatory as well as the voluntary burnt offerings. The peace or well-being offering, *shelamim* in Hebrew, differs in that it is not associated with the performance of any transgression, but is rather brought in consequence of a voluntary commitment, or in the form of a thanksgiving offering, as the result of being saved from a dangerous situation. Regarding the verse: "And this is the law of the sacrifice of peace offerings, which one may offer to the Lord" (Lev. 7:11), the Midrash asks the following question: Why is the extra phrase "which one may offer to the Lord" added, since it does not appear when describing the laws of the burnt offering (Lev. 6:2), sin offering (Lev. 6:18), or guilt offering (Lev. 7:1)? The answer given is: "A sin offering comes to atone for a sin and a guilt offering comes to atone for a sin; however, a thanksgiving sacrifice does not come to atone for a sin [but exclusively to thank the Lord]" (*Lev. Rabbah* 9:1). In other words, the peace offering may be considered to be the most altruistic of the sacrifices.

There are eight types of peace offerings, five of which are described below. For the remaining types, see APPENDIX I: THE DIFFERENT TYPES OF SACRIFICES.

1. Festal (*chagigah*) offering: The *chagigah* is one of three *mitzvot* which Israel was commanded on each of the pilgrimage festivals, as the Talmud states:

    > Three precepts are enjoined upon Israel when they make their pilgrimage at a festival: the pilgrimage offering, the festal offering, and to rejoice (BT *Chagigah* 6b).

    Interestingly, the Mishnah itself admits that the biblical requirement to bring these sacrifices is quite tenuous, when it says:

    > The laws concerning the [work permitted on] Sabbath, festal offerings, and [the prohibition of] benefiting from holy objects are like mountains hanging by a [single] hair, for they have minimal Scriptural basis and many laws (Mishnah *Chagigah* 1:8).

    In other words, the main source is the oral law, with only weak textual indicators. For example, the requirement to bring the festal sacrifice on Pesach[14] and Sukkot[15] derives from the use in the Pentateuch of the Hebrew word for festival (*chag*) as a verb (*ve-chagotem*), while the requirement to do so on Shavuot[16] is based on the use of the Hebrew word *mas*, meaning "tax," implying an obligation which the oral law interprets as referring to the festal sacrifice.

---

14. *Mechilta de-Rabbi Yishmael, Bo, Masechta de-Pascha, parashah* 7 in reference to Exod. 12:14.
15. BT *Chagigah* 10b in reference to Lev. 23:41.
16. BT *Chagigah* 8a in reference to Deut. 16:10.

2. Peace offerings of jubilation: As noted with respect to the festal offering, rejoicing was one of the three precepts obligated on holidays, based on the verse:

> And you should rejoice on your festival: you, and your son, and your daughter, and your man-servant, and your maid-servant, and the Levite, and the stranger, and the fatherless, and the widow that are within your gates (Deut. 16:14).

But how is the requirement to rejoice transformed into an obligation to bring sacrifices? The answer is found in the Talmud (BT *Pesachim* 109a), where it is stated:

> It was taught, R. Judah b. Beteira said: When the Temple was in existence, one could not rejoice without meat, for it says: "And you will sacrifice peace offerings, and eat there; and you will rejoice before the Lord your God" (Deut. 27:7).

Tosafot explains that although the verse cited does not refer to the holidays, it does indicate that rejoicing involves indulging in sacrificial meat. Having established the nexus between sacrifices and rejoicing, the Talmud states (in explanation of Mishnah *Chagigah* 1:4):

> Our Rabbis taught [it says]: "And you should rejoice on your festival" (Deut. 16:14). This includes all kinds of jubilation as [fulfillment of] rejoicing [on the festival]. From here the Sages said: Israelites may fulfill their obligation with vow offerings, freewill

offerings (Lev. 7:15), and the cattle tithe (Lev. 27:32); and priests [may fulfill it] with a sin offering and a guilt offering (Num. 18:9), and with the sacrifice of the first-born (Num. 18:18), and with the breast and the shoulder (Lev. 7:31-32). One might think also with bird offerings and meal offerings, [therefore] Scripture teaches: "And you should rejoice on your festival" only with those [offerings] from which the festal offering can be brought [i.e., meat of an animal, not a bird] (BT *Chagigah* 8a).

The peace offering of jubilation differs from the pilgrimage and festal offerings in that it is incumbent every day of the holiday, as opposed to the others, which must only be brought once on each holiday (Mishnah *Sukkah* 4:1; *Hilchot Yom Tov* 6:17). However, as noted above, one need not actually bring a special sacrifice. The main idea is to enjoy oneself by eating meat which may be from any other sacrifice or, in the case of a priest, from sacrificial meat which he receives as a priestly gift.[17]

A second distinction is that while the pilgrimage and festal offerings are incumbent on men alone, the jubilation offering is incumbent on women as well (BT *Chagigah* 6b), as women are mentioned twice (Deut. 14:26; 16:14) in connection with *simchah* (rejoicing), although Abaye explains that the obligation is actually on the husband to ensure that his wife rejoices (BT *Kiddushin* 34b).

The *mitzvot* of bringing the festal and jubilation offerings have an ethical facet as well, namely that eating their meat

---

17. R. Menachem Shach says that although one may fulfill the requirement to rejoice by partaking of any of the meat items mentioned, he must bring at least one peace offering of rejoicing (*Avi Ezri, Hilchot Chagigah*).

is meant to be done together with poor and lonely people who yearn for fellowship and hospitality. Rambam (*Hilchot Chagigah* 2:14) formulates this requirement as follows:

> When a person sacrifices festal and jubilation offerings, he should not eat alone with his wife and children, and imagine that he is fulfilling the command in the utmost sense, but rather he is required to gladden the indigent and forlorn, for it says "and the Levite, and the stranger, and the fatherless, and the widow" (Deut. 16:14). He must feed and give drink to them to the extent of his ability. Regarding he who partook of his sacrifices but did not pleasure the aforementioned in addition to himself, it says [concerning idol-worshipping Israelites]: "their sacrifices will be for them as the bread of mourners; all that eat of it will be polluted [since mourners are impure], for their bread will only satisfy their own appetite, it should not come into the house of the Lord [since it will not atone for their sins, which they continue to perform]" (Hos. 9:4). It is more of a mitzvah to host a Levite than anyone else, for he has "no portion or inheritance with Israel" (Deut. 18:1), and he does not receive gifts of meat [as does a priest], therefore Levites must be invited to one's table and entertained, or provided with courtesy meat portions with their tithes in order to meet their needs, and anyone who refrains from delighting the Levite and delays his tithes on the holidays transgresses a negative command, for it says: "Be careful not to forsake the Levite" (Deut. 12:19).

Even today, when there is no holy Temple and there are no sacrifices, the aspect of performing acts of loving-kindness on the holidays remains relevant, as Rambam states (*Hilchot Yom Tov* 6:16-18):

> Just as it is a mitzvah to honor the Sabbath and delight in it, so with regard to all of the holidays, for it says: "Call the Sabbath a delight, and the holy of the Lord honorable" (Isa. 58:13), and all of the holidays are referred to as "holy convocations" (Lev. 23:4)... and a person must be happy and kind-hearted— he and his children and his wife and the members of his household, and all who consort with him, for it says: "And you should rejoice on your festival: [you, and your son, and your daughter, and your man-servant, and your maid-servant, and the Levite, and the stranger, and the fatherless, and the widow that are within your gates]" (Deut. 16:14). Even though the rejoicing mentioned here refers to peace offerings, as we explain in *Hilchot Chagigah*, included in that rejoicing is to delight himself, his children, and the members of his household, each in the way that is suitable for him... and when he eats and drinks he must feed "the stranger, the fatherless, and the widow" (Deut. 16:11) together with other unfortunate paupers, but he who locks the doors of his yard and eats and drinks—he and his children, and his wife— and does not feed and give drink to the poverty-stricken and embittered, this is not a rejoicing which is a mitzvah, but rather a rejoicing of his belly... and such a rejoicing is a disgrace for them, as it says: "And

I will spread dung upon your faces, the dung of your [sacrifices brought on the] holidays" (Mal. 2:3).

3. Peace offering of the fourteenth (of Nisan): It was required to bring a special sacrifice on the day preceding Passover (*erev Pesach*) to be eaten before the Paschal lamb, in order that the latter "be eaten after the appetite is satisfied" (BT *Pesachim* 70a). The source of this obligation is found in the portion which deals with the sacrifice of the Paschal lamb, where it is written: "And you should sacrifice the Passover offering to the Lord your God, of the flock [sheep or goats, Lev. 1:10] and the herd [cattle]" (Deut. 16:2), whereupon the Talmud asks: "But the Passover offering is only from sheep or goats [Exod. 12:5, so why are cattle mentioned? The Talmud answers:] Rather 'flock' refers to the Passover offering, [while] 'herd' refers to the *chagigah* [i.e., the peace offering of the fourteenth]" (BT *Pesachim* 70b).

The Talmud (BT *Pesachim* 69b) explains that the peace offering of the fourteenth is not actually obligatory, since if the Paschal lamb is large enough to feed all of its participants to satiation, it is not necessary. Furthermore, if the fourteenth is Sabbath, it is not even permitted to bring it. Because of its conditional nature, the Sages argue whether it is even a Torah-based obligation, with Me'iri *in situ* saying that it is, since the Talmud derived it from a biblical verse. Tosafot (BT *Pesachim* 70a, s.v. *lav chovah hi*), on the other hand, considers it to be a rabbinical enactment, with the verse being no more than an intimation. Me'iri explains that because of the biblical restrictions on the specific animal to be brought as the Passover offering (male, unblemished, one-year-old lamb), there was a shortage and many people were enlisted for each lamb, more than could possibly eat to satiation from its meat, and so the peace offering of the fourteenth was used to almost fill them up, and then only a small portion of the Paschal lamb had to be eaten by each participant in order to complete the process.

4. *Bikkurim* (first fruits) peace offering: The first fruits of the seven kinds of produce for which the Land of Israel is praised (Mishnah *Bikkurim* 1:3)—wheat, barley, grapes, figs, pomegranates, olives, and dates (Deut. 8:8)—were to be brought to the Temple and given to the priests as described at length in Deuteronomy (26:1-11) and alluded to in Exodus (23:19; 34:26) and Numbers (18:13). The Mishnah (*Bikkurim* 2:4) states that simultaneous with the bringing of the first fruits, one also brings a peace offering, and Rambam (*Peirush ha-Mishnayot*; *Hilchot Bikkurim* 3:12) bases this law on the use of the word *simchah* (rejoicing) in connection with the bringing of the first fruits (Deut. 26:11). The word *simchah* appears in the context of the holidays (Deut. 16:14) and is the basis for requiring one to bring peace offerings of jubilation on the holidays.

5. Thanksgiving offering: This is an individual voluntary offering whose purpose is to indicate the contributor's gratitude to the Almighty for delivering him from a dangerous situation. It differs from other peace offerings in that, together with the animal sacrifice, one brought *matzot* of three different types (loaves, wafers, and loaves of scalded fine flour, Lev. 7:12)— ten of each, and ten loaves of leavened bread (*Menachot* 7:1). One of each of the four types was donated to the priest, and the remainder were eaten by the individual and his family and friends (Lev. 7:14; *Menachot* 7:2).

The Talmud enumerates the instances in which a thanksgiving offering should be forthcoming:

> R. Judah said in the name of Rav: Four [classes of people] should offer thanksgiving: those who have crossed the sea [and successfully completed their journey], those who have traversed the wilderness [as part of their journey], one who has recovered [from an illness], and one who was incarcerated in a prison and released (BT *Berachot* 54b).

Although the previous citation was said with regard to the special thanksgiving prayer *birkat ha-gomel*, Tosafot ha-Rosh *in situ* noted that the blessing was instituted as a replacement for the sacrifice after the destruction of the Temple, and this approach was accepted by Rashi and Rashbam (Lev. 7:12). The Talmud derived the requirement of these four to thank God from Psalm 107, where each of the four cases is alluded to, and at the end of each description the psalmist writes: "Let them give thanks to the Lord for His mercy, and for His wonderful actions for [the benefit of] mankind (Ps. 107:8, 15, 21, 31)." Modern applications of the thanksgiving prayer are as a blessing to be said by soldiers returning from dangerous assignments (*Shevet Levi* 9:45) and by survivors of serious traffic (or other) accidents (*Igrot Moshe, Orach Chayim* 2:59).

Rationale for the *Shelamim* Offering

Various opinions have been cited with regard to the significance of the *shelamim* offering.

View of Rashi – the *shelamim* offering is meant to emphasize the importance of peace:

According to one opinion, the word *shelamim* is based on the word *shalom*, meaning "peace," and so it says in the Midrash which is cited by Rashi (Lev. 3:1):

> Whoever brings a *shelamim* offering, brings *shalom* [peace] to the world. Another explanation is: *shelamim* — everyone feels completed [*shalem*] with it. The blood and the innards [are burned on] the altar, the breast and the shoulder [are given to] the priests, the skin and the meat [belong to] the owner (*Pesikta Zutrata*, Lev. 3:1).

It is possible to combine the two Midrashic derivations by saying that since all participants are satisfied with their portion, they have no reason to be jealous or quarrelsome, so that by default peace reigns among them.

In the view of Rambam, ensuring peace is the main task of Judaism. Rambam deals with a situation that might arise if a poor person has enough money for either Chanuka candles or Sabbath candles, but not for both. Regarding such a situation, he states (*Hilchot Megilla ve-Chanuka* 4:14):

> Sabbath candles take precedence, to promote peace within the household, since God's name is erased in order to advance peace between a man and his wife [to allow

a woman suspected of adultery to prove her innocence]. Great is peace, since the entire Torah was given to make peace in the world, as it says: "Her ways are ways of pleasantness, and all her paths are peace" (Prov. 3:17).

The following Midrash (*Gen. Rabbah* 1:4) says that the world was created only for Israel to fulfill the laws of the Torah:

> R. Bannai said: The world and its contents were only created in the merit of the Torah, as it says: "God founded the world with [in the merit of] wisdom; with understanding he established the heavens" (Prov. 3:19).

R. Bannai interprets the verse to mean that the world was created in order to promulgate Torah, which is the highest form of wisdom. If the world was created to spread Torah, and the essence of Torah according to Rambam is the development of a peaceful lifestyle, then the world was created in order for peace to reign.

View of Ramban – the *shelamim* offering is meant to encourage gratitude to God:

As noted, *shelamim* is a voluntary sacrifice. What motivates a person to make such a donation? R. David Zvi Hoffman (Lev. 1:116) suggests that one who brings a voluntary offering wishes to thank God that he is in a situation of physical and spiritual completeness or well-being (*shlemut*) as a result of his adherence to the Lord, or that he aspires to reach such a state, and for that reason this sacrifice is called *shelamim*.

The Midrash (*Gen. Rabbah* 14:9) stresses that one must thank God for every breath that he takes. Ramban proceeds in this direction by stating:

A person must be thankful for the concealed miracles which are the basis of the entire Torah, for man has no share in the Torah of Moses our teacher until we believe that all of our happenings and transactions are miracles—there is no such thing as nature and the way of the world (Ramban, Exod. 13:16).

Based on the Midrash and Ramban, one might have thought that *birkat ha-gomel* should be recited daily, a habit which would detract from its uniqueness. Instead, religious Jews attempt to thank God by saying a hundred blessings a day, and by repeating the silent prayer thrice daily, which includes the *Modim* (meaning "we are thankful [to You]") prayer.

Thanksgiving prayers are said not only by individuals upon delivery from danger, but by the entire *tzibbur* (public) upon salvation from peril. When the Maccabbes defeated the Syrian Greeks in 165 BCE, and the holiday of Hanukkah was established exactly three years after Antiochus erected a pagan altar in the Temple (1 Maccabees), the Talmud states: "the following year these [days] were appointed a festival with [the recital of] *Hallel* [a prayer of praise to the Lord] and thanksgiving." Interestingly, the American holiday of Thanksgiving is likely based on the decision of William Bradford, governor of Plymouth colony, to thank God for enabling the pilgrims to endure the first difficult years in the New World. Bradford had access to an annotated psalter with Rambam's summary of the laws regarding when *birkat ha-gomel* is to be said (based on the previously cited talmudic script) appended to Psalm 107.[18]

According to Ramban (Exod. 13:16), the world was created only for man to be grateful to God. In his words:

18. Meir Soloveichik, "God's Providence and the United States," *Torah To-Go Series* (Dec. 2014).

And the intention of all of the commands is that we believe in our God and thank Him for creating us, and this is the purpose of creation, for we have no other reason for the initial creation, and the Almighty does not desire the lower beings other than for man to know and be grateful that God created him.

But what will motivate man to feel grateful to the Almighty? To this question Ramban also has an answer, which is:

They [non-believers] say, "The Lord has abandoned the Earth." And when God favors a certain community or individual and does a miracle for them by changing the custom of the world and its nature, the nullification of these opinions becomes clear to everyone, for the amazing miracle shows that there is a God in the world Who innovated it, and Who knows and supervises and is able [to do whatever He wants].

MEAL OFFERINGS

The Rabbis noted a difference in formulation between the Torah's description of the burnt (animal) offering and the meal offering. Regarding the burnt offering it states: "When a *person* from among you brings an offering to the Lord" (Lev. 1:2), while with respect to a meal offering the verse reads: "And when a *soul* brings a meal offering to the Lord" (Lev. 2:1).

Regarding the change in words from *person* to *soul*, the Talmud states:

R. Isaac said: Why is the meal offering distinguished in that the expression "soul" is used [in connection with it]? Because the Holy One, blessed be He, said, "Who is in the habit of bringing a meal offering? A poor person [Rashi: It is his practice to bring a meal offering because he does not own animals]. I consider it as if he had offered his own soul to Me" (*Menachot* 104b).

The different kinds of meal offerings are described in detail in APPENDIX I: THE DIFFERENT TYPES OF SACRIFICES.

COMPARING THE PORTIONS OF *VAYIKRA* AND *TZAV*

The contents of the portion of *Vayikra* is as follows:
- ch. 1: burnt offering
- ch. 2: meal offering
- ch. 3: peace offering
- ch. 4, beginning of ch. 5: sin offering
- ch. 5: guilt offering

The portion of *Tzav* continues the discussion of sacrifices as follows:
- ch. 6: burnt offering, meal offering, sin offering
- ch. 7: guilt offering, peace offering.

One may ask the following three questions:

1. Why review the description of the sacrifices in the portion of *Tzav*, when they were already described in the portion of *Vayikra*?

2. If there is a reason to review, why is the order changed? Specifically, why does the peace offering precede the sin and guilt offerings in *Vayikra* and follow them in *Tzav*?

3. The portion of *Vayikra* starts with the words: "And the Lord called to Moses, and *spoke to him from the Tent of Meeting*, saying: Speak to the children of Israel, and say to them" (Lev. 1:1-2).

   The simple meaning of these verses would seem to be that the continuation of that portion was transmitted to Moses in the Tent of Meeting, i.e., after the *Mishkan* (Tabernacle) was built in the month of Nisan, and he proceeded to convey its contents to the Children of Israel. The problem is that in the portion of *Tzav*, after the description of all the sacrifices, the text states: "This is the law… *which the Lord commanded Moses on Mount Sinai*, on the day that he commanded the Children of Israel to bring their offerings to the Lord in the *Wilderness of Sinai*" (Lev. 7:37-38). In these verses, the sacrificial laws are said to have been given to Moses at Mt. Sinai almost a year before the Tent of Meeting was constructed, so where did the transmission actually occur? Furthermore, the passage is self-contradictory, initially speaking of Mt. Sinai as the site of the transmission, but switching to the Wilderness of Sinai at the end of the verse.

These questions may be answered by noting that there is an intrinsic difference between the contents of the portions of *Vayikra* and *Tzav*. In *Vayikra*, the designated audience is the Children of Israel. The objective is to acquaint them with what it is important for them to know about sacrifices, namely the different types, their purpose (some are voluntary, others are intended to atone for specific sins or certain categories of sins), their substance (animal, bird, or grain), and the physical details of animal sacrifices or the means of preparation of meal offerings. In the portion of *Tzav*, on the other hand, the designated audience is the priests, and not the Children of Israel, as stated explicitly in the second verse of the portion: "Command Aaron and his sons saying…" (Lev. 6:2). Accordingly, the burnt offering described in ch. 6 is the daily offering which is brought by the priests. The meal offering described next is for the initiation of new priests. The same offering is brought daily by the high priest. Sin offerings are eaten by priests only, and the focus at the end of the chapter is on which priests are permitted to partake of them, where they may do so, and what procedures must be observed. Similarly, in ch. 7, where the guilt offering and peace offering are spoken of, the focus is on the service demanded of the priests at the time of their sacrifice, the parts that are given to the priests, the time period allocated for eating the sacrifice and under what conditions. Completing the emphasis on priestly matters, the portion ends (ch. 8) with a detailed description of the consecration of Aaron and his sons at the inauguration ceremony of the sanctuary.

It is now possible to relate to the previously presented questions.

1. Indeed, the same sacrifices are described in both of these portions, but the emphasis is different and, as a result, the particulars included in each portion differ—in *Vayikra*, important details concerning those who bring sacrifices are presented, while *Tzav* deals with the activities and compensation of the priests who perform the sacrificial service.

2. In the portion of *Vayikra*, which is directed at the Israelite who brings an offering, the first sacrifices described are the burnt, meal, and peace offerings, all of which are voluntary, and afterwards the sin and guilt offerings, which are obligatory for

one who finds himself in certain situations. In *Tzav*, which is directed at the priests, the order is burnt, meal, sin, and guilt offerings—because they are all *kodshei kodashim* (most holy sacrifices), a factor which impinges on the conditions under which the sacrifice may be eaten by those who are permitted to do so, followed by the peace and thanksgiving offerings, which are *kodshim kalim* (less holy sacrifices), whose eating conditions are less stringent.

3. There exists an argument (BT *Chagigah* 6a) whether all of the commands including their most minute details were taught to Moses at Mt. Sinai (R. Akiva), or whether the commands were given to Moses in outline form at Mt. Sinai, while the myriad technicalities were filled in throughout the forty years of wandering in the desert (R. Yishmael). If one adopts the view of R. Yishmael, one may say that the laws in *Tzav*, which affect a relatively small group (the priests) were articulated in full to Moses at Mt. Sinai, to be transmitted to Aaron and his sons, while those in the portion of *Vayikra*, which were directed at the entire nation, were sketched to Moses at Mt. Sinai and only completed in the Tent of Meeting, and it is those which are referred to in the opening verse of the portion of *Vayikra*.

However, it is still not clear why the verse in the portion of *Tzav* mentions both Mt. Sinai and the Wilderness of Sinai, which would seem to imply two different locations. Ramban suggests that even regarding the laws included in *Tzav*, those relating to the inauguration ceremony (burnt, sin, and initiation offerings) were given at Mt. Sinai, while those relating to the peace and meal offerings, which were not urgent, were given in the Wilderness of Sinai, i.e. in the Tent of Meeting.

Ramban (Lev. 7:38), however, actually prefers the view of R. Akiva that a complete exposition of the laws was bestowed upon Moses at Mt. Sinai and repeated at the Tent of Meeting. He believes that both expressions—Mt. Sinai and the Wilderness of Sinai—really mean the Tent of Meeting. The term Mt. Sinai is used to stress that the repetition occurred before they left the Wilderness of Sinai altogether (Num. 10:12), while the Wilderness of Sinai is used to point out that these laws were not given on the mountain itself, but rather in the Tent of Meeting across from the mountain. All of the references in Leviticus thus refer to the Tent of Meeting, where these laws were repeated for the first time after being initially given at Mt. Sinai.

SUMMARY

Many people view sacrifices as an ancient means of appeasing the gods. In Judaism, their purpose is quite different. Most of the personal sacrifices are associated with the concept of *teshuvah* (repentance), and they serve as a means of atoning for various types of sins. Others are used as a means of thanking God for memorable events in the supplicant's life. Still others are used to help generate an environment of happiness and joy on the Jewish holidays. In addition to all of these purposes, many sacrifices were partially eaten by the priests, and thus served as an integral element of sustenance for those priests who were active in the Temple.

As far as communal sacrifices are concerned, some celebrated yearly agricultural milestones, others atoned for various unnoticed sins of the entire congregation, while they all enhanced the daily, Sabbath, and holiday priestly services in the holy Temple.

The *shelamim* sacrifice inculcates two of the most fundamental principles of Judaism. In the view of Rambam, the world was created in order for peace to prevail throughout civilization. According to Ramban, the world was created in order that man praise God and be thankful to Him for creating him with the ability to aspire to perfection, which in turn leads to a belief in personal providence, as does the ability to repent for one's sins. These principles are not at all contradictory, but complementary. One begins by being grateful to the Lord for creating a beautiful world, as stated by Ramban, which leads to a deepening of belief in God and His personal providence in the life of every being, and one continues by developing a strong will to fulfill His *mitzvot*, which according to Rambam are meant to establish peace among all the creations of the world.

It is now possible to appreciate the saying of the Sages: "In the future world, all sacrifices will be null and void except for the thanksgiving offering [a form of *shelamim*]" (*Lev. Rabbah* 96:9). Apparently, because of the cardinal principles of faith embedded in it, it will never be cancelled.

SHEMINI

The name of the portion, *Shemini*, means "eighth," inasmuch as the portion begins with a description of what took place on the eighth day of consecration of the Tabernacle. It is thus a continuation of the saga that started in the portion of *Tzav*, ch. 8, where the activities of the first seven days are detailed. These activities included washing and dressing Aaron and his sons in their priestly garments, and anointing the high priest[19] (Lev. 8:6-13); bringing a sin offering (a bull, to be burnt in its entirety outside of the Israelite camp), a burnt offering (a ram) and a consecration offering (a ram, a form of thanksgiving offering brought together with ten loaves each of three forms of unleavened bread[20]); sprinkling a mixture of the latter's blood and anointing oil on Aaron, his sons, and their priestly garments; cooking and partaking of the latter sacrifice together with the unleavened bread at the door of the Tent of Meeting; and burning any leftovers (Lev. 8:14-32). Sforno (Lev. 8:2) explains the order of the sacrifices by stating that when a sin offering and a burnt offering are both prescribed, the former always precedes the latter, since one must be cleansed of major sins before proceeding. The burnt offering precedes the consecration

19. In Rashi's view, Aaron's sons were also anointed (Exod. 40:15; 28:41, and Rashi thereon). Lev. 8:12 implies otherwise; see Ramban, Lev. 8:11.
20. Exod. 29:2, and Rashi thereon.

offering for similar reasons, since it too expiates for lesser sins (Lev. 1:4 and Rashi thereon). Only after full atonement was it proper for the priests to pursue their God-designated calling of being the spiritual intermediaries of the Nation of Israel. This entire process was to be repeated each day for seven days, during which time the priests were not to leave the Tent of Meeting (except in case of emergency – Ibn Ezra, Lev. 8:33-34).

Interestingly, this entire section is almost a verbatim repeat of Exodus 29:1-37 in the portion of *Tetzaveh*, where the entire installation process is described after having introduced the priestly garments. Rashi in fact notes this redundancy, saying as follows: "These are [the sacrifices] mentioned with regard to the commands concerning the inauguration in *Tetzaveh*. Now, on the first day of the inauguration, [He] once more alerted them at the time of implementation" (Rashi on Lev. 8:2). In other words, in Exodus the Bible has outlined the procedure in advance, while in Leviticus the process is described in real time.

The service on the eighth day, whose description opens this portion (Lev 9:1-22), is inherently different from that of the previous seven, and is revealed here for the first time. The consecration of the priests has been completed, so no sacrifice is needed for that purpose. Aaron is to bring a sin offering of a calf (to indicate that God has forgiven him for his involvement with the golden calf, Tanchuma *Shemini* 4), which will be burnt outside of the camp, and a burnt offering of a ram. At this stage, the priests will engage in their first acts of ministry for the benefit of the Children of Israel, who have been requested to bring a goat as a sin offering (to atone for the selling of Joseph, when a goat was slaughtered – Chizkuni, Lev. 9:3), a calf and a lamb as burnt offerings (possibly to atone for their much more substantial role than Aaron in the golden calf fiasco; see Ramban, Lev. 9:2), and an ox and a ram as peace offerings. However, the major event distinguishing this day will be the miraculous manifestation of the Divine Presence. In the words of Moses: "For today the Lord will appear to you" (Lev. 9:4). Mention of the expected occurrence of this spectacle is repeated when Moses instructs Aaron regarding the day's proceedings: "And Moses said: 'This is the thing which the Lord commanded you to do, in order that the glory of the Lord may appear to you'" (Lev. 9:6). The occurrence of this phenomenon had been described previously at the end of Exodus, where the Bible states: "and the glory of the Lord filled the Tabernacle" (Exod. 40:34). As will be explained in the next section, the result is outlined in Exodus before its denouement in Leviticus.

INAUGURATION OF THE PRIESTS

Rashi's View:

When were the first seven days of inauguration? Rashi (Lev. 8:2) states that they immediately preceded the erection of the Tabernacle (Exod. 40:17), and although this would imply that Scripture is out of order, this is not problematic, because the Torah is not arranged chronologically.

R. Eliyahu Mizrachi, *in situ*, proposes the following time-line according to this view:

1. 23-29 Adar: Moses consecrated the Tabernacle and the priests. Sacrifices were brought by the *kohanim*.[21] Moses set up the Tabernacle and dismantled it daily.[22]

---

21. Supported by numerous Midrashim, such as *Sifra Tzav, Mechilta de-Millu'im* 36; *Sifrei, Naso* 44.
22. *Sifra, Tzav, Mechilta de-Millu'im* 36; *Num. Rabbah, Naso* 12:15 cites opinions that Moses erected and dismantled it two or three times a day.

2. 1 Nisan: Eighth day of consecration. Moses set up the Tabernacle which would remain in place until it was time to travel (Num. 10:12). Sacrifices were brought both by the nation and the *kohanim*, and God's presence was manifested. Nadab and Abihu were burned to death (Lev 9:1-10:7).[23]

3. 1-12 Nisan: Each day one of the twelve princes brought his offering,[24] as stated in the book of Numbers: "And it came to pass on the day that Moses finished setting up the Tabernacle, and had anointed it and sanctified it, and all of its furniture, and the altar and all of its vessels, and had anointed them and sanctified them, that the princes of Israel... brought their offering before the Lord... each prince on his day" (Num. 7:1-11).

R. Eliyahu Mizrachi explains that the biblical source for Rashi's statement that the Tabernacle was erected on the first of Nisan is the verse in Exodus: "And it came to pass in the first month in the second year, on the first day of the month, that the Tabernacle was set up" (Exod. 40:17). This is the basis for Rashi's stressing that the Bible is not arranged chronologically, for otherwise, how is it that the Tabernacle's construction is already mentioned in Exodus, while the consecration ceremony, which preceded it, is only described in Leviticus?

Ordering the Torah by theme, as opposed to time, was not a new idea for Rashi. In Exodus, Rashi had stated:

Cited by Rashi on Lev. 9:23.
23. Based on a Midrash which appears in numerous collections, perhaps the earliest is *Seder Olam Rabbah* 7. Other locations include BT *Shabbat* 87b; *Sifra Shemini, Mechilta de-Millu'im* A; *Gen. Rabbah, Bereishit* 3; *Num. Rabbah, Naso* 13.
24. Ibid.

The incident of the [golden] calf [in the portion of *Ki Tissa*, ch. 32] occurred a long time before the commandment to work on the Tabernacle [in the portion of *Terumah*, ch. 25, which was intended to atone for the sin of the golden calf], for on the seventeenth of Tammuz the tablets were broken, and on the Day of Atonement God reconciled with Israel, and on the next day they began with the contributions for the Tabernacle, and it was set up on the first of Nisan (Exod. 31:18).

R. Mizrachi also explains that it was necessary to claim that the Tabernacle was erected and dismantled on each of the seven days of inauguration, since it would have been impossible to bring the ceremonial sacrifices if the altar was not yet functional. The Midrash[25] finds a source in the previously quoted verse (Num. 7:1), which includes the words: "on the day that Moses finished setting up the Tabernacle." The Midrash asks why doesn't the verse simply state "on the day that Moses set up the Tabernacle?" Apparently, the verse teaches that Moses set up the *Mishkan* many times, but on the first of Nisan, he set it up for the last time, i.e., he finished setting it up, as recorded in the previously quoted verse from Exod. 40:17.

R. Zvi Grumet[26] has suggested that the theme in Exodus is the return of the *Shechinah* to the Children of Israel, while the theme in Leviticus is the return of the *Shechinah* to Aaron the priest. Parts of the story are therefore repeated, with the emphasis changed. Eventually, both missions were accomplished.

---

25. *Num. Rabbah, Naso* 12:15.
26. Personal communication.

Ibn Ezra's View:

Diametrically opposed to Rashi's view that the order of events is not chronological, Ibn Ezra attempts to equate the sequential and chronological orders, arriving at the following time-line (Exod. 40:2):

1. 1 Nisan: the Tabernacle was set up.
2. 1-7 Nisan: the Tabernacle and the priests were consecrated.
3. 8 Nisan: the eighth day of consecration; Nadab and Abihu were burned to death (Lev. 9:1-10:7).
4. 8-19 Nisan: each day one of the twelve princes brought his offering.

The chronology proposed by Ibn Ezra seems to follow from a straightforward perusal of the relevant verses. Specifically, the *Mishkan* was erected on 1 Nisan (Exod. 40:2 in the portion of *Pekudei*), the priests were consecrated subsequently (Lev. 8 – *Tzav*), the special service of the eighth day took place (Lev. 9 – *Shemini*), and the princes brought their special offerings (Num. 7 – *Naso*). In doing so, Ibn Ezra avoids the need to conjecture that the Tabernacle was erected and dismantled every day during the week of inauguration, an occurrence nowhere explicated in Scripture.

Ramban's View:

With respect to the verse: "And it came to pass in the first month in the second year, on the first day of the month, that the Tabernacle was set up" (Exod. 40:17), at the end of the book of Exodus, which describes the erection of the *Mishkan* that occurred after the seven days of consecration, it was noted that Rashi had no problem with the verses in Leviticus which describe the first day of the consecration ceremony, namely: "Take Aaron and his sons with him... and assemble all of the congregation at the entrance of the Tent of Meeting" (Lev. 8:2). Rashi simply commented: "This section was said seven days before the erection of the *Mishkan*, because there is no earlier or later in the Torah." This flippant reaction was quoted by Ramban (Lev. 8:2), who was upset enough to state: "Why scramble [the order of] the words of the living God?"

In contrast to Rashi, Ramban agrees with Ibn Ezra that the order of the biblical text reflects the chronological sequence of events. He believes the story of the golden calf appears between the command to build the *Mishkan* and its actual construction for a very simple reason—that is when it actually occurred (Exod. 35:1). However, with regard to the date of its consecration, he feels that he has no choice but to agree with Rashi's timeline for two reasons. As quoted in connection with the latter timeline, a plethora of sources accept the first of Nisan as the eighth day of consecration. In addition, The only talmudic reference (BT *Sukkah* 25b) supporting Ibn Ezra is the view of R. Akiva, who says that Mishael and Elzaphan were impure on the fourteenth of Nisan, implying that Nadab and Abihu had died on the eighth of Nisan (or afterwards). However, the Talmud itself rejects this line of reasoning, saying that by the fourteenth they would have already become pure, implying that the tragedy had occurred earlier, such as on the first of the month.

In spite of the fact that Ramban takes the traditional approach that the first of Nisan was the eighth day of the consecration, which had started on the twenty-third of Adar, he still maintains that the Pentateuch does not diverge from chronological order. The questions which Ramban asks on his own theory are presented below, together with his proposed solutions.

1. At the end of Exodus, the Torah states: "And it came to pass in the first month in the second year, on the first day of the month, that the Tabernacle was set up" (Exod. 40:17). However, the portion of *Tzav* in Leviticus deals with the first seven days of consecration, which must have preceded this verse at the end of Exodus.

   Ramban answers that this particular verse is an introductory phrase, which informs the reader that what follows is the description of how the Tabernacle came to be set up in its final form on the first of Nisan. The next verse, which reads, "And Moses set up the Tabernacle," then starts unveiling the entire story from the twenty-third of Adar, all the time adding details and important information about sacrifices at the beginning of the book of Leviticus. The actual implementation is described in ch. 8 of Leviticus.

   Ramban, in Leviticus, adduces a proof to his view. He notes that Exodus ch. 40 is divided into two sections. Verses 1-16 speak of the events scheduled to take place on the first of Nisan, including the consecration of the priests; verses 17-38 speak of the actual implementation, but no mention is made of the involvement of Aaron and his sons, which was to have started from the twenty-third of Adar. Why would the implementation be split between the end of Exodus, where the last item is mentioned (final erection of the Tabernacle), and the beginning of Leviticus, where an earlier occurrence is described (anointing and clothing the priests on the twenty-third of Adar)? Ramban answers:

   > The correct interpretation is that he [Moses] was commanded to erect the Tabernacle on the twenty-third of Adar, and he erected it [then, as described in

the portion of *Pekudei*]. When the Tabernacle stood in its position, God—Who dwells among the Cherubs—called Moses and commanded him concerning the actions involved in bringing sacrifices—all those sections of Leviticus until here [ch. 8], because he wanted to teach him the actions involved in bringing sacrifices and the related laws before he offered them at all, since among the initiation offerings were a sin offering, a burnt offering, and a peace offering, and all of their laws could only be known from these sections which He placed before [bringing the sacrifices]. Afterward, He said to him: "Take Aaron and his sons with him," to direct him at the time of performing what He had told him initially: "And this is the thing that you must do to them to sanctify them to minister to Me as priests" (Exod. 29:1) and here he added "and assemble all of the congregation at the entrance of the Tent of Meeting" (Lev. 8:3), that it should be done in the presence of all of them, so that they know that God chose Aaron and his sons (Lev. 8:2).

2. Regarding the verse at the end of Exodus, "And the cloud covered the Tent of Meeting, and the glory of the Lord filled the Tabernacle," Ramban (Exod. 40:2) quotes a Midrash which states that this event also occurred on the first of Nisan, before the events at the beginning of Leviticus. The Midrash is based on the following verse: "And on the day that the Tabernacle was set up, the cloud covered the Tabernacle" (Num. 9:15). Since the *Mishkan* was set up on the first of Nisan, that must have been the day that the cloud covered the Tabernacle, and perhaps this is

the phenomenon referred to in the portion of *Shemini* by the phrase "for today the Lord will appear to you" (Lev. 9:4). But if the verse from the end of Exodus happened on the first of Nisan, and the events at the beginning of Leviticus happened on the twenty-third of Adar, the text is once more out of sequence. Ramban's rebuttal is that since Scripture had begun describing the unfolding of events from the twenty-third of Adar, it completed outlining the series before delving into the details, even though the last item described actually occurred after events in the next portion. This same approach was taken in the portion of *Vayishlach* in Genesis, which completes the narrative of Isaac's life. His death is described (Gen. 36:28), even though the sale of Joseph (described in *Vayeshev*, the following portion) actually preceded it. Ramban completes his analysis by saying: "This [adding events which actually occurred later, in order to complete a story and continue the narrative] is done frequently. Scripture returns to the beginning of the message which came to Moses from the Tent, and it says: 'And He called to Moses' (Lev. 1:1). All this is now in proper order" (Ramban on Exod. 40:2).

THE EIGHTH DAY OF CONSECRATION

It was noted that after the seven days of inauguration, the priests had been consecrated and were henceforth functional. During the first seven days, Moses himself had fulfilled the priestly role, while the priests were objects of Moses' ministration. By the eighth day, Aaron and his sons were themselves qualified, and so they were commanded to conduct the offering of sacrifices for the purpose of purifying and cleansing themselves and later the entire congregation. Afterwards, the verse states that "Aaron raised his hands toward the people and blessed them" (Lev. 9:22). What blessing did he give them? The Midrash (*Sifra Shemini, Mechilta de-Milu'im* 30) states:

> This blessing has not been elucidated, so one does not know [its contents]. At a later stage, Scripture specifies [it as being]: "May the Lord bless you and keep you. May the Lord's face shine upon you and be gracious unto you. May the Lord lift up His countenance to you, and grant you peace" (Num. 6:24-26).

Rashi understands the Midrash to be saying that the priestly blessing, which appears in its entirety in the book of Numbers, was actually transmitted to Aaron on the eighth day of consecration, although it only appears in writing at a later stage. It has been shown that Rashi believes that the Torah is not arranged in chronological order, so he has no problem with Aaron bestowing a blessing, even though it is only first stated in the book of Numbers.

Ramban, as previously indicated, assumes that the Torah is arranged chronologically. Accordingly, he distinguishes between the blessing here and that written in Numbers. One resolution of the Midrash which he provides (Lev. 9:22) is that Aaron actually gave the exact same blessing as is later recorded. However, it was given here by Aaron alone on an *ad hoc* basis, whereas in Numbers it is formalized as a daily requirement of all of the *kohanim* present in the Temple.

Another answer supplied by Ramban is that Aaron spontaneously prepared a prayer in much the same manner that King Solomon did many years later, when he dedicated the Temple he built (1 Kings 8:55-61).

According to this view, the Midrash wishes to explain that the blessing bestowed at this time was not specified, but that which the priests would be giving throughout the generations was presented in detail in the book of Numbers. There are three reasons to support this last theory of Ramban:

1. With regard to the sacrifices offered by Aaron, it says explicitly that he acted in accordance with the command of Moses (Lev. 9:10). With regard to Aaron's blessing, there is no indication that he did so as a result of Moses' command, allowing the possibility that Aaron's blessing was original.

2. The priestly blessing is formulated word for word in Numbers, but there is no hint of it being said in the present portion. One would expect it to appear in full on this occasion, since this is its first usage in the Bible.

3. The next verse (Lev. 9:23) says that Moses and Aaron blessed the people spontaneously. The Midrash (*Midrash ha-Gadol Shemini*) states, regarding that blessing:

> What was the blessing? R. Meir says they blessed them as follows: They told them: Let the Lord, the God of your fathers, make you a thousand times more [satisfied] than you are (Deut. 1:11). Just as you engaged in the work of the *Mishkan*, and the Divine Presence accompanied your actions, so should you merit to construct before Him the Temple with the Divine Presence accompanying the work of their hands [those who build it]. And they responded: "And let the graciousness of the Lord our God rest upon us and allow us to maintain the work of our hands [i.e., to reap the fruits of our work in our lifetimes], and

allow the work of our hands to be maintained [i.e., to exist even after our demise]" (Ps. 90:17).[27]

The verse from Psalms is in the chapter whose title is "A prayer of Moses" (Ps. 90:1), where Rashi comments that this is one of eleven psalms composed by Moses. Since this blessing was written by Moses (and preserved for generations, eventually finding its way into the book of Psalms), it would seem reasonable to assume that the blessing bestowed by Aaron in the previous verse was also of his own composition.

The Divine Presence descends:

As noted, the eighth day was meant to climax with the appearance of the Divine glory. Rashi (Lev. 9:23) explains that throughout the first seven days of the inaugurarion of the *Mishkan*, the Israelites were nagging Moses, asking to experience the presence of God. Their motive was quite admirable. It was not that they wished to view miraculous deeds as a means of entertainment. Rather, they wished to be assured that they had been forgiven for the heinous sin of worshipping the golden calf. Until the eighth day, Moses was able to procrastinate by saying that the Tabernacle had not yet assumed its final form, and so the time was not yet right for God to appear. On the eighth day he ran out of excuses. Instead of accepting the task of arranging this mini-revelation, Moses transferred the burden to his brother Aaron, telling the Israelites that Aaron was worthier than him because

---

27. *Sifra Shemini Mechilta de-Milu'im* 15 cites a second Tanna's version of the blessing as well. The *Sifra* relates the blessing to the verse in Exodus: "And Moses saw all the work, and behold, they had done it as the Lord had commanded, even so had they done it. And Moses blessed them" (Exod. 39:43). Rashi, who holds that the Bible is not arranged in chronological order, quoted the *Sifra* in both Exodus and Leviticus, apparently because he considers both to refer to the same instance. However, Rashi changes the Midrash slightly in that he has Moses reciting the verse from Psalms, while in the Midrash that verse is the response of the Israelites.

of his function in offering sacrifices and conducting the priestly service. Moses conveyed this idea to the Children of Israel when he said: "This is the thing [the priestly service] which the Lord commanded you to do, in order that the glory of the Lord may appear to you [to Aaron and the entire congregation]" (Lev. 9:6). The only problem with this arrangement was that it made Aaron anxious. What if the glory of the Lord did not manifest itself after he had completed the priestly service? Would he be blamed?

Aaron's uneasiness is the subject of verse 23, which states: "And Moses and Aaron went into the Tent of Meeting, and came out, and blessed the people; and the glory of the Lord appeared to all the people" (Lev. 9:23). The Midrash reflects Aaron's agitation:

> When Aaron saw that all of the sacrifices had been brought and all of the actions had been performed, and yet the Divine Presence had not descended upon the Israelites, Aaron was standing and sighing. He said: I know that the Lord is angry with me [apparently he still felt guilty concerning his role in the golden calf, even though most commentators downplay his culpability].[28] Because of me, the *Shechinah* did not descend upon Israel. This is [the result of] what Moses my brother did to me, for I entered [i.e., accepted upon myself the priestly service, but did not succeed in lowering the *Shechinah*] and [as a result] am embarrassed. Immediately, Moses entered [the Tent of Meeting] with him and prayed for mercy, and the Divine Presence descended upon Israel. That is why it says: "And Moses and Aaron went into the Tent of Meeting" (*Sifra Shemini Mechilta de-Milu'im* 19).

---

28. Abba Engelberg, *The Ethics of Exodus* (2016), pp. 224-244.

It is now clear why the beginning of verse 23 speaks of Moses and Aaron entering the Tent, and why the end speaks of the glory of God descending. The only remaining question pertains to the significance of the middle phrase, which relates that Moses and Aaron blessed the congregation. One might answer that for the *Shechinah* to rest upon Israel, it was necessary for purity and harmony to prevail among all segments of the nation. From their desire for the *Shechinah* to descend, it is clear that the congregation as a whole was eager to repent for the sin of the golden calf. From Aaron's agitation, it is clear that he too regretted any negative involvement that he had in the episode. However, Moses himself had possibly lost his faith in the nation, since he had certainly spoken very harshly to them (Exod. 32:27). Such an attitude could create a dissonance which would prevent the dwelling of the *Shechinah* among the people. By exiting the Tent with Aaron, the beloved defender of the oppressed, and jointly blessing the nation, Moses has at least partially restored the unity that last existed at the time of revelation, when the Jewish people was "as one man with one heart" (Rashi, Exod. 19:2).

A TRAGEDY OCCURS

One of the most shocking episodes in the Pentateuch is the story of Nadab and Abihu. A crowd of at least two million[29] had gathered to witness a revelational experience with miraculous events scheduled to transpire, as the verse states: "For today the Lord

29. The results of the census enjoined in the portion of *Ki Tissa* (Exod. 30:12-13) were 603,550 men above the age of 20 (Exod. 38:26). Since these men each had families with wives and younger children, the total would have been at the very least 3 or 4 times as many. According to the view that the sum includes men only up to the age of 60 (Num. Rabbah 5:2), the total number would be even greater.

will appear to you" (Lev. 9:4). When the heavenly scenario began unfolding, the congregation must have been ecstatic upon seeing the glory of God in the form of a lion made of fire (BT *Yoma* 21b[30]) descend from the heavens; emanate from the Holy of Holies; pass by the incense altar, setting the incense aflame;[31] and finally alight upon the outside altar, where it consumed the daily sacrifice. The setting was captured in the last verse of ch. 9:

> And there came forth a fire from before the Lord, and it consumed the burnt offering and the fat which were on the altar; and when all the people saw it, they exulted and fell on their faces [in gratitude] (Lev. 9:23).

And then, as the congregation broke out in song, a calamity occurred, when "two streams of fire issued from the Holy of Holies, branching off into four, and two entered into the nostrils of the one [Nadab] and two entered into the nostrils of the other [Abihu] and burned them" (BT *Sanhedrin* 52a; *Sifra Shemini, parsha* A), as described at the beginning of the next chapter: "And there came forth a fire from before the Lord, and it devoured them, and they died before the Lord" (Lev. 10:2).

The Talmud (BT *Sanhedrin* 52a) debates whether the words "it devoured them" imply that both body and soul were burnt, or whether just their internals were seared, leaving their bodies intact, as if they died of gas poisoning. According to both views, however, the burning sensation was initiated from within, entering through

---

30. According to Rashi, it was the glowing ember which took the form of a lion. Me'iri and Maharsha, however, say it was the fire itself which assumed that form, and the reason is that Solomon was from the tribe of Judah, which was compared to a lion (Gen. 49:9).

31. The incense offering preceded the continual burnt offering. See BT *Yoma* 33b.

the nostrils, which represent the spiritual connection between the body and the soul, as the verse in Genesis states: "and He breathed into his nostrils the breath of life, and man became a living soul" (Gen. 2:8).

One should note the resemblance between verses 9:23 and 10:2. According to Ibn Ezra, after a fire descended miraculously and burned the sacrifices (9:23), a second fire was issued for the express purpose of slaying Nadab and Abihu (10:2; Ibn Ezra on Lev. 10:1). Rashbam (10:2), on the other hand, perhaps because of the similarity between the two, considers them both to be referring to the same event, with the first serving as an introduction, and the second explaining in greater detail why this tragedy occurred.

THE SIN OF NADAB AND ABIHU

The Torah specifies the sin which brought about the terrible fate of Nadab and Abihu:

> And the sons of Aaron, Nadab and Abihu, each took his censer, and put fire in it, and laid incense on it [the fire], and brought a strange fire before the Lord, regarding which He had not commanded them (Lev. 10:1).

The simple meaning of this verse is that Nadab and Abihu performed an action which they were not authorized to do, namely the burning of incense, and were accordingly punished. A number of questions may be posed.

Question 1: Why was the punishment so severe?

The punishment seems to be out of proportion. To quote the Midrash:

> Titus the wicked entered the Holy of Holies with his sword drawn. He pierced the curtain and when he withdrew his sword, it was dripping with blood. Nevertheless, he entered in peace and exited in peace. The sons of Aaron entered in order to sacrifice and exited asphyxiated and charred (*Lev. Rabbah* 20:5).

Question 2: Does God desire human sacrifice?

Question 1 related to the lack of clarity with regard to the specific sin committed by Nadab and Abihu, but it was assumed that they had in fact sinned. Rashi on the third verse of ch. 10, however, gives the impression that Nadab and Abihu were completely innocent, which certainly contradicts the first verse of the very same chapter, which imputes a sin to them, even if its exact nature is undefined.

After the death of Nadab and Abihu, the Bible states: "And Moses said to Aaron: 'Concerning this the Lord spoke, saying: Through those who are close to me will I be sanctified, and before all the people I will be glorified.' And Aaron held his peace" (Lev. 10:3). Rashi wondered where, in fact, the Lord had said that he would be "sanctified" by the death of those close to him. In answer, Rashi quotes the following talmudic text:

> "And there [in the *Mishkan*] I will meet with the Children of Israel, and it will be sanctified by My glory [*bi-chevodi*]" (Exod. 29:43). Do not read *bi-chevodi*, but *bi-chevudai* [the *Mishkan* will be sanctified by My honored ones]. This [hinting at the death of Aaron's sons] the Holy One,

blessed be He, said to Moses, but he did not know [its meaning] until the sons of Aaron died. When the sons of Aaron died, he [Moses] said to him: "Aaron my brother! Your sons died only so that the glory of the Holy One, blessed be He, might be sanctified through them." When Aaron realized that his sons were God's honored ones, he remained silent, and was rewarded [for his silence], as it says, "And Aaron held his peace" (BT *Zevachim* 115b).

According to *Lev. Rabbah* (12:2),[32] Moses told Aaron that God had already informed him at Mt. Sinai that the Tabernacle would be sanctified through the death of a great person, and he had assumed that God was referring either to himself or to Aaron, but now that it turned out that Nadab and Abihu were intended, the implication is that the latter are even greater than Moses and Aaron.

The preceding Midrash is disturbing on a number of levels. Both Maharsha (BT *Zevachim* 115b) and *Torah Temimah* (Lev. 10:3) point out that the Midrash implies the complete innocence of Nadab and Abihu, in spite of the verse which says otherwise. But much more problematic is the implication that God's name would be sanctified by the death of innocent people. Does God savor human sacrifice? Is opposition to the cult of the Molech (Lev. 20:20) based more on jealousy of other gods than moral values? Was the binding of Isaac not a one-time occurrence, but rather a norm of worship in the Jewish religion? God forbid that this be the case!

Question 3: What was the sin?

Was there in fact no command to bring a "strange fire"? In actuality, the Torah states explicitly in the portion of *Vayikra*, which is

32. Quoted by Tosafot in *Zevachim*, as well as by Rashi on Lev. 10:3.

directed at the *kohanim*: "And the sons of Aaron the priest will put fire upon the altar" (Lev. 1:7), whereupon the Midrash (cited by Rashi) comments:

> Even when the fire descends from heaven, it is a mitzvah to bring fire kindled by man. The fire which descended in the time of Moses never left the copper altar until they arrived at the eternal house [the First Temple], the fire which descended in the time of Solomon never left the burnt offering [copper] altar until it was extinguished in the time of [King] Manasseh.[33]

In other words, Nadab and Abihu were merely following the biblical injunction to add a humanly ignited fire to that which descended from heaven, in order to stress the importance of man's involvement in the service of the Lord and the perfection of the world as an active participant, rather than as a passive recipient of the grace of God.

ANSWERING THE
FIRST AND SECOND QUESTIONS

The first question relates to the severity of the punishment, and the second to whether God approves of human sacrifice.

Regarding the sanctification of the Tabernacle by the death of holy people (question 2), Maharsha (BT *Zevachim* 115b)

33. *Sifra Vayikra – Dibura de-Nedava* 4:5:10; BT *Yoma* 21b. Ben Yehoyada states that the fire lit in the time of Moses continued burning on the altar until the fire in the time of Solomon descended. Me'iri claims that the fire miraculously descended daily. According to both views, the Talmud *in situ* says that the miracle continued also during the time of the Second Temple, but the fire was not potent enough to burn the sacrifices.

states explicitly that there is no such concept in Jewish law as punishment without guilt, and the notion of human sacrifice is totally abhorrent. What the passage is attempting to convey, in the view of Maharsha, is that in the case of righteous people, God is especially particular and He exacts a very severe punishment even, or perhaps especially, from the righteous. By doing so, God's name is elevated and sanctified in this world, because obedience to His word becomes more prevalent. When one sees that the righteous are punished for their wrongdoings, using *a fortiori* logic he realizes that the less righteous, namely the average and wicked people, will most certainly be punished.

Were Nadab and Abihu righteous?

There are a number of sources for the tradition that Nadab and Abihu were considered to be very righteous. In the previously quoted Midrash, it was seen that Moses considered them to be greater than he and Aaron, while the *Zohar* (section 3, p. 61b) says that there were none like them (in terms of greatness) other than Moses and Aaron, and accordingly they were called nobles (Exod. 24:11). The Jerusalem Talmud states:

> Said R. Chiya son of Ba: The sons of Aaron died on the first of Nisan, and why is their death mentioned on [in connection with] Yom Kippur (Lev. 16:1)? To teach you that just as Yom Kippur atones for Israel, so the death of the righteous atones for Israel (JT *Yoma* 1:1).[34]

Finally, the Tanna R. Yirmiyah b. Elazar says:

> The death of the sons of Aaron is recorded in four places,

---

34. Also found in *Tanchuma* (Buber), *Acharei Mot* 10.

and in each location their transgression is recorded. Why so many times? To inform you that this sin is the only one they were guilty of (*Lev. Rabbah* 20:8).

The four sources referred to are:

1. In the present portion (Lev. 10:1).
2. In the opening verse of the portion of *Acharei Mot*: "And the Lord spoke to Moses, after the death of the two sons of Aaron, when they drew too near to the Lord and died" (Lev. 16:1).
3. In the census conducted a year after leaving Egypt, at the beginning of the book of Numbers: "And Nadab and Abihu died before the Lord, when they offered a strange fire before the Lord, in the wilderness of Sinai, and they had no children; and Eleazar and Ithamar [their brothers] ministered in the priest's office in the presence of Aaron their father" (Num. 3:4).
4. In the census conducted at the end of the forty-year sojourn in the desert, in the portion of *Pinchas*: "And Nadab and Abihu died, when they offered a strange fire before the Lord" (Num. 26:61).

It should be noted that there are other sources which indicate that the sins of Nadab and Abihu were somewhat more extensive. One of these sources relates to an event which culminated in the making of a sacrificial covenant between God and the Israelites, which is described at the end of the portion of *Mishpatim*. The text states:

> Then Moses, and Aaron, Nadab, and Abihu, and seventy of the elders of Israel ascended; and they saw the glory of the God of Israel; and under His feet was the likeness of a brick of sapphire stone, which was as clear as the

heavens. And He did not lay His hand upon the nobles of the Children of Israel; and they gazed at God, and they ate and drank (Exod. 24:9-11).

Rashi, based on the Midrash,[35] explains that the nobles, in the last verse, refers to Nadab, Abihu, and the elders. The text says that God did not punish them, implying that they deserved to be punished, because they gazed at God light-heartedly, as if associating with God were a matter of eating and drinking. However, God did not wish to diminish the joy and merriment at the occasion of receiving the Torah, so He delayed the punishment of Nadab and Abihu to the eighth day of the inauguration, and the punishment of the elders to the massacre at Taberah (Num. 11:1-3) and Kibroth ha-Ta'avah (Num. 11:4-34).

The *Zohar* (*Acharei Mot* p. 57a) provides a basis for the claim that Nadab and Abihu were punished for more than one sin. Recall the first verse of *Acharei Mot*: "And the Lord spoke to Moses, after the death of the two sons of Aaron, when they drew too near to the Lord and died" (Lev. 16:1). The *Zohar* asks: Why are the last two words of the verse (and died) necessary? It is stated at the beginning of the verse that they died. The *Zohar* answers that they were culpable for two sins that carried the death penalty.

It should be noted that the story at the end of *Mishpatim* does not have to be interpreted to the detriment of Nadab and Abihu. Onkelos (Exod. 24:11) translates the last phrase as follows: they perceived God's magnificence and rejoiced in their sacrifices, which were accepted as if they had eaten [them] and drunk [with them].

However, even if Nadab and Abihu had more than one sin, they could still be considered righteous. In addition, even if they were

---

35. *Tanchuma* (Buber) *Beha'alotcha* 27; *Targum Yonatan*, Exod. 24:11; *Exod. Rabbah* 3:45; *Num. Rabbah* 15.

not exemplary, they were central figures in the biblical narrative. Exacting punishment of important people has a strong effect on the public not only if those punished are otherwise righteous people, but just because they are well-known public figures, as Nadab and Abihu certainly were.

Maharsha's justification for the severity of the punishment had to do with instilling basic discipline in the nation. Torah Temimah (Lev. 10:3) provides a specific reason for why the additional exhortation was necessary at this point. The concept of the Tabernacle with its associated sacrifices was new to the fledgling nation. The populace associated it with atonement for sins, and indeed, according to many views, the *Mishkan* was built as a means of overcoming the great sense of guilt espoused by the sin of the golden calf. There was a real fear that the masses would come to the conclusion that there is no need to meticulously observe the *mitzvot*, since there exists a magical charm which cleanses all transgressions. It was thus necessary to inform the Israelites that neither the Taberancle nor the sacrifices are meant to atone for willfully ignoring Jewish law. Rather, they offer absolution for inadvertent or accidental transgressions. By imposing the death penalty on Nadab and Abihu for purposeful violation of God's command, even though they were known as *tzaddikim* (righteous people), an important message is being transmitted, namely that in spite of their intimate involvement with the the priestly service, the Tabernacle, and its concomitant sacrifices, they were not exempted from the same punishment for volitional violation of the Torah that would befall any other member of the community.

ANSWERING THE THIRD QUESTION: WHAT WAS THE SIN?

After explaining that Nadab and Abihu were castigated because they sinned, and why it was necessary to do so publicly, it is appropriate to examine in detail what exactly was the sin. It has already been pointed out that in addition to the sin performed on the eighth day of the inauguration, there are views that they were also being punished for a prior sin, transgressed at a time when highlighting the penalty would have been undesirable.

The potential sins are of two types. Since the text says that their transgression was bringing "a strange fire," and since it has been demonstrated that doing so was not necessarily forbidden, various possible interpretations of the textual description will be examined. The second type of sins to be considered will be those attributed to Nadab and Abihu from alternate sources, having nothing to do with the accusatory verse heretofore discussed.

Sins of the First Type:

It was noted earlier that the Torah actually requires the priest to bring a "strange fire," so that could not possibly be the transgression of Nadab and Abihu. The Talmud and Midrash accordingly came to the conclusion that the sin wasn't the act of lighting the fire itself, but rather the fact that they did so in front of Moses without first conferring with him. In the words of the Talmud: "R. Eliezer stated: The sons of Aaron died only because they made a legal decision in the presence of their teacher Moses" (BT *Eruvin* 63a),[36] a concept elucidated in APPENDIX II: MAKING DECISIONS IN THE PRESENCE OF ONE'S TEACHER.

---

36. Additional sources are: BT *Yoma* 53a; *Lev. Rabbah Acharei Mot* 20:6; *Sifra Shemini* 1:32.

Question of Maharsha:

Maharsha (BT *Eruvin* 63a) asks a number of questions on the claim that the sin of Nadab and Abihu was that they made a decision in the presence of their teacher (Moses).

1. It has been noted that it is a mitzvah for the *kohen* to light the fire himself.
2. This law, which appears in Leviticus, was certainly taught to Nadab and Abihu by Moses.
3. In fact, they must have heard this law, as well as all other laws, four times, as described in the Talmud:

> Our Rabbis learned: What was the procedure of the instruction in the oral law? Moses learned from the mouth of God. Then Aaron entered and Moses taught him his lesson. Aaron then moved aside and sat down on Moses' left. Then Aaron's sons entered and Moses taught them their lesson. His sons then moved aside, Eleazar taking his seat on Moses' right and Ithamar on Aaron's left. R. Judah stated: Aaron was always on Moses' right. Then the elders entered and Moses taught them their lesson, and when the elders moved aside all the people entered and Moses taught them their lesson. It follows that it [the lesson] was transmitted to Aaron four times, to his sons three times, to the elders twice, and to all the people once. Moses left and Aaron taught them [everyone else] his lesson. Then Aaron left and his sons taught them their lesson. His sons left and the elders taught them their lesson. It follows that everybody heard the lesson four times. From here R. Eliezer inferred: It is a man's duty to teach his pupil [his lesson] four times. Using *a fortiori* logic: If Aaron, who

learned from Moses, while Moses [had learned it] from God, had to learn his lesson four times, how much more so an ordinary pupil who learns from an ordinary teacher (BT *Eruvin* 54b).

Summarizing, Maharsha says that in this case there was certainly no need to ask Moses, because Nadab and Abihu had in fact already heard the law from him. It was thus in the category of a well-known law which does not require the student to consult his teacher.

Ra'avad (quoted in Ritva, *Eruvin* 63a) answers that the situation was not at all simple. It is true that in addition to the heavenly fire, the *kohen* was also instructed to light one, but that was said with respect to the outer copper altar, upon which the animal offerings were brought. The incense, on the other hand, was brought on the inner golden altar. The proper procedure was to take a burning ember from the outer altar and transfer it to the inner altar. Since their mistake was inadvertent, they would not have been punished so harshly, except for the fact that they should have referred the question to Moses, and thus they transgressed the rule to not make such decisions on one's own.

Tosafot (BT *Eruvin* 63a, s.v. *mai darush*), on the other hand, considers it unlikely that Nadab and Abihu, who were after all great scholars, would have erred to such an extent. He therefore says that there was a one-time decision that the incense on the eighth day would be offered on the copper altar.

Basing himself on this Tosafot (assumedly), Maharsha then explains that the situation was nevertheless not that straightforward. Although the verse in Leviticus said explicitly that the *kohen* should put fire on the altar, it does not mention the source of the fire. It may be that the verse requires the priest to take an ember from the heavenly fire and transfer it to a different location on the outer altar (in this case), just as he is required to transfer it to the inside altar in the routine case. Although that is incorrect, and Nadab and Abihu actually acted properly by lighting an external fire, they still should have clarified the issue with Moses rather than acting on their own. The phrase "which he had not commanded them" (Lev. 10:1) refers to the fact that Moses had not commanded them to bring the fire, rather they brought it on their own. The word "he" thus refers to Moses, rather than the Almighty, and this approach fits the Talmud's statement that they were punished so harshly for not first discussing the topic with Moses.

OTHER SUGGESTIONS FOR SINS OF THE FIRST TYPE: BRINGING "A STRANGE FIRE"

Rashbam:

It has been noted that Rashbam (Lev. 10:1) believes that the fire which descended at the end of ch. 9 and beginning of ch. 10 refer to the same event, i.e., there was only one fire, and it descended after Nadab and Abihu had lit the incense in their own pans. Although the priests had indeed been commanded to kindle their own fire, that was on typical days. This was a special day in that the fire was to descend from heaven in a spectacular manner, creating an epiphanal experience which would be engraved in the memories of the entire congregation. Moses did not want the effect to be diluted by Nadab and Abihu lighting a second fire. Rashbam compares the wish of Moses to the words of Elijah the prophet, "do not place fire" (1 Kings 18:25), when he wished to impress the nation by the miraculous descent of the fire on his sacrifice, as opposed to that of the prophets of Baal.

Rashbam does not clarify whether Moses had specifically commanded them not to kindle a fire, but he definitely implies that they should have waited for the heavenly fire (which they and all of the congregation knew about).[37] The meaning of the phrase "which he had not commanded them" is thus a fire which Moses did not order nor want on this particular day. Unfortunately, Nadab and Abihu were more intent on focusing the attention of the multitude on themselves than on enabling the Lord's name to be sanctified.

Da'at Zekenim mi-Ba'alei Tosafot does not go quite as far as Rashbam in that it says that the *kohanim* were to add their own fire even on the eighth day of consecration. However, it was to be done only after the heavenly fire descended, and Nadab and Abihu decided on their own to do it before (or perhaps simultaneously), and in that sense they made a halachic decision without consulting their mentor.

Sforno:

The commentators until now have all assumed that the fire lit by Nadab and Abihu was in connection with the daily incense offering. Sforno (Lev. 10:1) considers the fire ignited by Nadab and Abihu to be a totally extraneous fire, whose necessity was a figment of their imagination.

In connection with the daily burnt offering, the Bible states: "It should be a continual burnt offering throughout your generations [brought] at the door of the Tent of Meeting before the Lord, where I will meet with you, to speak to you there" (Exod. 29:42). Nadab and Abihu concluded that since God spoke of meeting Moses

37. Although the incense is generally offered before the parts of the morning burnt offering (Mishnah *Yoma* 3:5), the fire on the outside altar is already lit, but here Nadab and Abihu lit their fire before there was fire on the outside altar.

every day after sacrificing the burnt offering, and since incense was brought after that sacrifice, this implies that after any form of revelational activity, incense was to be offered. Since the presence of God was meant to appear on the eighth day of consecration, they deduced, of their own volition, that incense should be brought. This, then, was the "strange fire which He had not commanded them" (Lev. 10:1).

Abarbanel – many sins alluded to in the same verse:
Unlike the previous commentators, each of whom suggested a specific sin which was transgressed, Abarbanel (Lev. 10:1) suggests that Nadab and Abihu were guilty of many sins, all of which are hinted at in the text, an approach which makes their harsh punishment more acceptable. The verse "And the sons of Aaron, Nadab and Abihu, each took his censer, and put fire in it, and laid incense on it, and brought before the Lord a strange fire, regarding which He had not commanded them" (Lev. 10:1) is parsed so that it hints at a series of sins, as follows:

1. **And the sons of Aaron, Nadab and Abihu:** Nadab and Abihu were merely "the sons of." Even if Nadab and Abihu made no mistakes, who invited them to actively participate?

    On the eighth day, Moses would not have allowed anyone other than Aaron to perform the service, as the verse states: "And Moses said to Aaron: 'Draw near the altar, and offer your sin offering… and make atonement for yourself, and for the people… as the Lord commanded'" (Lev. 9:7).

    As far as incense is concerned, the Mishnah (*Yoma* 1:2) explains that the high priest would offer it when he chose to, and otherwise it was raffled among the priests (Mishnah *Yoma* 2:4), and the Talmud (BT *Yoma* 26a) adds that since by tradition the one who offered the incense would become wealthy, no priest was allowed more than one turn.

If Aaron was designated to conduct the animal sacrifices, how much more so would he have brought the incense, which was much more spiritual in nature? Furthermore, the eighth day of consecration, concerning which the Bible states: "today *the Lord will appear to you*" (Lev. 9:4), was comparable to the Day of Atonement, concerning which it says that the high priest would "place the censer... *before the Lord* " (Lev. 16:12), and indeed on that day all of the service was performed by the high priest exclusively.

2. **each took his censer:** the incense service is meant to be performed by one priest alone, not by more than one as in the case of the congregation of Korah, and doing so is a serious offense. Interestingly, Alshich (Lev. 10:1-2), basing himself on *Lev. Rabbah* 20:8, explains the transgression in the opposite manner. They were punished for not acting jointly—each took his own censer independently of the other. Had they discussed the matter, perhaps they would have seen the folly of their actions.

3. **and put fire in it, and laid incense on it:** Abarbanel understands this phrase as follows: *and put fire in it* [inside of the incense], *and* [after having] *laid incense on it* [the pan]. They placed fire (charred wood) in the incense after the incense had already been placed on the censer, when the order should have been reversed.[38]

---

38. Abarbanel attributes this view to Ramban, although the version of Ramban in front of us says that the sin was that the incense was placed entirely on top of the fire without any part touching the pan, i.e., he understands the verse as follows: and put fire in it [the pan], and laid incense [only] on it [the fire].

4. **brought before the Lord:** hints at the fourth sin, which was that they improperly entered the Holy of Holies, which is the meaning of "before the Lord." This is explicated in the next verse, which says "and they died before the Lord," upon which the Midrash comments: "they stretched out a metal spear and dragged them out [of the Holy of Holies]" (*Sifra Shemini Mechilta de-Millu'im* 35).

5. **a strange fire:** the fire for the incense was supposed to have been brought from the outer altar, as the verse states: "And he will take a censer full of coals of fire from off the [Rashi: outer] altar (Lev. 16:12). Instead, Nadab and Abihu brought an extraneous fire, which is commanded only for animal sacrifices on the burnt offering altar, not incense offerings on the inner altar, as explained in the previous section.

6. **regarding which He had not commanded them:** It was previously noted that the incense offering belonged to the high priest. Aaron was meant to become the high priest, and not his sons. However, Moses served as high priest during the first seven days of the inauguration (Lev. 8) as well as on the eighth day, although he appointed Aaron to fulfill those functions which were specific to the last day (Lev. 9:7; Rashi, Exod. 40:29). Aaron completed these tasks with great success, as noted in the Jerusalem Talmud (*Yoma* 1:1):

> R. Tanchum b. Yuden said: All of the seven days of consecration, Moses served as high priest, and the *Shechinah* did not rest [upon Israel] through his efforts. When Aaron wore the priestly garments and served, the *Shechinah* rested [upon Israel] through his efforts. What is the proof? "For today the Lord will appear to you" (Lev. 9:4).[39]

---

39. Also appears in *Lev. Rabbah* 11:6; *Pesikta Rabbati* 14 – *Parah*; *Tanchuma: Chukat* 21.

That Moses was still functioning as high priest on the eighth day of consecration is stated explicitly in the portion of *Pekudei*, where the consecration is described as follows: "And he [Moses] put the golden altar in the Tent of Meeting before the curtain [of the Holy of Holies]; and he burnt the incense of sweet spices on it, as the Lord had commanded Moses" (Exod. 40:26-27).

If the first sin was that Nadab and Abihu should have given precedence to their father, the sixth sin is that the offering of incense during this period was reserved for Moses alone, and not Aaron. Perhaps this is what was meant when the rabbis accused them of "making a decision in the presence of their teacher," i.e., the decision to usurp the offering of the incense.

Sins of the second type:

The Midrash cites a number of other possible sins committed by Nadab and Abihu not even remotely derivable from Lev. 10:1, the source of most of those listed previously. In fact, these items are associated with the first verse of *Acharei Mot*, which states: "And the Lord spoke to Moses after the death of the two sons of Aaron, when they came near to the Lord and died" (Lev. 16:1).

Additional lessons are based on the redundancy of the second half of the verse. After all, the reason for their demise had already been written in *Shemini*. Apparently, a new rationale for their death is being implied, and it must have something to do with the way that they "came near to the Lord."

1. They offered the incense in a state of inebriation (*Lev. Rabbah* 20:9; *Tanchuma Acharei Mot* 6). The motivation for this reason is probably the contiguity of the description of the death of Nadab and Abihu to the prohibition of drinking before entering the Tabernacle, as expressed in the following verses:

And the Lord spoke to Aaron, saying: "Do not drink any wine or strong drink, neither you nor your sons who are with you, when you go into the Tent of Meeting, in order that you not die; it will be a statute forever throughout your generations" (Lev. 10:8-9).

Ibn Ezra notes that these verses were said to Aaron, rather than Moses, as if to say: This is a warning to protect you and your sons, so that you do not die like your older sons.

Etz Yosef (*Tanchuma Acharei Mot* 6) comments that even though this section is written after the death of Nadab and Abihu, they should have realized on their own that one does not disgrace the Divine service by behaving in such a manner. The following Midrash makes the same point:

This is comparable to a king who had a loyal housekeeper, whom he found one day standing near the door of the local bar [an embarrassment for the king]. He secretly [in deference to his previous loyalty] beheaded him and appointed a replacement, but it was not known why he had executed the first one. However, when he ordered the second one not to enter a bar, we know why he killed the first one (*Lev. Rabbah* 12:1).

The *Matnot Kehunah* (*Lev. Rabbah* 20:9), on the other hand, says that the prohibition to drink wine was actually given before the incident, just that the Torah does not follow chronological order, and so it appears afterward.

In *Gittin* (60a-b), it is stated that eight Torah portions were given on the first of Nisan (the eighth day of consecration), one of them including the command not to drink before performing the Godly service. According to Ibn Ezra (Exod. 40:2), who holds that Nadab and Abihu died on the eighth of Nisan, this would imply that the prohibition was already in effect when they sinned. According to Rashi, however, who holds that they were killed on the first of Nisan, there is no way of knowing whether the law was given before or after Nadab and Abihu were executed, so either of the previously cited views remains possible.

2. They were not wearing one of the official garments that priests were required to wear when officiating (Exod. 28), specifically the robe (*Tanchuma Acharei Mot* 6; *Lev. Rabbah* 20:9). A high priest was required to wear the following eight garments: robe, apron, breastplate, gold plate (on the forehead), tunic, turban, belt, pants. The regular priest wore only the latter four. Two questions present themselves:

    a. Since this transgression is not explicit in the Bible, how was it derived?

    b. Since Nadab and Abihu were not high priests, they were not supposed to be wearing the robe in the first place. In fact, if they wore the robe, they would be deserving of punishment—not if they didn't.

In answer to the first question, it was noted that the opening verse of *Acharei Mot*, "And the Lord spoke to Moses after the death of the two sons of Aaron, when they came near to the Lord and died" (Lev. 16:1), mentions the death of the brothers twice. The death penalty is also applied to a priest who is not properly attired, as stated in the portion of *Tetzaveh*: "And they [the priestly garments] will be on Aaron, and his sons, when they enter the Tent of Meeting, or when they approach the altar to minister in the holy place, in order that they not bear iniquity and die" (Exod. 28:43). However, in addition to this inclusive warning, there is a specific warning that not wearing the robe is a capital offense: "And it [the robe] will be upon Aaron to minister; and its sound [caused by the bells hanging on its hem] will be heard when he enters the holy place before the Lord, and when he comes out, in order that he not die" (Exod. 28:35). By not wearing the robe, a high priest would be susceptible to a double penalty. By mentioning the death penalty twice at the beginning of *Acharei Mot*, the sin of not wearing the robe is being hinted at (*Etz Yosef*, *Lev. Rabbah* 20:6).

Another motivation is supplied by R. David Luriah (Radal, *Lev. Rabbah* 20:22), who cites the verse describing how Moses asked Aaron's cousins, Mishael and Elzaphan, to remove the bodies: "And they drew near, and carried them in their tunics out of the camp, as Moses had said" (Lev. 10:5). He notes that it says they were wrapped in their tunics (which weren't burned), but not their robes—which apparently they weren't wearing.

In answer to the second question, it was previously mentioned that the high priest's robe had bells along its hem, about which the verse states "its sound will be heard when he enters the holy place before the Lord, and when he comes out, in order that he not die" (Exod. 28:35). *Matnot Kehunah* (*Lev. Rabbah* 20:9) takes the verse to mean that not only will the sound be heard, but that it is required that it be heard; hence it is required that the entering priest wear his robe. *Imrei Yosher* (ibid.) goes even further and explains that it is the robe which protects the priest from dying when he enters the holy area, as the verse says, "in order that he not die." Also noted previously was that one of the sins which can be derived from the verse describing their offense is that they improperly accessed the Holy of Holies. Accordingly, since they were intent on entering the Holy of Holies, they should have done so wearing robes, and if they didn't, they were missing a garment.

3. They neglected to wash their hands and feet before performing the priestly service. Once again, this sin is not mentioned in the text, and it is derived, as in the case of not wearing the robe, by virtue of the death penalty being inscribed twice with regard to washing, just as it is mentioned twice in the first verse of *Acharei Mot* (*Etz Yosef, Tanchuma Acharei Mot* 6). With regard to hand washing, it first says: "When they go into the Tent of Meeting, they should wash with water, so that they do not die" (Exod. 30:20).

    This verse is immediately followed by another mention of the death penalty: "And they will wash their hands and their feet, so that they do not die" (Exod. 30:21).

4. They did not have children. This is derived from the reference to their death when the next census of the tribe of Levi was taken, where it says:

> And Nadab and Abihu died before the Lord, when they offered a strange fire before the Lord, in the Wilderness of Sinai, and they had no children; and Eleazar and Ithamar ministered in the priest's office in the presence of Aaron their father (Num 3:4).

If Nadab and Abihu had children, their names would certainly have been mentioned in this verse, since they would have taken precedence over Eleazar and Ithamar in the priestly service (*Lev. Rabbah* 20:11). That being the case, there was no need to specifically mention that "they had no children." By noting this fact, the verse apparently means to enumerate it as a possible cause of their death. R. Ze'ev Wolf Einhorn (Maharzo) notes that had they been married, they would not have been faulted for being childless, since that would be an act of God. But since they didn't marry, they were not fulfilling the mitzvah to be fruitful and multiply, concerning which it states: "He who spills a man's blood, by man his [own] blood should be shed; for man was made in the image of God. And you should be fruitful and multiply" (Gen. 9:6-7).

The juxtaposition between murder and having children equates the former with the lack of the latter. *Etz Yosef* (*Tanchuma Acharei Mot* 6) says that, admittedly, not having children is not a capital offense; however, together with other sins, they were deserving of the death penalty. Another possibility proposed by him is that even a minor sin is punishable by death for a priest who serves in the presence of God and is thus held to a higher standard.

5. They were not married, apparently because they were quite conceited and felt that no woman was good enough for them. The Midrash states:

> What did they say? Our father's brother is a king. Our mother's brother is a prince. Our father is a high-priest, and we are two assistant priests. What woman is [possibly] suitable for us? (*Lev. Rabbah* 20:10).

A number of commentators (e.g., Maharzo and *Yefat To'ar*) question the attribution of their vainglory to the appointment of their father as high priest, and themselves as asssitants, since that only occurred on the day of their death. Perhaps one could say that the looming of the appointment was known well in advance. Alternatively, Maharzo explains that their smugness stemmed from the fact that their grandfather Amram was the head of the Sanhedrin and one of the outstanding scholars of his generation; their father Aaron was already a prophet in Egypt; their uncles were Nachshon b. Aminadav—who, on that very day was the first among the princes to offer consecration sacrifices (Num. 7:12)—and Moses; and they themselves were considered to be greater than any of the elders, which may be noted by the ordering of the names in the verse at the end of *Mishpatim*: "And to Moses He said: 'Come up to the Lord, you, and Aaron, Nadab, and Abihu, and seventy of the elders of Israel; and worship from a distance" (Exod. 24:1).

The language of the Midrash is especially harsh, claiming that many outstanding women wasted their younger years waiting in vain for them to choose wives. The word used to describe these women is *agunot,* meaning "chained women."

6. The Midrash continues to point out what seems to be a character flaw, namely that they openly said (or at least thought) that they were eager for the day when Moses and Aaron would die, so that they would be able to rule over the congregation. Maharzo explains that they were actually superior to Moses and Aaron in their conceptual ability (as previously cited from *Lev. Rabbah* 12:2, and Rashi on Lev. 10:3), but were inferior in their personality traits, especially with regard to modesty, as opposed to the well-known verse that Moses was very meek, more than any man upon the face of the earth (Num. 12:3). The Slonimer Rebbe, R. Shalom Noach Berezovsky, taking a Chasidic approach, explains that even if a student is greater than his teacher, he should retain his subservience to him and

accept his decisions, because it is through his teacher that he establishes and develops his attachment to the Divine spirit.

SUMMARIZING THE REASONS

Many different reasons for the untimely death of the sons of Aaron have been recorded. Some have to do with the technicalities of their offering, such as whether it could be offered jointly by two priests, what should be placed on the pan first—the coals or the incense or even what should be the source of the fire. Others had to do with their personality flaws, in particular the haughtiness which led them to denigrate others, be they members of the congregation or even Moses and Aaron themselves. Some of the reasons combined their bad traits with their performance as priests, by saying that because of their arrogance they usurped a task without permission, namely the offering of the incense, which was not meant for them. It was pointed out that this behavior was understandable, because they were apparently of superior intelligence and knowledge, but it was still not justifiable.

The most commonly quoted explanation is that they made a legal decision concerning the source of the fire to be used for the incense offering in the presence of their teacher. R. Kook has explained the predominance of this reason as resulting from its combination of two factors: the pure halachic aspect, namely the proper source of the fire to be used, and the moral aspect, namely displaying proper respect for one's teachers and elders. Of course, laxity in following the proper procedural instructions in administering the holy service manifests a lack of respect for the highest authority. R. Kook goes on to say that as important as the ministerial details are, one's moral behavior takes precedence, even if it might lead to a diminution of the absolute correctness from a halachic point of view.

TAZRIA

After dealing with the laws of the Sanctuary— sacrifices and the inauguration of the Tabernacle—in the first ten chapters of Leviticus, the text proceeds to enumerate the laws of purity. Ch. 11 in *Shemini* lays out the dietary laws, whose non-observance leads to a state of impurity through consuming or even touching carcasses of unclean creatures. Ch. 12 in the portion of *Tazria* speaks of the impurity caused by childbirth, while ch. 13 (and ch. 14 in *Metzora*, the next portion) deals with the impurity of someone who contracts leprosy. Ch. 15 in *Metzora* deals with impurities resulting from bodily secretions.

The Midrash explains the sequence of these chapters as follows (*Lev. Rabbah* 14:1):

> R. Simlai said: Just as the creation of man (Gen. 1:27) follows that of animal, beast, and fowl (Gen. 1:25), so his laws follow those of animal, beast, and fowl. That [explains] what is written: "This is the law of the animal, [and of the fowl, and of every living creature that moves in the waters, and of every creature that swarms upon the earth]" (Lev. 11:46), and afterwards: "When a woman conceives" (Lev. 12:1).

R. Zalman Sorotzkin (*Oznayim la-Torah*, Lev. 12:1) explains that since the continued existence of the world was conditional upon Israel's acceptance of the Torah, the enumeration of its laws was in a way equivalent to creation, and accordingly the Law was presented in the same order as creation. Laws relating to animals, which were created first, precede those relating to human beings, once again reinforcing the idea that man is the pinnacle of creation.

Observing the laws of purity allows each Israelite as an individual and the congregation as a whole to complete one of the steps necessary for the achievement of holiness, which is (roughly) the translation of the title of the seventh portion of Leviticus: *Kedoshim*. The entire subject will be discussed in the context of that portion.

PURITY AND IMPURITY: DEFINITIONS

The states of being impure and pure are called, in biblical Hebrew, *tum'ah* and *taharah*, respectively, and one who is in one of those states is said to be *tamei* or *tahor*.

Malbim (*Vayikra* 306) points out that there are two usages of the word *tum'ah* in the Bible. One he calls *tum'at ha-nefesh* (spiritual impurity), which is used to express disgust with various activities but does not symbolize a halachic state of being, and accordingly has no associated ritual means of purification. The second is called *tum'at ha-guf* (bodily impurity), and it indicates a halachically well-defined state with clear-cut rules of behavior while impure, and pre-determined actions to extricate oneself and regain one's purity. Spiritual impurity results from the commission of serious sins, such as murder or incest. Physical impurity results from certain conditions or actions, e.g., leprosy or contact with items considered detestable, such as corpses or carcasses. A thorough discussion is presented in Appendix III: Spiritual and Physical Impurity.

Motivation for the Laws of Purity

A number of different explanations for the detailed laws of purity have been proposed. Some have translated *tamei* as "unclean" and *tahor* as "clean," which would imply that these laws have something to do with hygiene, along the lines of the well-known maxim "cleanliness is next to Godliness." Indeed, the cause of *tum'ah* is contact with possibly infected items, such as the disintegrating corpse of a human being or an animal; a person suffering from leprosy; or bodily secretions, some of which result from sexual disorders. Furthermore, the purifying ritual was composed of commonly accepted techniques of disinfection, namely allowing a certain amount of time to lapse and bathing oneself in clean water. In short, *tum'ah* devolves on one who is infected or has been in close proximity to infection; he is separated (or even secluded) in order to prevent the spreading of the infection, and is then disinfected by means of immersion in water.

However, there are reasons to reject the hygienic motivation. First, the Torah relates *tum'ah* to *kedushah* (holiness), which relates to spiritual health rather than physical health. Consider the following verses, which follow the listing of forbidden foods:

43. Do not make yourselves detestable with any swarming thing that swarms; do not make yourselves unclean (*tamei*) with them, that you should become defiled (*tamei*) thereby. 44. For I am the Lord your God; sanctify

yourselves and be holy, for I am holy; do not make your souls unclean (*tamei*) with any manner of swarming thing that moves upon the earth (Lev. 11).

If sanctification results in part from refraining from eating prohibited foods, the consequences of avoiding *tum'ah* must be spiritual and not merely hygienic (even if one accepts the view of Rambam, *Guide for the Perplexed* 3:48, that the dietary laws are health-based, holiness is certainly spiritually-based). Furthermore, the distinction which Malbim made between spiritual and physical impurity indicates that a significant portion of the states-of-being associated with the word "impurity" relate to metaphysical wrongdoing, and it is thus reasonable to assume that the remaining portion—that associated with physical impurity, is no different.

Another point which negates the health connection is the fact that according to *halachah*, Gentiles are exempted from the demands of ritual impurity. The Talmud (BT *Nazir* 61b) bases this on the verse that one who enters the Temple when impure "will be ostracized from the community" (Num. 19:20), which implies that only those who are in the community in the first place (i.e., Jews) are subject to the laws of purity and impurity. In a similar vein, the Mishnah (*Negai'm* 3:1) states that heathens and resident aliens in the Land of Israel cannot be declared to be ritual lepers. If ritual purity had anything to do with cleanliness, it could be spread by any person. But if it is meant to impart a lesson, it is relevant only to those whose mission is to promulgate that lesson.

THE VIEW OF RAMBAM

A statute devoid of reason:

In one location, Rambam has taken the easiest path and avoided the necessity to rationalize the entire system of tum'ah and taharah by stating:

> It is clear and obvious that the defilements and purifications are Divine decrees, and are not among those things which man's knowledge can determine, and behold they are among the statutes. Similarly, ritual bathing for [cleansing] defilement is among the statutes, for defilement is not mud or excrement that is cleansed by water, but rather a Scriptural decree (*Hilchot Mikva'ot* 11:12).

A simulatory reason:

Nonetheless, Rambam does give a hint as to the reason for the entire system. The previously quoted text continues:

> This act [ritual bathing] depends on the heart's intention. Therefore, the rabbis said: If he bathed without intent, it is as if he didn't bathe (BT *Chagigah* 18b). And even so, there is a hint regarding this: Just as one who readies himself to be purified, once he immerses is purified, even though nothing was renewed in his body; similarly, one who readies his heart to purify himself from spiritual impurity, which is [composed of] wicked thoughts and bad traits—since he accepted upon himself to withdraw from that [evil] counsel and brought his soul to the waters of knowledge—he is pure. It [the Bible] says: "And I will sprinkle clean water upon you, and you will become clean;

of all your uncleanness, and of all your idols, will I cleanse you" (Ezek. 36:25).

Rambam's explanation relates physical impurity to spiritual impurity. He is saying that when cleansing himself of his physical uncleanness, one may imagine that he is cleansing himself of his evil behavior and bad traits, and with enough effort, it may succeed.

To teach respect:

Another rationale may be derived from Rambam's words in *Hilchot Tum'at Ochlin* (16:8), where he clarifies that all of the prohibitions in the Torah concerning being *tamei*, spreading impurity, or eating impure foods relate to two very specific situations: entering the Temple and touching/eating holy food—whether sacrificial meat, the heave offering. or the second tithe—which must be consumed in Jerusalem. He bases this on the verse in *Tzav* which explains the disposition of meat from a peace offering which has become *tamei*: "And flesh that touches any unclean thing may not be eaten; it should be burnt with fire" (Lev. 7:19). Rambam says that since this verse refers specifically to holy meat, the clear implication is that no such prohibition exists when the meat is not intrinsically holy.

Furthermore, it is permitted for a non-priest to touch a dead body or any other impure object from the outset, thereby becoming *tamei*, a ruling which the Talmud (BT *Rosh Hashanah* 16b) derives from the verse in which God tells Moses: "Speak to the *priests who are the sons of Aaron*, and say to them: 'Nobody should defile himself [by coming in contact] with the dead among his people'" (Lev. 21:1). Likewise, regarding a Nazirite it states: "All the days that he has consecrated himself to the Lord he should not approach a dead body" (Num. 6:6), implying that he may do so at the culmination of his vows.

Levites and Israelites, in other words, are unconditionally permitted to allow themselves to become impure. After all, how would the dead be buried? In fact, Rambam (*Hilchot Tum'at Ochlin* 16:9) points out that even priests and Nazirites are permitted to allow themselves to become *tamei* from any kind of impurity other than the dead, since, as *Kesef Mishneh* points out, there is no verse which prohibits such contamination.

There are occasions during the year when one is advised to purify himself, as the Talmud states:

> R. Isaac further said: A man should purify himself for the festival, as it says, "[Of their flesh you should not eat] and their carcasses you should not touch; [they are unclean to you]" (Lev. 11:8). It has been similarly taught: "and their carcasses you should not touch." I might think that [ordinary] Israelites are cautioned not to touch carcasses…. If in the case of a serious uncleanness [i.e. touching a corpse] priests are cautioned, but Israelites are not cautioned, how much more so [would they not be cautioned] in the case of a light uncleanness [touching a dead animal]! Why does it say "and their carcasses you should not touch?" [It must be] on a festival (BT *Rosh Hashanah* 16b).

However, even on holidays, according to Rambam (*Hilchot Tum'at Ochlin* 16:9), the prohibition is not intrinsic, but rather because on holidays one wishes to be fit to enter the Temple premises and partake of the holy meat of sacrifices, which must be eaten in purity. Accordingly, Rambam states that if one does not purify himself for the holiday, he is not punished.[40]

---

40. *Kesef Mishneh* bases this on his interpretation of the *Sifra* on Lev. 11:8.

It is now possible to propose a reason for the rules of purity. It has been shown that there is no comprehensive requirement to be in a state of purity; it is only required when entering the Temple, on holidays, and when eating certain holy foods. It is thus seen to serve as a method for generating respect for holy places, times, and objects. It serves as a means of distinguishing between the mundane and the holy. By proferring special treatment to various times, places, and objects, one allows oneself to be inspired by them throughout the year, when engaged in routine activities.

Rambam fleshes out this idea in his *Guide for the Perplexed* (3:47), where he states:

> The object of the Sanctuary was to create in the hearts of those who enter it certain feelings of awe and reverence, in accordance with the command, "You must reverence my sanctuary" (Lev. 19:30). But when we continually see an object, however sublime it may be, our regard for that object will be lessened, and the impression we have received of it will be weakened. Our Sages, considering this fact, said that we should not enter the Temple whenever we liked, and pointed to the words: "Make your foot rare in the house of your friend" (Prov. 25:17). For this reason, the unclean were not allowed to enter the Sanctuary, although there are so many kinds of uncleanliness, that [at one time] only a few people are clean. For even if a person does not touch a beast that died of its own accord (Lev. 11:27), he can scarcely avoid touching one of the eight kinds of creeping animals (Lev. 11:29-31), the dead bodies of which we find at all times in houses, in food and drink, and upon which we frequently tread wherever we walk; and, if he avoids touching these, he may touch a woman

in her separation (Lev. 15:18), or a male or female that have a running issue (Lev. 15:2-13, 15:25-27), or a leper (Lev. 13:46), or their bed (Lev. 15:5). Escaping these, he may become unclean by cohabitation with his wife, or by an emission (Lev. 15:16), and even when he has cleansed himself from any of these kinds of uncleanliness, he cannot enter the Sanctuary till after sunset; but not being enabled to enter the Sanctuary at night time, although he is clean after sunset, as may be inferred from [Mishnah] *Middot* and [Mishnah] *Tamid*, he is again, during the night, subject to becoming unclean either by cohabiting with his wife or by some other source of uncleanliness, and may rise in the morning in the same condition as the day before. All this serves to keep people away from the Sanctuary, and to prevent them from entering it whenever they liked. Our Sages, as is well known, said, "Even a clean person may not enter the Sanctuary for the purpose of performing Divine service, unless he previously takes a bath." By such acts, the reverence [for the Sanctuary] will continue, the right impression will be produced, which leads man, as is intended, to humility.

Rabbis Hirsch and Soloveitchik:
Both R. Samson Raphael Hirsch and R. J.B. Soloveitchik feel that *tum'ah* represents the opposite of life, and since life is a positive value which man is urged to make the most of, it follows that death and those phenomena which are reminiscent of it are negative values from which one must distance himself as much as possible. While according to R. Hirsch death, and hence *tum'ah*, represent the loss of free will, R. Soloveitchik stresses the resulting inability to lead the religious life.

According to R. Hirsch, the purpose of life is for man to perfect his spiritual being and ethical behavior by performing actions which enable him to properly mold his personality and exhibit his moral character. Nature itself has no values, so natural forces and instincts which impinge upon man, and to which he is subject, represent powers which oppose man's striving to achieve his desired goals. Death represents such a force, and for that reason death in all of its manifestations is considered inimical to a Jew's *raison d'etre*, hence the special treatment. In his own words:

> … a dead human body… is called *tum'ah*. For, in fact, there lies before us actual evidence that Man must—willy-nilly—submit to the power of physical forces; that this corpse that lies before us is not the real human being; that the real human being, the actual Man, which the powers of physical force cannot touch, had departed from here before the body—merely its earthly envelope—could fall under the withering law of earthly Nature. More, that as long as the real Man, with his free-willed, self-determining Godly nature, was present in this body, the body itself was freed from forced obedience to the purely physical demands, and was elevated into the sphere of moral freedom in all its powers of action and also of enjoyment, when the free-willed ruling of the higher part of Man decided to achieve the moral mission of his life. In short… that in life, thinking, striving, and accomplishing Man can master, rule, and use even his sensuous body with all its innate forces, urges, and powers, with God-like free self-decision, within the limits of, and for the accomplishment of, the duties set by the laws of morality. All these are Truths which, in face of human frailty and the powers of the forces

of Nature which the appearance of Death preaches, are to be brought again and again to the minds of living people, so that they remain conscious of their unique position of freedom in the midst of the physical world, and remain forever armed in proud consciousness of their freedom, armed against the doctrine of materialism.[41]

R. Hirsch goes on to extend this symbolism to all of the variations of *tum'ah*. The formation of the body of large animals is similar to that of men, and therefore their carcasses can simulate the idea of subjection to Nature and the lack of spiritual freedom, and can hence cause uncleanness when touched or carried. Even the eight swarming creatures are vertebrates, and thus do not vary greatly in formation from the human body, just in their size, so their carcasses have been declared to be impure, but only if touched.

R. Hirsch explains that after dealing with carcasses, which awaken the idea of human lack of freedom, at the end of *Shemini*, the Torah proceeds to examine "conditions which are capable of endangering the consciousness of moral freedom to an even higher degree, as they present living Man succumbing to physical necessity." These conditions, dealt with in the portion of *Tazria*, he calls "impurities which emanate from the body," and they include menstrual women (*niddah*), gonorrhoeists (*zav* and *zava*), men having sperm emissions, women giving birth, and victims of *tzara'at*. Because of the danger of these cases having an even stronger influence on human behavior, their treatment is more severe, causing one to be unclean for seven days or longer (as in the case of exposure to a corpse), and requiring one to bring special sacrifices at the end of the period of impurity, as opposed

---

41. Samson Raphael Hirsch, *The Pentateuch*, Vol. 3 (*Vayikra*), New York (1971), p. 308, based on the translation by Isaac Levy.

to the impurity of carcasses which causes *tum'ah* for only one day and has no associated sacrificial requirement. The exception to this rule is menstruant women, who are exempt from bringing sacrifices, and men with spermal emissions, who are free of both the sacrificial and extended time demands. These exclusions relate to more routine occurrences, so it may have been impractical to impose frequent, additional burdens.[42]

R. Soloveitchik, like R. Hirsch, sees *tum'ah* as essentially connected with death, and he says explicitly (*Ish ha-Halachah*, pp. 36-37):

Judaism has a negative view of death and the dead. A corpse defiles, a grave defiles, a person who is defiled by a corpse is impure for seven [days] and is prohibited from eating holy foods and from entering the Temple, a Nazirite who becomes defiled by a corpse loses the previous days of purity and must shave himself and bring a sacrifice. Priests are forbidden to be exposed to the dead. Whoever's holiness is greater than that of his friend, his prohibition to become *tamei* is stricter. A regular priest can allow himself to become defiled to the seven [close] relatives, [but] a high priest (and similarly a Nazirite) cannot become defiled even to them. And when many religions viewed the phenomenon of death in a positive light, which supports and nurtures religious "feeling" and awareness, and they therefore sanctified death, the dead, the grave, for here is the threshold to transcendentalism, the gate to the world to come, a window full of light open to a higher and supreme sphere, Judaism declared impurity with regard to the dead, and detested death,

42. Ibid., p. 320.

destruction, and dying, and chose life and sanctified it. Authentic Judaism, which echoes *halachah*, sees in death a powerful negation and frightening contradiction to the entire religious life-style. Death contradicts the essence of the glorious experience of the man of religion… *halachah* has no affinity to death and burial. On the contrary, it looks upon these pheneomena in a negative manner. "One whose dead [relative] is lying before him is exempt from the recital of *Shema* and from prayer [the *Amidah*] and from [wearing] phylacteries, and from all of the *mitzvot* said in the Torah" (Mishnah *Berachot* 3:1).

While R. Hirsch stresses the importance of the soul, and denigrates the corpse specifically because the "real human being" has departed and all that is left is the "earthly envelope," so that the person can no longer continue to develop his "Godly nature," R. Soloveitchik places the emphasis on perfecting and achieving goals in this world - which is the only playing field for mankind at large. The *mitzvot* are meant to enable one to achieve these goals for the living, and are thus cancelled when one is immersed in dealing with the dead. One may assume that these goals are what has been termed *tikun olam*.

According to these approaches, the various forms of impurity symbolize death in reality or potentiality. Menstruation and seminal emission are the result of the potential for life which did not materialize. As for a leper, the Talmud (BT *Nedarim* 64b) states:

Four are considered as if dead: A poor man, a leper, a blind person, and one who is childless… A leper, as it is written, "[And Aaron looked upon Miriam, and behold, she was leprous. And Aaron said unto Moses…] let her not be as one who is dead" (Num. 12:10-12).

Those mentioned in the talmudic extract are unable to increase the amount of life on earth, either because they did not reproduce or because they are isolated by virtue of their blemish (the blind person), their malady (the leper), or their total absorption in providing for their own needs (the poor).

Although giving birth is a joyous occasion which, on the face of it, adds to the quantity of life on earth, the woman herself must separate from what she has come to consider an integral part of her body. Rabbi Frand (*Rabbi Frand on the Parsha, Tazria*) bases himself on this concept in explaining why the period of impurity when giving birth to a girl (fourteen days, Lev. 12:5) is longer than for a boy (seven days, Lev. 12:2). Specifically, because the degree of holiness associated with a daughter, who herself will in the future become pregnant and add holiness to the world, is greater than that of a boy, also the severance from it represents a greater temporary reduction of the mother's holiness than the birth of a son. Perhaps the symbolic loss of life in the mother's body can help one understand the ostensibly contradictory phenomenon of post-partum depression.

Circumcision

As noted, the portion opens by describing the impurity associated with childbirth in the verse: "If a woman conceives and bears a male, then she will be unclean for seven days" (Lev. 12:2). The following verse is: "And on the eighth day, the flesh of his foreskin should be circumcised" (Lev. 12:3).

Or ha-Chaim asks a simple question. Why is the subject of circumcision broached in this section, which is focused on— and in the middle of the treatment of— the subject of purity and impurity? In addition to being out of context, it has already been presented in the book of Genesis in the portion of *Lech Lecha* (Gen. 17:10), where it is counted by both Rambam and *Sefer ha-Chinuch* as one of the three *mitzvot* commanded in that book (in addition to the commands to be fruitful and multiply,[43] and not to eat the sciatic nerve).[44]

A possible answer to this question may be derived from the *Tanchuma*, which describes a meeting between R. Akiva and the wicked Turnus Rufus, a Roman governor posted in Judea during the first half of the 2nd century CE, who frequently challenged the famous talmudic scholar to debate. One subject concerning which he repeatedly harangued R. Akiva was circumcision, since altering the human body, and specifically the male physique, was anathema to Greco-Roman culture. The Midrash (*Tanchuma, Tazria* 5) states:

> Said Turnus Rufus to him [R. Akiva]: Since He desires [that male children undergo] circumcision, why does it [the baby] not come out circumcised from its mother's womb? Said R. Akiva to him: And why does its umbilical chord come out with it [the baby], hanging from its stomach? Will its mother not cut it off? Regarding what you say, why does it not come out circumcised, because the Lord only gave the *mitzvot* to Israel to purify them [Israel] by means of them. Accordingly, David said: "the word of the Lord is pure" (Ps. 18:31).

It has been noted that according to the views of R. Hirsch and R. Soloveitchik, the purpose of the laws of purity is to stress

---

43. Gen. 1:28, 9:7.
44. Gen. 32:33.

the importance of life and the requirement to use it to achieve holiness, and all that the latter entails. Circumcision symbolizes the same concept, namely that man was not created perfect, just as the world was not created perfect, and the purpose of creation is to give man the opportunity to use all of his talents in efforts to move society and the world at large towards utopia by means of *tikun olam*. In short, both the laws of purity and the mitzvah of circumcision emphasize man's task in this world, and are thus appropriately juxtaposed.

The joint goal of the laws of purity and circumcision may help one understand the following passage (BT *Niddah* 31b):

> And why did the Torah ordain circumcision to be on the eighth day [Rashi: rather than the seventh]? So that everyone [i.e. the guests] should not be happy [Rashi: eating and drinking at the festive meal (given in honor of the circumcision)] while his father and mother are sad [Rashi: on account of the prohibition of intercourse (which remains in force until the conclusion of the seventh day)].

Since both the laws of purity and the command to circumcise stress the same idea—the requirement to be enthusiastic about life and to make the most of it to accomplish the goal of spreading joy to all the inhabitants of the world—it is understandable that on the day of the *brit* (circumcision), all parties should be as happy as possible. In keeping with this view, it is not surprising that the Talmud has a positive attitude toward all kinds of pleasure, including sexual.

Since circumcision emphasizes the task of man in this world, one of the most central themes in Judaism, it is understandable why the penalty for its transgression is the severe punishment of *karet* (excision, Gen. 17:14). Breach of only one other positive commandment— sacrificing the Paschal lamb (*korban Pesach*)— has such a dire consequence.

THE MEANING OF HOLINESS

The sixth portion in the book of Leviticus is *Kedoshim* (which literally means "holy"), where it is written: "Speak to all of the congregation of the Children of Israel, and say to them: 'You should be holy, for I, the Lord your God, am holy'" (Lev. 19:2). In the portion of *Shemini*, holiness was associated with properly obeying the dietary code (Lev. 11:44). In the portion of *Kedoshim*, holiness will be associated with successful fulfillment of a number of other commands, namely those connected to correct sexual behavior and the attainment of a philosophical understanding of Jewish theology, and those social laws which enable the proper functioning of a just society.

From a global point of view, holiness may be said to be composed of three elements:

1. Separation of the Jewish nation from all others by observance of ritual laws which apply to them exclusively, such as the dietary laws.
2. Perfecting themselves as a model nation, which will be dealt with extensively in the portion of *Kedoshim*.
3. Serving as a light unto other nations, as described in numerous places in the book of Isaiah (42:6, 49:6, 60:3).

Although there seems to be some overlap between the concepts of purity and holiness, the latter may be looked upon as being broader and more proactive, while the former may be considered to be narrower and more passive in nature, but a necessary prerequisite for achieving holiness.

METZORA

As noted in the portion of *Tazria*, the notion of impurity in Judaism is generally connected to the concept of death, and it represents the absence of the potential to live, to create, and to improve conditions in the world (*tikkun olam*). This is true whether one is referring to a dead body; an egg or sperm cell which has not been transformed into new life; or even the birthing process, in which new life that was part of the mother's body is detached and ostensibly lost to her. The portions of *Tazria* and *Metzora* deal with impurity related to a dermatological condition, *tzara'at*, commonly translated as leprosy. The question arises: how does this conflate with the conceptual explanation of impurity? If it is because the disease is potentially life-threatening, then everyone suffering from a serious disease should be rendered impure. Furthermore, the Sages never refer to the health-related aspects of *tzara'at*.

As previously indicated, the Talmud states (BT *Nedarim* 64b):

Four are considered as if dead: A poor person, a leper, a blind person, and a childless person... A leper, for it says [when Aaron beseeched Moses to help cure Miriam's leprosy]: "Let her not be as one who is dead" (Num. 12:12).

In what way is a leper equivalent to a dead person? After all, he can still engage in improving the world. The following talmudic text may shed some light on the matter:

> R. Samuel b. Nachmani said in the name of R. Jonathan: As a result of seven sins leprosy comes: slander, bloodshed, lying, incest, arrogance, robbery, and envy [*tzarut ha-ayin*] (BT *Arachin* 16a).

Note that the seven sins enumerated are all *bein adam le-chaveiro* (between man and his fellow man). These are the laws that epitomize the ultimate goal of the Pentateuch, and they may be divided into three groups. One group is composed of internal personality faults, namely arrogance and envy. Another group is composed of major crimes, namely bloodshed, lying, incest, and robbery. In between is slander, which is the first step in translating one's innermost thoughts of the type generated by the first category into actions of the second category. Leprosy is traditionally associated with slander, as it is the first outward manifestation of the dangerous potential embedded in such a person's character, and the procedure which a leper undergoes represents a metaphorical call to examine his personality and make every effort to steer his mind in a more positive direction.

As noted in the portion of *Tzav*, R. Moshe Botschko explains that not only is it prohibited to sin, but one must also refine his personality to the point that he does not have the urge to do so, since otherwise it is difficult to restrain oneself. This is why emotions of the type listed in the first category are also forbidden.

The incidence of leprosy is the Bible's way of indicating that there are situations, other than a person's death, which prevent him from engaging in *tikkun olam*. It can also be negated by decadent behavior, which causes *tzara'at*, which in turn generates *tum'ah*.

The Midrash (*Gen. Rabbah* 9:7) explains that although the evil inclination incessantly tempts one to sin, it is a necessary part of man's makeup, since without it a person would not build a home, marry a wife, father a child, or engage in commerce. In short, it is responsible for lust and ambition, two required ingredients for the successful functioning of the world.[45] On the other hand, when man totally subjugated himself to the dictates of his evil inclination, it became necessary to filter out the villains, and God brought about the great flood. Afterwards, God promised that such a calamity would never again occur (Gen. 8:22). In order to regulate the world, he selected the Jewish nation to excel in moral behavior and serve as an example,[46] but how could God prevent the Jewish nation from degenerating? The answer is by constantly stressing not only moral behavior, but also the evolution of a moral outlook by avoiding sins of the first category. When individual Israelites allowed themselves to develop malicious personalities, *tzara'at* was an instrument that the Almighty could use to tweak the system and avoid the spread of negative behavior to the extent that He would once again be tempted to reign calamity on the entire nation or even the entire world.

Avoiding sins of the first type is also stressed in the Mishnah: "R. Joshua says: Envy, the evil inclination [unbridled], and hatred of mankind remove man from the world" (*Avot* 2:11). The Hebrew word used for envy in this Mishnah is *ayin ha-ra* [literally, "the evil eye"], which is understood to be similar in meaning to *tzarut*

---

45. BT *Yoma* 69b describes the disastrous result of temporarily disabling the evil inclination.

46. According to Prof. Yehuda Levi (*Mul Etgarei ha-Tekufah*, p. 48), their chosenness was not because of their superiority. They were actually considered more rebellious and stubborn than the Gentiles, and so it was necessary for them to receive 613 laws in order to constrain them, rather than the seven which sufficed for the Gentiles.

ha-ayin, one of the seven possible causes of leprosy. The Talmud (BT *Arachin* 16a) defines *tzarut ha-ayin* in connection with the following verses:

> When you have come to the land of Canaan, which I am giving you for a possession, and I put the plague of leprosy in a house on the land of your possession, then he for whom the house is his [who owns the house] should come and tell the priest, saying: "There seems to me to be a plague in the house" (Lev. 14:34-35).

The Talmud wonders why Scripture uses the awkward expression "for whom the house is his," rather than the relatively simple phrase "who owns the house," and it gives the following answer:

> Why does it say "[for whom the house] is his"? [It means to say that] if one devotes his house to himself exclusively, refusing to lend his vessels by saying he has none, the Holy One, blessed be He, publicizes [his belongings] when he empties his house. Thus "is his" excludes [from house leprosy] those who lend their belongings to others (BT *Yoma* 11b).

In the end, *tzarut ha-ayin* may be defined to include dissatisfaction with one's lot in life, envy, (Bartenura, *Avot* 2:11), and selfishness (BT *Arachin* 16a), as well as looking askance at the achievements of others and being unwilling to enjoy their successes (*Tiferet Yisrael, Avot* 2:9, note 91).

Interestingly, the Mishnah cited (*Avot* 2:11) extends the biblical prohibition of not hating one's brother (i.e., another Jew, Lev. 19:17) to not hating any human being. After all, every human being is created in God's image, and one should adopt a positive attitude towards everyone independent of race, religion, or creed.

The phrase "remove man from the world" is also of interest. The simple meaning is that these bad traits shorten a man's life. Rambam precociously notes that socially isolated people develop psychosomatic illnesses and die young. He might have based himself on the talmudic description (BT *Bava Metzia* 107b) of Rav's supernatural ability to visit a cemetery and determine the cause of death of those buried there. Rav concluded that of every one hundred, ninety-nine died of "the evil eye" and only one of natural causes. Another possible explanation of "remove man from the world" is that such behavior will lead to the eventual destruction of mankind in general.

Various authorities, and even the Talmud, have detected hints for the causes of leprosy in the Hebrew words used to describe the disease, *tzaraat* (*tzoraas* in Ashkenazic pronunciation), and the afflicted person, called a *metzora*. The former sounds like the well-known skin disease psoriasis, but also like *tzarut ha-ayin*, "envy." As for the latter, the Talmud sees an equivalence between *metzora* and *motzi shem ra*, "slander" (BT *Arachin* 15b). *Torah Temimah* views the motivation for this explanation as being the unique use of the word *metzora* in this portion, while in all other citations the leper is called a *tzarua* (e.g. Lev. 13:44, 13:45, 14:3, 22:4; Num. 5:1).

BIBLICAL OCCURRENCES

The snake:
The first Midrashic reference to leprosy as a punishment for slander occurs in connection with the story of the tree of knowledge in the Garden of Eden. The Bible states:

2. And the woman said to the serpent: "Of the fruit of the trees of the garden we may eat; 3. but of the fruit of the tree which is in the middle of the garden, God said: You should not eat of it, and you should not touch it, lest you die" 4. And the serpent said to the woman: "You will not die, 5. for God knows that on the day that you eat of it, your eyes will be opened, and you will be like God, knowing good and evil" (Gen. 3).

The Midrash explains the words of the snake as follows:

He [the snake] said: He [God] ate of this tree and created the world, and He has told you not to eat of it, so that you will not create other worlds. Every craftsman hates other craftsmen of the same trade (*Gen. Rabbah* 19:4; quoted by Rashi, Gen. 3:5).

The snake's slander thus consisted of three elements: minimizing God's ability; accusing God of being jealous of His own creatures; and implying that God's threat to kill Eve upon eating the fruit was empty, and thus that God's commands should not be taken seriously.

With respect to the snake's punishment, the Torah states: "Because you did this, you are cursed more than all animals and all beasts of the field" (Gen. 3:14). The Midrash (*Gen. Rabbah* 20:4) says that the curse was leprosy,[47] explaining that the scales on the snake's back are the scars which remained.

---

47. The derivation is explained in *Exod. Rabbah* 3:13, where it is noted that the Hebrew word for "cursed" is *arur*, while leprosy is described in Hebrew as *tzara'at mameret* (Lev. 13:51), the two words having the same root.

Moses:

Regarding God's initial conversation with Moses, the text states (Exod. 4):

1. And Moses answered and said: "But they will not believe me nor hearken to my voice, for they will say: 'The Lord did not appear to you.'" 2. And the Lord said to him: "What is that in your hand?" And he said: "A staff." 3. And He said: "Cast it on the ground." And he cast it on the ground, and it became a serpent, and Moses fled from before it. 4. And the Lord said to Moses: "Stretch out your hand, and take it by the tail." And he stretched out his hand, and held it, and it became a staff in his hand. 5. [This sign was performed] so that they will believe that the Lord, the God of their fathers, the God of Abraham, the God of Isaac, and the God of Jacob, has appeared to you. 6. And the Lord said to him in addition: "Put your hand in your bosom." And he put his hand in his bosom; and when he took it out, behold, his hand was leprous, as white as snow. 7. And He said: "Put your hand back in your bosom." And he put his hand back in his bosom; and when he took it out of his bosom, behold, it returned [to look] like his other flesh.

In the first verse, according to the Midrash (*Exod. Rabbah* 3:12),[48] Moses slandered the Israelites when he said that they would not believe that he was God's messenger. In fact, states the Midrash, they did believe him, as it says further, "and the people believed" (Exod. 4:31); and they already had a tradition of being believers from the time of Abraham, as it says: "And he believed in the Lord" (Gen. 15:6). God hinted to Moses that he had sinned by having his

48. Cited by Rashi on Exod. 4:2-3.

staff turn into a snake, as if to say: By slandering the Israelites, you adopted the habit of the snake in the Garden of Eden.

After informing Moses that he sinned in the same manner as the snake, verse 4 makes it clear, according to the Midrash (*Exod. Rabbah* 3:13),[49] that he would also be punished in the same way that the snake was, by contracting leprosy. The symbolism of placing his hand in his bosom is that he was stricken when his hand was hidden, just as slander usually occurs in secret behind the victim's back.

Miriam: Described in detail in Num. 12.

King David:

If incest, lying, and bloodshed are all possible causes of *tzara'at*, then King David should certainly have been a candidate for being stricken, in that he committed adultery with Bath-sheba (2 Sam. 11:4), lied to her husband Uriah (v. 8), and then had him murdered (v. 15). Although one opinion in the Talmud attempts to justify (rationalize) his behavior (BT *Shabbat* 56a), the simple meaning of the text and the condemnation of Nathan the prophet (2 Sam. 12:6) would indicate that he did seriously sin. His greatness lay not in his being immaculate, but rather in his straightforward, sincere repentance (v. 13).

The Bible does not explicitly say that he contracted leprosy. Nevertheless, the Rabbis infer that he did from David's plea for forgiveness for his tryst with Bath-sheba, upon being approached by Nathan. David writes: "Cleanse me with hyssop, so that I will be clean; wash me, and I will be whiter than snow" (Ps. 51:9).

---

49. Rashi on Exod. 4:6 also relates his leprous hand to his slander of the Israelites, but brings the example of Miriam rather than the snake in the Garden of Eden.

Later it will be described that, as part of the purification process for leprosy, the priest takes hyssop and dips it in the blood of a bird which has been slaughtered. Maharsha (BT *Sanhedrin* 107a) reads the second half of the verse as follows: "wash me from snow, and I will be white." He explains that one of the forms of biblical leprosy has the appearance of snow. The implication of the verse is thus that the king is suffering from the disease and praying for the day that it will clear up sufficiently for the purification ceremony to be performed.

The Psalm continues: "Restore to me the joy of Your salvation, and let a gracious spirit support me" (Ps. 51:9). The Talmud (BT *Sanhedrin* 107a) explains that in the past, the Divine presence had rested upon David, but that can transpire only when one is in a state of joy, which cannot co-exist with leprosy. David asks God to cure him of his leprosy so that he may once more attain a state of bliss, thus allowing the Divine Presence to return.

In a different location, the psalmist writes: "Let those that fear You return to me, and they that know Your testimonies" (Ps. 119:79). But who are those that fear the Lord and know His testimonies? They are the members of the Sanhedrin, who had also separated themselves from David during this period. Maharsha explains that the first part of the verse refers to David's pain at not being able to pray with a quorum (*minyan*), while the second refers to his discomfort at being unable to study with a partner.

Although explicit reference to a bout of leprosy is absent, is there any hint in the biblical description of King David's reign that it might have occurred? The following talmudic segment implies that is indeed the case:

R. Judah said in Rav's name: For six months David was smitten with leprosy, the *Shechinah* deserted him, and the Sanhedrin held aloof from him… How do we know that it was for six months? Because it is written: "And the days that David reigned over Israel were forty years. Seven years he reigned in Hebron, and in Jerusalem he reigned thirty-three years" (1 Kings 2:11), while [elsewhere] it is written: "In Hebron he reigned over Judah seven years and six months" (2 Sam. 5:5). Thus, these six months are not counted [in the first passage quoted], indicating that he was smitten with leprosy [since a leper is considered as dead, those six months were not counted in 1 Kings] (BT *Sanhedrin* 107a-b).

Gehazi:

Gehazi, the servant of the prophet Elisha, is first mentioned in connection with the Shunamite woman who provided the prophet with room and board gratis (2 Kings 4:12). When the prophet asked the woman how he could repay her for her kindness, it was Gehazi who interceded on her behalf by saying that she was childless and her husband was old (v. 14). The prophet promised that she will give birth in a year (v. 16), which indeed happened (v. 17). On the other hand, when she beseeched Elisha at Mt. Carmel on behalf of her son who had died suddenly, Gehazi thrust her aside rudely (v. 27). Elisha, however, told him to hurry to Shunem with the former's staff, not to speak to anyone on the way, and to lay the staff on the child's face (v. 27). In the end, this approach did not succeed (v. 31), and Elisha himself had to revive the child (v. 35).

Gehazi next appears in connection wth Naaman, an Aramean general who was sent to the king of Israel (Jehoram son of Ahab, or perhaps Jehu son of Nimshi) to seek a cure for his leprosy (2 Kings 5:6), which was effected by means of immersion in the Jordan River (v. 14). In gratitude, he offered generous gifts to Elisha, but the latter refused to accept them (v. 16). Gehazi, moved by cupidity, ran after Naaman in order to obtain the gifts which were refused by his master (v. 21), inventing a story about two needy prophets (v. 22). Elisha became aware of Gehazi's activities, and when the latter denied them (v. 25), he smote him with leprosy until he was "as white as snow" (v. 27). Gehazi appears once more in conversation with the king, describing the miracles which Elisha had performed (2 Kings 8:5).

Maharsha (BT *Sanhedrin* 107b) explains that Gehazi's punishment was "measure for measure." Naaman initially thought that he had been cured in a natural fashion, and thus offered payment as one would to any doctor. Elisha refused the payment because it was through prayer that he was miraculously cured, for which there is no fee. By Gehazi demanding compensation, it was as if he was acquiescing to Naaman's claim that he was cured by natural means, and for that reason he was cursed in kind, by striking him with leprosy, for which there is no medical antidote.

The Jerusalem Talmud (*Sanhedrin* 10:2) characterizes Gehazi as a Torah scholar. However, he is said to have had three weaknesses: he was envious, immodest sexually, and in denial of resurrection of the dead. All of these faults are based on the biblical description of his activities.

That he was envious is derived from 2 Kings 6:1, which states that the number of Elisha's disciples grew tremendously. Since this verse appears immediately after Gehazi is smitten with leprosy at Elisha's behest, the assumption is that in the past, Gehazi had been responsible for there being a much smaller group of students. The Talmud explains that when Elisha lectured, Gehazi would sit outside the study hall. Potential students did not enter, saying to themselves that if his own servant Gehazi didn't find the lectures to be beneficial, they probably wouldn't either.[50]

---

50. See also BT *Sanhedrin* 107b.

That Gehazi was promiscuous was derived from the previously quoted verse (2 Kings 4:27) telling how Gehazi had brusquely thrust the Shunamite aside. The Talmud (BT *Berachot* 10b) states that he placed his hand on the glory of her beauty between her breasts.[51]

As far as his lack of belief in resurrection, the Talmud derives this from the fact that when Gehazi lay the staff on the face of the child who had collapsed, he was not revived (2 Kings 4:31). The Talmud says that this was because he had not followed instructions. He had been told not to speak to anyone, but in actuality he derisively told everyone he met that he was on his way to resurrect a dead child by placing a staff on his face, obviously mocking the possibility of doing so.

In describing Elisha's miracles to the king at a later stage, Gehazi had said: "My lord the king, this is the woman, and this is her son, whom Elisha restored to life" (2 Kings 8:5). The Talmud considers Gehazi to have been impertinent in mentioning his master Elisha by his first name (BT *Sanhedrin* 100a).

Finally, the Talmud (BT *Sanhedrin* 107b) accuses him of aiding and abetting idol worship by hanging a magnet above the golden calf constructed by Jeroboam (I Kings 12:28-30), making it look as if it were magically suspended in the air, or by engraving the Divine name in the calf's mouth making it continually repeat the phrase: I am the Lord your God.

The Talmud (BT *Sanhedrin* 107b) indicates that the punishment imposed on Gehazi by Elisha was too harsh, being that a leper is quarantined and not permitted to enter the community, thus preventing him from coming under the good influence of Torah scholars and eventually mending his ways. In fact, after his ex-communication, the Bible tells of the four lepers

51. See also *Pirkei de-Rabbi Eliezer* 32.

who saved the nation from hunger (2 Kings 7:3), with the Talmud (BT *Sanhedrin* 107b) maintaining that they were Gehazi and his three sons (who were complicit in his rapaciousness, according to Radak [2 Kings 5:27]).

Gehazi's sins thus included promiscuity, envy, selfishness, and idol worship—each of which have been mentioned as potential causes of leprosy. King David had also performed some of these sins, but his ostracism was limited in time and he was thus able to repent, and so Elisha was faulted for not offering the same opportunity to Gehazi.

King Uzziah:

In the line of Judean kings, about half-way between the righteous kings Jehoshaphat and Hezekiah, reigned Uzziah (or Uzziyahu, or Azariah). The Bible states that "he did that which was right in the eyes of the Lord" (2 Kings 15:3), but he was nevertheless stricken by leprosy (v. 5).

The Bible attributes Uzziah's leprosy to the fact that as a result of his great accomplishments, "his heart was lifted up so that he acted corruptly, and he trespassed against the Lord his God; and he went into the Temple of the Lord to burn incense upon the altar [which is permitted for priests only]" (2 Chron. 26:16). In fact, this verse is used as a proof-text for the talmudic statement that *tzara'at* may result from arrogance (BT *Arachin* 16a). In addition, according to a legend recorded by Josephus (*Antiquities of the Jews* 10:4), upon Uzziah's entering the holy sanctuary, a powerful earthquake erupted, destroying many of the roads, edifices, and gardens which had so filled the king with pride and were perhaps the stumbling blocks which led to his grave transgression. The earthquake made such a tremendous impression that it was referred to in the books of Amos (1:1), Isaiah (6:4),[52] and Zechariah (14:5).

Since it is clear that he sinned greatly, why is he referred to both in 2 Kings 15:3 and 2 Chron. 26:4 as having done "that which was right in the eyes of the Lord"? One may learn an important lesson from these references, namely that more important than the severity of one's sins is the intensity of one's repentance. That Uzziah was strongly affected by the rebuke administered by God is hinted at in 2 Chron. 26:20, which describes how Uzziah was practically pushed out of the Temple when it became apparent that he was leprous, and the verse adds the phrase: "and also he himself made haste to leave." In other words, Uzziah was aware that he sinned, and was very embarrassed and upset with himself. Furthermore, in his subdued state, he quietly accepted his punishment by living out the rest of his life in quarantine and appointing his son as regent (2 Kings 15:5; 2 Chron. 26: 21). Josephus (*Antiquities of the Jews* 10:4) portrays his mood in greater detail:

> Now, as soon as the priests saw that the king's face was infected with leprosy, they told him of the calamity he was under, and commanded that he should go out of the city as a polluted person. Hereupon, he was so confounded at the sad distemper, and sensible that he was not at liberty to contradict, that he did as he was commanded, and underwent this miserable and terrible punishment for

---

52. The verse in Isaiah reads "And the doorposts shook at the sound of their shouting, and the house was filled with smoke" (Isa. 6:4), which *Seder Olam Rabbah*, ch. 20 (Leiner edition) takes to refer to the earthquake which occurred on the day Uzziah entered the Temple and died, but this would seem to contradict 2 Chron. 26:21, where it says he died later. Radak, on the other hand, believes that the verse refers to an earthquake which Isaiah saw in a prophetic dream, not an actual event.

an intention beyond what befitted a man to have, and for that impiety against God which was implied therein. So he abode out of the city for some time, and lived a private life, while his son Jotham took the government; after which he died with grief and anxiety at what had happened to him, when he had lived sixty-eight years, and reigned of them fifty-two; and was buried by himself in his own gardens.

Apparently, the nation was aware of his sincere regret, and allowed him to retain his title as a "tainted monarch" (*Seder Olam Rabbah* 19), with his son Jotham serving as regent and administering the kingdom.

The power of whole-hearted repentance is illustrated by other biblical figures as well, most outstandingly by King David, whose sins were of the highest degree, yet his repentance was equally sublime (2 Sam. 12:13). Even more amazing is the story of King Menasseh, who was said to have been the worst king who ever ruled Israel, and whose sins were considered to be more severe than those of the Amorites, whom the Israelites had replaced because of their defilement of the Land of Israel (2 Kings 21:11). Regarding the verse: "And also Menasseh shed very much innocent blood, until he had filled Jerusalem from one end to the other (v. 16)," the Talmud states:

Here [in Babylon], it is interpreted to mean that he killed Isaiah [who was his mother's father]. In the West [Palestine], they said: [It means] that he made an image as heavy as a thousand men, and every day it slew all of them [by falling on them. Then another thousand would be needed to stand it up, and they too would be crushed the next day] (BT *Sanhedrin* 103b).

In spite of his great sins, when he suffered serious military reverses, he resolved to repent, regarding which Scripture states:

> And when he was in distress, he entreated the Lord his God, and he humbled himself greatly before the God of his fathers. And he prayed to Him; and He acquiesced to him, and He heard his supplication, and He brought him back to Jerusalem to his kingdom. Then Menasseh knew that the Lord, He is God (2 Chron. 33:12-13).

Once more, it has been shown that when one repents in earnest, atonement is forthcoming, independent of the severity of the transgression.

THE BIBLICAL SOURCE PROHIBITING SLANDER (*LASHON HA-RA*)

The prohibition of slander is based on the following verse: "You should not circulate as a tale-bearer among your people; you should not stand by [idly, when] the blood [i.e. the life] of your neighbor [is in danger]" (Lev. 19:16). This prohibition is counted by Rambam (*Sefer ha-Mitzvot*) as the 301st prohibition, and by *Chinuch* as the 236th command. The Hebrew word for tale-bearer is *rachil*, which is derived either from *meragel* ("spy" — Rashi, Saadiah Gaon), or from *rochel* ("peddler" — Ibn Ezra, *Sifra Kedoshim* 2:4). In the former view, tale-bearers enter their friends' houses, spy on their activities, and share those details which they find to be distasteful with their social peers. In the latter view, the tale-bearer is similar to a peddler who takes his merchandise (in this case personal information) from the seller, and passes it on (as gossip) at the marketplace to a buyer.

A third interpretation is that *rachil* derives from *rach* (soft), meaning that one should not speak negatively of his adversaries, yet be soft on his cohorts who behave similarly (*Sifra Kedoshim* 2:4). In short, the Torah legislates against the formation of cliques whose members slander the uninitiated out of pure spite, but treat their own favorably.

Rambam (*Sefer ha-Mitzvot*) stresses the gravity with which the Torah treats this transgression by noting that the Torah adjoins it with a command relating to the saving of life, which when disobeyed leads to loss of life, implying that what the tale-bearer does is comparable to murder. However, since no physical act is associated with it, it is not even punishable by flogging (*Hilchot De'ot* 7:1, based on BT *Makkot* 16a).

DEFINING SLANDER (*LASHON HA-RA*)

Rambam (*Hilchot De'ot* ch. 7) defines four incrementally more serious levels of slander, all of which are included in the prohibition against *lashon ha-ra*.

1. Tale-bearing (*rechilut*), in the words of Rambam:

    > Who is a tale-bearer? One who carries reports, and goes from one to another and says "So-and-so said this;" "Such and such I heard about so-and-so." Even if what he says or repeats may be true, the tale-bearer ruins the world (*Hilchot De'ot* 7:2).

The prohibition includes *a fortiori* the case that a tale-bearer tells his collocutor what others said about him. The admonition refers not only to talking about what another said, but also about what he did. The danger in doing so is that one can never be sure of the attitude of one's partner in conversation. He might be antagonistic to the person being described and conspire against him.

The classic example is the story of Doeg the Edomite. David had found refuge from King Saul in the priestly city of Nob, where he told their leader Achimelech b. Achituv that he was on a secret mission ordered by the king, but found himself without food or weapons. Achimelech was able to give him holy showbread[53] and the sword of Goliath (1 Sam. 21:1-10). When Saul tried to determine where David was hiding, he was informed by one of his chiefs, Doeg the Edomite,[54] who was aware of the deeds of David and Achimelech. King Saul then commanded Doeg to kill the priests in Nob. In addition to slaying eighty-five priests, he smote the entire city—men, women, children, and even livestock (1 Sam. 22:6-19).

In this case, Doeg told the truth, and described the actions of Achimelech, who was quite proud of having the opportunity to help the son-in-law of the king; but Doeg must have realized that this information would lead to the loss of innocent lives, and so Rambam describes tale-bearing as having the potential to ruin the world.

---

53. Rashi explains that although forbidden to non-priests, it was permitted in this case because they were starving to death. Radak says it was from the loaves of a thanksgiving sacrifice, which are permitted to non-priests.

54. Rashi, based on *Midrash Tehillim* 3:4, says he was a great scholar (see also BT *Chagigah* 15b; *Sanhedrin* 106b) and the head of the Jewish court. Radak says he was called an Edomite because he resided in Edom. *Midrash Tehillim* 52:4 says he reddened the faces of others by his vast Torah knowledge (Edomite is derived from *adom*, which means red in Hebrew), or he acted toward David like Esau (Edom), who was jealous and vengeful.

It follows that if the tale-bearer is certain that his tale maligns nobody, will have no negative consequences, and might even lead to a positive outcome (such as the recipient forming a positive attitude toward the person described), then there is no sin in such behavior.

2. The evil tongue (*lashon ha-ra*) means, in the words of Rambam, "he who speaks disparagingly of his friend, even if what he says is true" (*Hilchot De'ot* 7:2). This practice, a greater offense than mere *rechilut*, refers to one who generally guards his tongue, but every once in a while errs. The biblical precedent is the case of the spies (Num. 13), who were sent to search out the land and returned with a negative report.

Ramban says that the spies told the truth, which was a requirement of the task they were given, and they sinned by saying the word *efes* (however) in the verse: "However, the people that dwell in the land are fierce, and the cities are fortified and very great" (Num. 13:28). The name of the sin that Ramban is referring to is *lashon ha-ra*, as is clear from the following Mishnah (BT *Arachin* 15a):

> We find that the judgment against our fathers in the wilderness was sealed only because of their evil tongue, as it is written [with respect to the spies, who slandered the Land of Israel, leading to God's decision to prevent all those men who were adults at the time of the exodus from seeing the Promised Land (Num. 26:64, and Rashi thereon)]: "and [you] have tested Me these ten times" (Num. 14:22).

The Talmud disputes the imputed seriousness of *lashon ha-ra* as follows:

Perhaps it was due to the fact that their measure [of guilt] was not full yet, for R. Hamnuna said: The Holy One, blessed be He, does not punish man until his measure [of guilt] is full, as it is said: "When his lust [for wealth, interpreted here as his quota of sins] is filled, he will suffer" (Job 20:22). Resh Lakish replied: Scripture said, "and [you] have tested Me these ten times," i.e. because of "these" was the judgment against them sealed (BT *Arachin* 15a).

The Talmud raises the possibility that *lashon ha-ra* is a relatively minor infraction, but being the last of ten sins, it was the one that tipped the scales. The answer is that the verse quoted contains the extra word "these" which, according to Rashi, implies that even if the first nine sins hadn't occurred, this sin by itself would have been sufficient to deprive them of entry into the land. The Talmud continues:

Come and see how great is the power of an evil tongue! From where [do we know its power]? From the spies, for if such [happens] to those who spread an evil report against wood and stones, how much more [will it happen to] he who spreads an evil report against his neighbor!

It is now clear that the Talmud comes down very hard on those who speak *lashon ha-ra*, and specifically on the spies, but from Ramban's explanation it is not at all clear what the *lashon ha-ra* in fact was. He justifies everything they said except for the word "however," which is simply a conjunctive adverb.

The answer is that one must understand the essence of *lashon ha-ra*. The tale-bearer tells the truth about a specific item. If his intention were to confine himself to that item exclusively, it would be perfectly legitimate to pass on such information. For example, if someone is looking for a good doctor, it would be completely acceptable to express one's true opinion, and totally improper to praise a poor doctor, thereby misleading the questioner. By doing so, one would surely transgress the prohibition of "you should not... place a stumbling-block before the blind" (Lev. 19:14). The problem arises when the information being passed on is of no immediate concern, and its only purpose is to create an overall aversion to the subject of the calumny. This is completely unfair, since nobody is perfect, especially the tale-bearer, and the only result of such speech is to create social friction, while the Torah strives for social harmony. By saying "however," in the case of the spies, they were implying that it would be impossible for the Israelites to overcome a strong enemy – a judgment they were not requested to make, and so they were guilty of generating a negative environment, which could only have harmful repercussions with respect to the task at hand.

3. Rambam's third category is the slanderer, *motzi shem ra*, which he defines as one who tells lies about others (*Hilchot De'ot* 7:2). As in the case of *lashon ha-ra*, the source of this infraction is in the Bible (Deut. 22:13-21), where the case of a man who falsely accuses his fiancée of unchaste behavior during the period of betrothal is described. Such a person is whipped (Rashi on Deut. 22:18; *Ketubot* 46a), fined 100 shekels, and prohibited from ever divorcing her (Deut. 22:19).

The seriousness of *motzi shem ra* is stressed in the following Mishnah:

[The law regarding] *motzi shem ra* is sometimes lenient and sometimes stringent. How so? Both one who is *motzi shem ra* on the greatest of priestly stock and on the lowest in Israel pays one hundred *sela*. It is seen [lit., found] that he who speaks is [punished] more than he who commits an act (BT *Arachin* 15a).

Rashi explains that the act being referred to is rape, for which the rapist is fined only fifty shekels (Deut. 22:28-29).

The Talmud questions whether *motzi shem ra* is as serious an offense as the Mishnah has implied, by asking:

Perhaps it [the larger penalty in the case of *motzi shem ra*] is because he wanted to cause her death, as it is written: "But if this thing is true... then they will take out the damsel... and the men of her city will stone her with stones and she will die." Raba answered: Scripture said "because he has spread an evil name" (Deut. 22:19), i.e., [only] because of the evil name that he has spread [and not because of the threat of capital punishment] (BT *Arachin* 15a).

Rambam's third level of slander, *motzi shem ra,* is thus seen to be quite similar to the second level, except for the fact that the specific content which the slanderer promulgates is false, making him one degree nastier than one who spreads embarrassing information which is at least true and not a fabrication. In the general case, the sinner is not flogged, because no act is involved.

Of course, there is also the specific form of *motzi shem ra* referred to earlier, where the husband accuses his wife of immorality after having relations with her upon entering the marital state. Unlike the more general case, here the husband is fined and flogged (since an act was involved[55]), but the initial prohibition derives from the same verse which warns against circulating as a tale-bearer (Lev. 19:16).[56]

4. The habitual slanderer (baʿal lashon ha-ra): Rambam defines this category of slander as the fourth and most serious (worst) type. In his own words (Hilchot Deʿot 7:2):

> Baʿal lashon ha-ra is a person who sits [in company] and says "That person did such a thing, so-and-so were his ancestors, and I have heard this about him, and he spoke derogatory words." Of such a person, Scripture says: "May the Lord cut off all smooth-speaking [fluent] lips, the tongue that speaks haughty things" (Ps. 12:4).

Rambam apparently understands "smooth-speaking" to describe a person whose main subject of conversation focuses on the failings of other people, moving continuously and smoothly from one to another, haughtily placing himself on a pedestal in a position to criticize others.

After listing the four types of slander, Rambam relates to avak lashon ha-ra, literally "dust of lashon ha-ra," i.e., a diluted form (just as dust is a diluted form of dirt) which is a derived strain of slander. The concept is first mentioned in Bava Batra (165a), immediately after telling the following story:

---

55. According to R. Yehudah (BT Ketubot 45b), even if he did not have relations and no act was involved he is flogged, either because R. Yehudah does not require an act for flogging (Rashi), or it is a rabbinic enactment (Rabbeinu Tam).
56. BT Ketubot 46a, according to R. Elazar.

One time he [R. Simeon the son of R. Judah the Prince] was sitting before him [R. Judah] and he finished [reading or studying] a section of the book of Psalms. Rabbi [Judah the Prince] said to him: "How correct is the writing [i.e. the script of the scribe who produced the manuscript]!" He said to him: "I did not write it, Judah Hayyata wrote it." He said to him: "Distance yourself from tale-bearing"... What tale-bearing is there? [There is tale-bearing] based on [the teaching] of R. Dimi, for R. Dimi, brother of R. Safra, taught: A man should never tell of the goodness of his friend, for by talking of his goodness, he comes to his bad deeds [Rashbam: when specifying his praise, we also mention his disgrace] (BT *Bava Batra* 164b).

Rambam, in recording R. Dimi's dictum, makes two assumptions:

1. This story provides an example of *avak lashon ha-ra,* not full-scale *lashon ha-ra,* because of the proximity between the recording of the story and the first mention of *avak lashon ha-ra* (although the Talmud does not explicitly link the two).
2. The prohibition to speak positively about someone is applicable when one is addressing people who are hostile to him. When providing examples of *avak lashon ha-ra,* Rambam includes "anyone who speaks of the goodness of his friend *before his enemies*" (*Hilchot De'ot* 7:2). The last words do not appear in the talmudic text. Rambam certainly realized that the Talmud records numerous cases of the Sages praising one another, such as when R. Yochanan b. Zakkai spoke of the positive attributes of each of his students (*Avot* 2:8) or when Issi b. Judah specified the distinctive merits of the various Sages (BT *Gittin* 67a).

Rashbam (BT *Bava Batra* 165a) references the segment from the Talmud cited below as an example of *avak lashon ha-ra*:

> What constitutes evil speech? Rabbah said: For example, to say there is fire in the [oven of the] house of so-and-so [Rashi: implying that he is rich and there is always a fire burning in his house to cook food]. Abaye said to him: What did he do? He just gave information [Rashi: to people seeking fire]. Rather, when he utters it in an insolent manner, saying: "Where else should there be fire if not in the house of so-and-so? There is always meat and fish [i.e. he is very rich]" (BT *Arachin* 15b).

Finally, Rambam (*Hilchot De'ot* 7:2) gives two more examples:

1. Saying that nobody could have imagined that so-and-so could have gotten to where he is;
2. Saying "do not talk about so-and-so, I do not want to even mention what happened to him [in the past]."

Although these cases are not mentioned in the Talmud, *Be'er Mayim Chaim* (*Hilchot Lashon ha-Ra* 9:1) explains that they are derived from the prohibition to praise a person before his enemies, since that can lead to saying negative things, so certainly opening a discussion with leading remarks that could turn critical is forbidden, even before friends.

A number of examples of *avak lashon ha-ra* have been given. What is missing is a unifying principle, and that is provided by Rambam in his commentary on *Avot* 1:16, where he says: "*Avak lashon ha-ra* refers to hinting at a person's defects without explaining." In other words, if one does not actually make derogatory comments, but just hints at their existence, or alternatively lays the groundwork which will eventually lead to such comments, that is *avak lashon ha-ra,* as opposed to complete *lashon ha-ra,* where one explicitly derogates another person.

Seriousness of *lashon ha-ra*:

Although not a punishable prohibition (no physical act having been involved[57]), the Talmud goes out of its way to stress the gravity of slander (category 3 of leprosy-inducing sins, which bridges between the other categories, as previously described), as well as its negative consequences, and speaks very harshly of those who engage in it. It is possible that the most extreme statements refer mainly to the habitual slanderer,[58] but they certainly may serve as a warning against any level of slander. To cite some of the talmudic exhortations (BT *Arachin* 15b):

1. "Speaking slanderously is comparable to denying the existence of God." One certainly wouldn't have spoken in such a manner had he felt the Presence of God monitoring all of his actions.
2. "One who slanders deserves to be stoned."
3. "In the West [Land of Israel] they say: Talk about third [parties] kills three persons: It kills the slanderer, he who accepts it, and he whom they are talking about."

    Midrash Tehillim 12:4 (also JT *Pe'ah* 1:1) illustrates this saying with the story of Saul in pursuit of David. The Midrash explains that Doeg was the slanderer; Saul the one who accepted the slander; and all of Nob, the city of priests, the object of the slander. They all died prematurely: Saul in battle (1 Sam. 31:6); Achimelech and the inhabiants of Nob by the

---

57. BT *Makkot* 16a; *Zevachim* 29b.
58. Implication of *Yalkut Shimoni* 938.

hand of Doeg (1 Sam. 22:16-19); and Doeg at the age of thirty-four, based on the verse: "Bloody and deceitful people will not even live out half of their days [which would have been thirty-five]" (Ps. 55:24), as detailed in the Talmud (BT *Sanhedrin* 106b). The Midrash (also BT *Sanhedrin* 20a) goes on to point out that in this case, there was even a fourth victim, Abner, Saul's cousin and chief of staff, who died treacherously at the hand of Joab (2 Sam. 3:27), since he could have prevented the massacre at Nob, but failed to do so. Actually, the Bible explains that no member of Saul's army was willing to kill Achimelech (1 Sam. 22:17), ostensibly including Abner. Nevertheless, as chief of staff, Abner would have been in a position to object more strenuously, which he did not do, and for that reason he was punished.

4. "The School of R. Yishmael taught: Whoever speaks slander increases his sins to the level of the three [cardinal] sins: idolatry, incest and adultery, and bloodshed."

It may be noted that of these three cardinal sins, two (incest and bloodshed) are on the list of sins punishable by *tzaraat* which have been grouped in the first category. Only idolatry is not on that list. Perhaps the reason is that the Torah stresses actions, not philosophy. True, idol worship leads to corruption and immorality; however, the essence of sin is the *result* of the pagan beliefs (and not the beliefs themselves), and if it would be possible to lead a moral life in spite of one's mistaken belief (which Judaism considers to be impossible in the long-run), then God would be relatively satisfied, as it says in the Jerusalem Talmud: "Would that they forsake Me and observe My commandments" (JT *Chagigah* 1:6).

On the other hand, it should be noted that in a more exhaustive list of eleven sins which can cause *tzaraat*, paganism is included (*Tanchuma Metzora* 4), possibly because of the fact that moral foibles are, in the long run, the inevitable result of denying the existence of the Creator. In addition to idol worship, the eleven causes include the desecration of God's name. Together, they may be said to compose another category, preliminary to those previously catalogued. The *Tanchuma* also extends the first category (internal personality faults) by adding evil thoughts as a cause, and the third (serious crimes) by adding strife-generating activities.

Inevitability of *lashon ha-ra*:

As serious as slander was considered to be, the Talmud had no illusions as to people's ability to avoid it entirely. From the following talmudic text, one obtains an impression of how the Amora'im rated both themselves and others, religious as they might be:

> R. Amram said in the name of Rav: [There are] three transgressions which no man escapes every day: sinful [unchaste] thoughts, examination of prayers [Rashbam: thinking how God will respond positively to his prayers, since he said them in earnest; Tosafot: failing to focus on the meaning of his prayers] and slander [*lashon ha-ra*]. Slander? Could you imagine that [people are that bad]? Rather, implied slander [*avak lashon ha-ra* is meant]. R. Judah said in the name of Rav: most [people are guilty] of robbery [Rashbam: by delaying payment to their employees][59] a minority of lewdness, and all of slander. Of slander? Could you imagine that? Rather, implied slander (BT *Bava Batra* 164b-165a).

59. If robbery includes lying, this result is confirmed by modern research, which shows that people are exposed to as many as 200 lies per day, as reported in Jerald Jellison's *I'm Sorry, I Didn't Mean To, and Other Lies We Love To Tell* (1977).

The Talmud metaphorically describes God as making every effort to limit man's ability to slander, but to no avail. To graciously (but not accurately) absolve mankind from guilt, the Talmud, in the following text, pretends that the tongue independently initiates its nefarious works:

> R. Johanan said in the name of R. Joseph b. Zimra: What is the meaning of the verse: "What can be given to you, and what can be done more for you, you deceitful tongue" (Ps. 120:3). The Holy One, blessed be He, said to the tongue: All limbs of a person are standing, you are lying [making it more difficult to activate]; all limbs of a person are on the outside, you are on the inside [making it more difficult to activate]; not only that, but I surrounded you with two walls, one of bone [the teeth] and one of flesh [the cheeks] (BT *Arachin* 15b).

Apparently, even God is at a loss as to how to control the tongue.

In fact, the following passage (BT *Ta'anit* 8a) implies that slander is as instinctive to humans as devouring other creatures is to animals of prey:

> In the future, all the animals will assemble and come to the snake and say: "The lion attacks and eats [Rashi: its prey immediately and is not afraid]; the wolf tears and eats [Rashi: because it fears the other creatures, it drags its prey to its lair]; [both the lion and the wolf enjoy their prey] but what pleasure do you have [Rashi: from killing a person (since you do not eat him)]?" He [the snake] will say to them: "What benefit accrues to he who uses his tongue?"

The point being made is that slander is of no tangible benefit to a human being, and although in the short-run one might actually enjoy maligning others, in the long-run not only is it not beneficial, but it leads to suffering and strife.

Although the Talmud has stressed the serious results of *lashon ha-ra,* the afore-cited texts wish to empathize with the individual Jew who has great difficulty, and often does not succeed, in behaving properly, with the hope that this assurance will renew his confidence and enable him to improve his performance in the future.

Related laws – extending the framework:

A number of Torah laws are directly related to the prohibition of slander, either because they attempt to remove the motivation to slander, or because they forbid one to malign his neighbor in an equally painful way. These laws are found in the portions of *Kedoshim* (mainly) and *Behar*, and will be dealt with there.

Source	Definition	Rambam	*Chinuch*
You should not hate your brother in your heart (Lev. 19:17).	Do not hate—removes motivation.	Neg. 302	238
You should rebuke your neighbor (Lev. 19:17).	Correcting someone directly is preferable to slandering him.	Pos. 205	239
You should rebuke your neighbor and not bear sin because of him [i.e. by insulting him] (Lev. 19:17).	Do not publicly embarrass, insult, or shame; similar to slander, with stronger effect.	Neg. 303	240
And you should love your neighbor as yourself (Lev. 19:18).	Loving one's neighbor—removes motivation.	Pos. 206	243
And you should love the stranger, for you were strangers in the land of Egypt (Deut. 10:19).	Loving the stranger—removes motivation.	Pos. 207	431
And you should not [verbally] vex one another (Lev. 25:17).	Do not to insult—similar to slander, with stronger effect.	Neg. 251	338

Conclusion

The laws of purity and impurity in general, as well as those specifically associated with *tzara'at*, at first blush seem to be of the mystical and eschatological variety. The goal of the commentary on the present and previous chapters is to show that although the associated laws seem to be highly technical and picayune, while the details of the accompanying rituals and rites seem to be very arbitrary and even paganistic, their overall purpose is to inculcate important philosophical concepts which are part of the Jewish worldview and important modes of behavior which outline the ideal demeanor expected of a religious Jew. The classical texts themselves intimate that acheiving perfection is not realistic for even the most righteous of people. Nevertheless, the purpose of the legislation is to allow every Jew to set up a target which he will spend most of his life aiming at.

Acharei Mot

The portion of *Acharei Mot* is spread over three chapters, each of which deals with a different subject. Ch. 16 deals with the Yom Kippur ritual in the Tabernacle and later the Holy Temple, presenting in detail the activities of the high priest and his assistants on the Day of Atonement, with a focus on the individual and communal sacrifices which were to be brought. Ch. 17 supplements earlier portions in the book of Leviticus by adding certain general rules which apply to all sacrifices (as opposed to those in the portions of *Vayikra* and *Tzav*, which relate to specific types), as well as certain general laws relevant to the consumption of meat in general (beyond those presented in *Shemini*, which enumerate the different permitted species). Ch. 18, on the other hand, deals with moral uncleanness, in contrast to ritual uncleanness, which is discussed in the latter part of *Shemini*, *Tazria*, and *Metzora*. A list of incestuous and adulterous relationships is presented, but the chapter also lays the basis for normative sexual functioning within marriage, which may be generalized to serve as an outline for appropriate social and sexual behavior. Since the subjects of the first two chapters are not applicable after the destruction of the Temple, the present discussion will enlarge upon the content of the third chapter.

INTRINSIC HOLINESS OF THE LAND OF ISRAEL

Ch. 18 begins with the following verse:

> You may not follow the practices of the land of Egypt
> where you dwelt, nor may you follow the practices of the
> land of Canaan to which I am bringing you, neither may
> you walk in their statutes (Lev. 18:3).

The Midrash (*Sifra* 8:13) makes it quite clear which common
practices of both the Egyptians and the Canaanites are being
referred to, namely "idol worship, incest, and murder." Why were
Egypt and Canaan specified by name? One view (Ra'avad, *Sifra*
8:12:3) is that the behavior of these two nations was worse than
that of other nations, possibly because their sinful treatment of
Israel eased them into the performance of additional sins, as
the Sages have stated: "One sin drags another after it (*aveirah*
goreret aveirah)." Interestingly, both nations were descended from
Noah's evil son Ham (Gen. 10:6). In particular, Egypt was said
to be "totally immersed in ugly ways and inappropriate customs"
(*Tanna de-Vei Eliyahu* 8).

Another view (*Bereishit Rabatti, Miketz* 41:39) is that the
situation is comparable to a king who had only one daughter. He
found her a place to live, but soon realized that the neighbors
indulged in prostitution and witchcraft. He thus decided to find
her an alternative domicile, but the neighbors turned out to be no
better, so he told his daughter to be very careful until he is able to
sanitize her surroundings.

The Torah does not wish to discourage the adoption of the
positive aspects of non-Jewish cultures, just those which it views
as being corrupt. The Midrash states:

You may not follow the practices of the land of Egypt [where you dwelt], nor may you follow the practices of the land of Canaan [to which I am bringing you] (Lev. 18:3). You might think that they [Israel] may not build buildings or plant vegetation as they do; therefore, the verse says: "neither may you walk in their statutes." I only said the statutes which have been legislated for them and for their fathers and for the fathers of their fathers. And what did they do? A man would marry a man, and a woman a woman; a man would marry a woman and her daughter, and a woman would marry two [husbands]. Therefore, it says: "neither may you walk in their statutes" (*Sifra* 8:12:8).

The Torah proceeds to note that the Land of Israel has been sanctified as a holy place which cannot tolerate the behavior of the Canaanites. In the words of Scripture:

It is because of such [behavior] that the nations that I am casting out before you defiled themselves. And the land became defiled, and I called it [the land, i.e. its inhabitants] to account for its iniquity, and the land vomited out its inhabitants [through harsh physical conditions and military defeat] (Lev. 18:24-25).

INTERACTION BETWEEN THE SEXES

An important aspect of any society is the nature of relationships between members of the opposite sex (as well as of the same sex). Men and women may engage in both social and sexual intercourse, but the rules must be defined. The Jewish religion has definite views on these subjects, and some of the sources are to be found in *Acharei Mot*.

The items to be discussed are the following religious concepts:

1. *negi'ah* (touching)
2. *yichud* (seclusion in a private place with a member of the opposite sex who is not one's spouse)
3. *tzni'ut* (modesty)
4. conversation
5. homosexuality.

NEGI'AH (PHYSICAL CONTACT)

Ch. 18 opens with the general admonition: "No person should *approach* a close relative for the purpose of uncovering their nakedness. I am God" (Lev. 18:6).

"Uncovering nakedness" is the Bible's term for sexual relations and, as the verse implies, the continuation of the chapter proceeds to list relatives whom one is prohibited from marrying and with whom sexual contact is classified as incest. However, there are five verses (18:19-23) which specify relations which are forbidden not because of blood relationships, but for other reasons, two of which state:

> **19** Do not approach a woman during her menstrual period to uncover her nakedness. **20** Do not have carnal relations with your neighbor's wife and defile yourself with her.

From the phrase "do not approach," the Midrash cited below (*Sifra Acharei Mot* 8:13:2) derives that not only is sexual intercourse prohibited, but also even "approaching":

I only know that he should not uncover [her nakedness]. From where does one know that he may not approach [come close to her]? The verse (18:19) says "do not approach." I only know that he should not uncover or approach a menstrual woman. From where does one know regarding all of the incestuous relations that one may not approach or uncover? The verse (18:6) says: "no person should approach."

Malbim (Lev. 18:19) explains that verse 6 applies to incestuous relationships, while verse 19 relates to the menstrual woman and to the adulterous relationship of verse 20, which is even stricter, since *yichud* is also forbidden in the latter case.

But what does "approaching" mean? The answer is found in the following Midrash:

What hedge [protective decrees] did the Torah make for its words? Behold it says "Do not approach a woman during her menstrual period" (Lev. 18:19). You might think that he [her husband] may embrace her and kiss her and engage in idle chatter with her. The verse says "do not approach" (*Avot de-Rabbi Natan* A:2).

Rambam (*Sefer ha-Mitzvot*, prohibition 353) considers the prohibition against embracing and kissing to be part of the Torah's definition of the law, as he explains in *Mishneh Torah*:

Anyone who has intercourse with a forbidden partner through one of the limbs, or who hugs and kisses in a lustful way and pleasures himself from the physical intimacy, receives lashes for a Torah level transgression (*Hilchot Issurei Bi'ah* 21:1)

Ramban (*Hasagot*, prohibition 353), on the other hand, feels that the extension is only rabbinical, and the apparent biblical derivation is only an *asmachta* (a support verse, not to be taken literally). *Siftei Cohen* (*Shach*) elucidates the view of Rambam as follows:

> Even Rambam is only speaking when embracing and kissing is done for carnal pleasure, for we find in the Talmud in a number of places that Amora'im embraced and kissed their daughters and sisters [and it was permissible because it was platonic in nature]... and this is explicit in the words of Rambam... and these are his words: "Anyone who has intercourse with a forbidden partner through one of the limbs, or who hugs and kisses in a lustful way and pleasures himself from the physical intimacy, receives lashes for a Torah level transgression" (*Shach, Yoreh De'ah* 157:10).

A typical example of familial embracing is found in the following talmudic segment: "Ulla, when he would come from the house of his teacher, would kiss his sisters on their chests, and some say on their hands" (BT *Shabbat* 13a).

Since platonic physical contact between the sexes is permitted, one would imagine that routine hand-shaking would not pose a problem from a religious point of view. Indeed, R. Elimelech Bar Shaul[60] reports that such was the custom even among the most pious, and others[61] have noted that it is strictly forbidden to embarrass a woman by failing to respond to her outstretched hand, based on such talmudic excerpts as:

---

60. In a letter which appears in Shmuel Katz, *Kedoshim Tihiyu*, p. 245.
61. R. Chaim Berlin, *Responsa Nishmat Chaim, Even ha-Ezer* 135:6; R. Shlomo Karlbach in *Le-David Zvi: Sefer ha-Yovel le-Rav David Zvi Hoffman*, p. 218.

1. Great is human dignity [e.g., not shaming a person], as it overrides a prohibition in the Torah [specifically the law requiring one to obey rabbinical decrees] (BT *Berachot* 19b).

2. "And you should love the Lord your God" (Deut. 6:5), [which means] that you should make the name of Heaven beloved. [How?] One should read Torah, and learn Mishnah, and serve Torah scholars, and be pleasant when interacting with people. What do people say about he [who acts thusly]? ... So-and-so, who studied Torah, see how pleasant are his ways, how proper are his deeds. The verse (Isa. 49:3) states about him: "You are My servant, Israel, in whom I will be glorified" (BT *Yoma* 86a).

Nevertheless, R. Moshe Feinstein[62] prohibits hand-shaking with members of the opposite sex, apparently because he sees it as a sexually imbued gesture. If that is correct, according to Rambam it would be prohibited by Torah law, and adhering to God's commands takes precedence even over human dignity.

YICHUD (SECLUSION)

The prohibition of improper seclusion is stated explicitly in the Mishnah:

> A man may not be secluded with two women [who could easily be persuaded to sin, and certainly not with one woman], but one woman may be secluded with two men [Rashi: for one is embarrassed in the presence of his friend]. R. Shimon says: Even one man may be secluded

---

62. *Responsa Igrot Moshe, Even ha-Ezer* 4:32:9.

with two women when his wife is with him, and he may [even] sleep with them in an inn, because his wife guards him. A man may be secluded with his mother and with his daughter and sleep alongside them with bodily contact [i.e., without clothes]. And when they have grown up, this one sleeps in her garment and that one sleeps in his garment [but they may share a bed] (Mishnah Kiddushin 4:12; BT *Kiddushin* 80b).

The Talmud seeks the source of the law presented in the Mishnah:

R. Yohanan says in the name of R. Yishmael: From where is there an allusion from the Torah to the prohibition against seclusion? For it says [concerning one who incites others to idolatrous worship]: "If your brother, the son of your mother, entices you" (Deut. 13:7). But is it only the son of a mother who entices? Does the son of a father not entice? Rather, [the verse means] to tell you: A son may be secluded with his mother [Rashi: that is why the verse says "the son of your mother," to tell you that the son may be with the mother], but it is prohibited to be secluded with those [other than a mother] with whom relations are forbidden by the Torah (BT *Kiddushin* 80b).

The law of the Mishnah thus prohibits seclusion with many of the potentially incestuous partners; however, there are a number of exceptions to this rule. A man is permitted to be alone with his wife even during her menstruation, in spite of the fact that sexual relations are prohibited at that time (BT *Sanhedrin* 37a), as well as with his mother and daughter.

The law was extended to include non-related single women at the urging of Tamar. It will be recalled that Tamar, the daughter of King David, found herself alone in a room with her brother Amnon, who wished to have relations with her. Tamar begged him to desist, saying: "Please, speak to the king; he will not withold me from you" (2 Sam. 13:13).[63]

The following extensions are accordingly stated in the Talmud:

> David came and decreed [at the behest of Tamar] against seclusion even with an unmarried woman; and the disciples of the schools of Shammai and Hillel came and decreed against seclusion even with a heathen woman (BT *Avodah Zarah* 36b).

Why is seclusion prohibited? Three possibilities may be suggested:

a. to prevent baseless gossip,
b. to prevent engaging in forbidden sexual relations,
c. to prevent well-based gossip, i.e., combining the first two reasons.

The first reason is found in *Avot de-Rabbi Natan* (A:2), which also supplies another source for the prohibition of *yichud*:

---

63. The Talmud (BT *Sanhedrin* 21a) wonders how King David could possibly allow two siblings to marry, and answers that Tamar was actually the daughter of a captive woman, whose mother was pregnant with her before she was captured (according to the view that one may not cohabit with a captive woman until after she converts) or after she was captured, but before her mother converted (according to the view that cohabitation was permitted on the battlefield). Either way, she was not considered David's daughter by Jewish law and would have thus been permitted to marry Amnon.

No person should approach a close relative (Lev. 18:6). Hence it was said: "A man should not be alone with a woman in an inn, even with his sister or his daughter or his mother-in-law, because of public opinion."

The second reason is delineated in the same source, which continues:

It says "no person should approach" (Lev. 18:6) and it says "do not approach" (Lev. 18:19). Do not approach something which may lead to transgression. Keep a distance from that which is offensive and from whatever seems offensive. The Sages said: "Keep a distance from a minor sin lest it lead you to a major sin; hastily fulfill a minor commandment for it will lead you to a major commandment."

The third reason is adopted in *Kiddushin*, where it is stated: "Rav said: 'One is flogged [Rashi: a rabbinical enactment] but not prohibited [from continuing to live with her husband] for committing *yichud*'" (BT *Kiddushin* 81a).

The implication is that there is at least a strong suspicion that illicit behavior was engaged in, and for that reason it was necessary to state that nonetheless, since there is no proof of immorality, her marital status is unaffected. The Talmud proceeds to strengthen the likelihood of misbehavior by bringing examples of great Sages who succumbed to temptation. Two examples will suffice.

a. These captive women, who were brought to Nehardea, were brought up to the house of R. Amram the Pious [Rashi: who ordered that they be redeemed and placed in his attic].

They removed the ladder from before them [to make them inaccessible]. When one of them passed by, a light shone through the aperture [Rashi: her face shone]. R. Amram took a ladder that ten [men together] could not lift. He lifted it on his own and began climbing. When he was halfway up the ladder, he spread his legs [i.e. he stopped], raised his voice [and cried out]: "There is a fire in the house of Amram [Rashi: he alerted the neighbors to come and extinguish the fire in order to assuage his evil inclination, for he would be ashamed before them]." The Sages came [Rashi: as they thought there was a fire there]. They said to him: You have embarrassed us [by calling us for no reason and allowing us to see what you had intended to do]. R. Amram said to them: It is better that you be shamed in Amram's house in this world, and not be ashamed of him in the world-to-come (BT *Kiddushin* 81a).

b. R. Hiyya bar Ashi was accustomed to say, whenever he would fall on his face [in prayer]: "May the Merciful One save us from the evil inclination." One day his wife heard him. She said: "Let us see. It has been several years since he has withdrawn from [having intercourse with] me [Rashi: due to his advanced years, so why is he afraid of his evil inclination?]. What is the reason that he says this [prayer]?" One day, while he was studying in his garden, she adorned herself and repeatedly walked past him. He said: "Who are you? She said: I am Haruta [Rashi: the name of a well-known local prostitute], returning from my day at work. He propositioned her. She said to him: Give me that pomegranate from the top of the tree [as payment]. He leapt up, went, and brought it to her [and they engaged in intercourse].When he came home, his wife was lighting a fire in the oven. He ascended and sat inside it [Rashi: to kill himself]. She said to him: "What is this?" He said to her: "Such and such an incident occurred." She said to him: "It was I." He paid no attention to her [thinking she was merely trying to comfort him], until she gave him signs [i.e., the pomegranate]. He said to her: "I, in any event, intended to transgress." All the days of that righteous man's life he would fast [for the transgression he intended to commit], until he died from it (BT *Kiddushin* 81b).

The point of these stories is that if even great talmudic Sages can cave in to desire, how much more so simple folk. On the other hand, the Talmud (BT *Sukkah* 52a) claims that the situation may be reversed, i.e., the unlearned may be less prone to sinning than scholars. The famous Amora Abaye secretly followed a couple through the forest and noticed that although they enjoyed absolute privacy (as far as they knew), they maintained their distance. Abaye feared that he would not have been able to control himself, and was quite upset until an elder came along and told him: "He who is greater than his friend, has an evil inclination which is greater."

What is the meaning of that saying? Perhaps it wishes to stress that the simple faith of the uneducated frequently allows them to fulfill the spirit of the *mitzvot*, while the expertise of great scholars (who are aware of all the technical details and loopholes associated with *halachah*) may actually present a stumbling block. At any rate, it is clear that secluding oneself with a member of the opposite sex presents a challenge for both rabbis and laymen.

TZNI'UT (MODESTY)

The Torah does not relate directly to the question of modest dress and behavior. There is, however, a talmudic source which discusses the proper environment for saying the daily prayer called *Kri'at Shema*, from which basic principles may be derived. The Talmud states:

> R. Yitzchak stated: An exposed tefach [handbreadth of skin] in a woman constitutes nakedness. Regarding which law was this said? If you say that it comes to prohibit looking at her, did not R. Sheshet say: Why did the verse (Num. 31:50) enumerate [in the phrase "ankle-bracelets and arm-bracelets, breast-shaped ornaments, and kumaz[64] (womb-shaped ornament, placed in the womb)"] jewelry that is worn externally [e.g., bracelets] together with jewelry worn internally [kumaz]? To tell you: anyone who gazes upon a woman's little finger is considered as if he gazed upon her genitals [if his intentions are impure, even less than a handbreadth is forbidden]. Rather, it is referring even to his wife, with regard to the recitation of Kri'at Shema [i.e. one may not recite Shema before an exposed handbreadth of his wife. Rosh 37: "in a place which is normally covered in a woman"] (BT *Berachot* 24a).

The verse cited describes the women's jewelry captured in the fight against Midian, which was, according to the text, offered to the Lord "to make an expiation for our souls." The Talmud asks what sin had they [who fought in Midian] committed, and quotes them as answering: "If we have avoided committing an actual sin, we have not avoided thoughts (*hirhur*) [of sin]" (BT *Shabbat* 64a). More specifically, "they nourished their eyes on nakedness." By doing so, they transgressed the following sin, as described in the Talmud:

---

64. BT *Shabbat* 64a.

"And you should guard yourself from every evil thing"
(Deut. 23:10) — from here R. Pinchas b. Yair said: A
person should not think [impure thoughts] during the day
and [as a result] become impure [by emissions] at night
(BT *Ketubot* 46a).

A similar law is derived from the verse concerning ritual fringes,
which states: "And you will look at it and remember all of the
commandments of the Lord and observe them, rather than
lustfully following after your heart and after your eyes" (Num.
15:39), concerning which the Talmud states: "'After your eyes' -
this is thoughts of sins [of licentiousness]" (BT *Berachot* 12b).

These verses (Deut. 23:10, Num. 15:39) refer to two different
prohibitions. The first prohibits improper enjoyment of a woman's
beauty, while the second involves imagining immoral acts (*Sefer
Mitzvot Katan* 30).[65]

The upshot of this talmudic passage is that inappropriate
gazing upon a woman's body is forbidden, but a man may look
at a woman in normal circumstances, and even say prayers in her
presence. However, one is forbidden to read *Shema* in the presence

---

65. Rambam only counts the verse from Numbers as a negative command
(*Sefer ha-Mitzvot*, Prohibition 47), and apparently includes "enjoyment
of beauty" as part of this command (*Hilchot Issurei Bi'ah* 21:2). *Bet
Shmuel* (*Even ha-Ezer* 21:2) believes that Rambam considers "enjoyment
of beauty" to be prohibited only rabbinically, perhaps because he does
not count the verse from Deuteronomy as a mitzvah, and also because
he stated in *Hilchot Issurei Bi'ah* 21:2 that it is not punishable by lashes.
However, the latter point is moot, because even Torah-level commands
are not punishable by lashes if no act is involved. Tosafot (BT *Avodah
Zarah* 20b) says explicitly that *hirhur* based on the verse in Deuteronomy
is a Torah-level prohibition (although he does not clarify which type of
hirhur). Ramban (*Sefer ha-Mitzvot*, forgotten prohibition 11) counts each
of the two verses as a separate command, from which one may derive that
he considers both forms of *hirhur* to be forbidden by the Torah.

of an improperly attired woman, even if it is his wife.[66]

The Talmud's prohibition to gaze at a woman's body, as a means of sexual stimulation or simply to enjoy her beauty, manifests a surprisingly modern concept. Only in the latter part of the 20th century was it realized that women should not be objectified, i.e., they should not be related to merely as sex objects, but rather as intelligent counterparts to the male population. Orthodox Judaism, together with 21st-century feminists, find beauty contests and the like to be degrading to members of both sexes.

Furthermore, the traditional approach which holds that viewing immodestly dressed women is likely to lead men to have sinful thoughts has been empirically confirmed by experiments which have shown that men respond more to visual sexual stimuli than women.[67]

To summarize, the Talmud discusses two prohibitions, and implies a third:

1. For a man to look intensely at any part of a woman's anatomy (R. Sheshet).

2. To say the *Shema* prayer in the presence of an improperly clad woman, not only as a sexual violation (if she is not his wife), but because it exhibits a lack of respect for the prayer and the God to Whom one prays (R. Yitzchak). It is likewise forbidden to say *Shema* in the presence of excrement, or an unclothed man or child (BT *Berachot* 25a).

---

66. The implication is that if the improperly attired woman is not his wife, he should not look at her altogether.

67. Heather A. Rupp; Kim Wallen. *Sex Differences in Response to Visual Sexual Stimuli: A Review*, "Archives of Sexual Behavior" 37, 2 (Apr 2008) 206–218.

3. Rashba states:

> Her face, hands, legs, speaking voice, and uncovered
> hair protruding from her braids we do not fear [as a
> source of sin], because he is used to them and they do
> not stimulate [sexual feelings] (BT *Berachot* 24a).

From Rashba's explanation, it is clear that the prohibition
to gaze lasciviously is prohibited even upon areas generally
uncovered (e.g. the little finger), but routine looking is
permissible. By the same token, one may derive that upon
private areas, even normal gazing is not permitted. The
reasoning behind the prohibition is quite straightforward—
even casually observing hidden areas of a woman's body may
generate a titillating experience in a man.

At this stage, the talmudic discussion proceeds as follows:

> R. Chisda said: A woman's leg [Hebrew *shok*. Rashba: which
> is a private part and is normally covered] is considered
> nakedness, for it says: "Uncover the leg and pass through
> the rivers" (Isa. 47:2), and it says [Rashi: right after]: "Your
> nakedness will be revealed and your shame will be seen"
> (Isa. 47:3). Shmuel stated: A woman's voice is considered
> nakedness, as it says: "For your voice is sweet and your
> looks are pleasant" (Song of Songs 2:14). R. Sheshet
> stated: A woman's hair is considered nakedness, for it says:
> "Your hair is like a flock of goats [trailing down from Mt.
> Gilead]" (Song of Songs 4:1).

The first item to be dealt with concerns the exact meaning of *shok*. In describing the *shok* of a sacrifice, which is given to the priest when bringing a peace offering, the Mishnah (*Chullin* 10:4) makes it quite clear that it is the part of the leg above the knee. On the other hand, in describing a person's limbs, the Mishnah (*Ohalot* 1:8) places the *shok* between the ankle and the knee, implying that it is the lower leg. Tosafot (BT *Menachot* 37a, s.v. *kiboret*) distinguishes between animals, where it refers to the upper leg, and humans, where it refers to the lower. Accordingly, Rashbah (BT *Berachot* 24a) assumes that R. Chisda is referring to the lower leg. *Pri Megadim* (*Mishbetzot Zahav* 75:1, adopted by *Mishnah Berurah* 75:2), however, based on the Mishnah in *Chullin*, understands that here too the upper leg is meant.

The question that arises is whether these additional restrictions are general in nature, comparable to the law of R. Sheshet barring gazing on a woman's body, or specific to the saying of *Shema*, as described by R. Yitzchak. If the former is the case, then the laws introduced by R. Chisda prohibit hearing a woman's voice or seeing her hair in any situation. If the latter is the case, then in general one is permitted to hear a woman sing or see her hair, just not in the context of saying the *Shema* prayer. Rosh (*Berachot* 3:37) and Rambam (*Hilchot Issurei Bi'ah* 21:2) generalize them, while Ra'avya (Part 1, *Berachot* 76) confines the law to the reading of *Shema*. R. Yosef Karo (based on Rashi on BT *Berachot* 24a, s.v. *ervah*) applies it in general (*Even ha-Ezer* 21:1) and also to *Shema* (*Orach Chayim* 75:3).

Another question which arises was posed by Bach (*Orach Chayim* 75:2): since R. Yitzchak has already stated that it is prohibited to read *Shema* when a *tefach* of normally covered skin is exposed, what is added by saying that a woman's leg may not be exposed? One already knows that, since the leg is normally covered. A number of answers have been proposed:

1. Rashba (BT *Berachot* 24a) says that the leg was chosen simply because it is a sexually neutral limb which is not necessarily covered for men, and one might not have realized that for women it has a different status.

2. *Tosafot ha-Rosh* (BT *Berachot* 24a) says that even among women the leg is frequently displayed, and hence one may not have enumerated it among the normally covered organs.

3. *Bach* (*Orach Chayim* 75:2) claims that the *shok* is more erotically suggestive than other normally covered areas, and hence a man may not say the *Shema* in the presence of a woman whose *shok* is uncovered even if the amount showing is less than a handbreadth.

4. *Bach* brings a second explanation which is diametrically opposed to his first. He cites Rashi (s.v. *ervah*), who says that R. Chisda is stating that one may not *gaze* at the *shok*, which *Bach* finds totally superfluous, being that one may not even gaze at the smallest finger. He answers that the *shok* has a tendency to be dirty, being so close to the ground. Being so repulsive, one might have thought that even gazing at it would not be sexually stimulating, but R. Chisda explains that this is not the case, and the *shok* is in the same category as any other limb.

5. *Mishnah Berurah* (75:2) states "but [saying *Shema* where] her [upper] arms and [upper] legs [are revealed], even [in a place] where [they are] accustomed to walk [with those limbs] uncovered—like the prostitutes—is prohibited." *Mishnah Berurah* apparently believes that R. Chisda singled out *shok* because it is a limb which prevents one from saying *Shema* even if the custom is not to cover them.[68]

---

68. Since *Mishnah Berurah* holds that *shok* refers to the leg above the knee, he would only require skirts to cover the knee, but according to those who consider the *shok* to be below the knee, a woman would have to cover her entire leg, and in a parallel manner, her entire arm until the hand (*Responsa Minchat Yitzchak* 6:10).

It was noted that there are different opinions as to whether *shok* refers to the leg above or below the knee. The *Mishnah Berurah* said it refers to the upper knee, but it is clear from the answers of *Tosafot ha-Rosh*, *Bach*, and probably Rashba that they understood it to refer to the lower leg.

Most of the commentators cited would prohibit a man from viewing a woman whose clothes expose areas normally covered. Mishnah Berurah goes one step further and says that the *shok* may not be exposed even in locations where it is normal to reveal it, although his definition of *shok* is more limited.

Of course, even if R. Chisda's prohibitions are general, according to most commentators they are rabbinical in origin (*Nishmat Adam* 4:1)[69] and only forbidden if comparable to gazing, i.e., when sexual feelings are aroused. For example, Ra'avya (Part 1, *Berachot* 76) says that the hair of an unmarried woman is not sexually arousing, since it is not normally covered. Similarly, both Rambam (*Hilchot Issurei Bi'ah* 21:2) and R. Yosef Karo (*Even ha-Ezer* 21:1) do not speak of a woman's voice, but rather of "the voice of lewdness,"[70] which would imply that the prohibition is only when her singing (or even speaking) is sexually arousing (*Kachva de-Shavit*, *Berachot* 24a; *Mishnah Berurah* 85:17). Similarly, in discussing the degree of lewdness generated by a woman's voice, Rama (*Orach Chayim* 75:3) says that "hearing a voice which he is familiar with is not considered nakedness." On the other hand, Chatam Sofer (*Choshen Mishpat* 190) considers a woman's singing to be "an abomination comparable to nakedness" in all instances.

---

69. *Divrei Chefetz* 34, however, claims that these restrictions are Torah-based.

70. This is according to the second explanation of *kol ervah* in *Perishah* on *Even ha-Ezer* 21:2. In *Orach Chaim* 75:3, R. Yosef Karo limits the prohibition to hearing the "singing voice of a woman."

It is interesting to note that with regard to those situations which lead to *hirhur*, whether as a result of seeing or hearing women, the main obligation is on the man, who—after all—is the one who would be thinking the improper thoughts, and it is his duty to avoid such situations. On the other hand, a woman should not act or dress improperly, since by doing so she will enable and even stimulate men to sin, thus transgressing the prohibition to "place a stumbling block before a blind person" (Lev. 19:14).

R. David Bigman[71] has attempted to adapt Rambam's prohibition to hear a "voice of lewdness" to the contemporary scene, and has concluded that one may hear a woman singing under certain conditions which take into account the context and atmosphere, the lyrics and musical style of the song, and the singer's dress and body language. Since the purpose of the halachic prohibition is to avoid sinful thoughts (*hirhur*), the conditions are fulfilled when the presentation is innocent and asexual.

As far as dress is concerned, it is clear that Jewish law favors conservative dress, since a Jewish man is prohibited from seeing a woman whose clothing reveals bodily areas normally covered. The earlier commentaries seem satisfied to allow the laws to be dictated by local custom, but Mishnah Berurah has defined certain absolutes, positing that Jewish women should not dress "like prostitutes," leaving unanswered the question of how to dress if there is a conflict between normative apparel and his pre-defined absolute boundaries.

CONVERSATION

Although the status of women in both the narrative and the legal rulings of the Bible reflect the attitudes of the contemporary

71. "A New Analysis of 'Kol B'Isha Erva,'" Jewishideas.org.

civilization, there seems to be no interdiction of men and women engaging in conversation. The Bible records dialogues between single women and their interlocutors (Rebecca and Abraham's servant [Gen. 24:17-27], Rachel and Jacob [Gen. 29:11-12], the daughters of Zelophehad and Moses [Num. 27:2-4], Ruth and Boaz [Ruth 2:8-14]); married women and their husbands (Sarah and Abraham [Gen. 16:5-6; 21:10], Rebecca and Isaac [Gen. 27:46], Rachel and Jacob [Gen. 30:1-3], Rachel, Leah and Jacob [Gen. 31:4-16]); married women and their male relatives (Esther and Mordechai[72] [Esther 4:6-16]); and married women and other men (Deborah and Barak [Jud. 4:6-9], Yael and Barak [Jud. 4:622]; and Hulda the prophetess with Hilkia et al. [2 Kings 22:14-20]). Although there is a paucity of women in leadership positions in the Bible, those who were—such as Deborah and Hulda—would certainly have come in contact frequently with the male populace, and the Bible seems to consider such behavior to be completely normative.

When Shmuel said "A woman's voice is considered nakedness" (BT *Berachot* 24a), he explained in tractate *Kiddushin* (70a) that he was referring even to the *speaking* voice of a woman. Although Rashba (BT *Berachot* 24a) limited Shmuel's proscription to extending greetings, which display a greater degree of intimacy, R. Eliyahu Mizrachi (Gen. 18:9) took it quite literally and prohibited all dialogue, *Meshaneh Halachot* (7:254) permitted only short transactions, and even *Mishnah Berurah* (75:18) disallowed verbal interaction if the male listener finds it to be enjoyable or entertaining.

---

72. According to Esther 2:7 and 2:15, Mordechai and Esther were cousins. According to Josephus (*Antiquities of the Jews* 11:6), Mordechai was Esther's uncle. The Midrash sees both Mordechai and Esther (BT *Megillah* 13b), and Barak and Deborah (Radak, Esther 4:4) as married couples, although in *Eliyahu Rabbah* 10, Deborah's husband is described as being pious, but ignorant.

Another source apparently allows for conversations between men and women as long as it is not overdone. The Mishnah states:

> Do not engage in too much conversation [*sichah*] with women. They said it with regard to one's own wife. How much more so does it apply to one's neighbor's wife. From this the Sages said: "Any time that a person engages in too much conversation with women, he brings evil upon himself, neglects the study of Torah, and in the end will suffer purgatory" (*Avot* 1:5).

In order to understand how this Mishnah relates to today's reality, it is necessary to examine the reasons suggested by the various commentators and to judge the relevance and scope of each. The Mishnah itself says explicitly that by spending time speaking to women, one deprives himself of free time which might be devoted to Torah study. However, this could not be the principal reason, since it follows the warning that one who speaks to women will bring "evil upon himself." Moreover, that reason would apply to idle conversation in general, even between two men.

Two approaches have been taken. Rambam and Rabbeinu Yonah believe that communication between the sexes should be severely limited. Me'iri and R. Samson Raphael Hirsch exclude only certain types of interactions.

Limited communication:

Rambam (*Perush ha-Mishnayot*) feels that conversation between men and women generally revolves around sexual matters, and as such, inflames the desires of the participants and can easily lead to *hirhur* or possibly even acting out those evil thoughts. Along the same lines, the French version of *Avot de-Rabbi Natan* (ch. 7) says that the prohibition is with respect to one's menstruant wife, or one's neighbor's wife, because it looks suspicious and could at the very least lead to slanderous accusations by the neighbors. Rabbeinu Yonah (*Avot* 1:5) elaborates, explaining that with respect to his own wife, he is more likely to be able to control his passion, since at the end of her menstrual cycle she will be permitted to him, whereas his neighbor's wife will never be permitted and is especially alluring since "stolen water is sweet" (Prov. 9:17).

Rabbeinu Yonah himself takes a very strict approach, stating that in principle a man's relationship with his wife is solely for the purpose of procreation and not for mutual enjoyment. Man is distinguished from animals in that he seeks purity and holiness, which are engendered by abstinence, as the Sages said: "Torah scholars should not be with their wives like roosters" (BT *Berachot* 22a).

With regard to the verse "Behold, He Who forms the mountains, and creates the wind, and declares to man what it is that he has spoken" (Amos 4:13), the Talmud tells the following story:

> What is the meaning of [the phrase] "[declares to man] what it is that he has spoken?" Rav said: Even superfluous [frivolous] speech that is between a man and his wife is declared to a person at the time of death [and he will have to account for it]. Is that so? Was not Rav Kahana lying beneath Rav's bed, and he heard Rav chatting and laughing and then he performed his needs [had relations with his wife]? He [Rav Kahana] said: "The mouth of Rav is like one who has never eaten a cooked dish [his behavior is lustful]." Rav said to him: "Kahana, leave, as this is not proper conduct" [but the implication is that Rav himself

did engage in frivolous talk before relations]. This is not difficult. Here [where such speech is permitted] it refers to a situation where he must appease his wife before relations, and there it refers to a situation where he does not need to appease her (BT *Chagigah* 5b).

Expanded communication:

According to Me'iri (*Avot* 1:5), husband and wife may communicate as much as is necessary concerning the details of running a household and covering its expenses. However, areas of knowledge which are not directly relevant to her daily functioning, such as current events, history, and general knowledge, should not be shared with her, because her husband is better off spending more time working or studying Torah.

R. Hirsch (*Avot* 1:5, in the Hirsch Prayer Book) goes much farther in terms of the range of topics, saying that her husband "will want to discuss with her the serious concerns of life and will derive enjoyment from the resulting exchange of views and counsel." According to R. Hirsch, the word *sichah* symbolizes chatter and trifling talk, and is referred to negatively later in *Avot*, where one is advised to avoid *sichat yeladim* ("children's talk," in 3:14) and to aspire to *mi'ut sichah* (limiting idle conversation, in 6:6). In fact, the latter two references refer to both men and women, as do the following citations:

1. Why do talmudic scholars die when they are minors? Not because they are adulterers and not because they are robbers, but rather because they cease studying Torah and indulge in idle conversation (*divrei sichah*) (*Avot de-Rabbi Natan* A:26).
2. R. Chananiah b. Ya'akov says: If one wakes up in the night in the midst of words of Torah, it is a good sign for him; in the

midst of words of idle conversation (*divrei sichah*), it is a bad sign for him (*Avot de-Rabbi Natan* A:29).

One type of interaction between spouses which is universally condemned by all of the exegetes on this Mishnah is gossip, as described in the following Mishnah:

> If a man came to the study house and was not treated with honor, or if he had a dispute with his friend, he should not go and tell his wife, "This is how I fell out with my friend; he said this to me and I said that to him." For [in doing so] he disgraces himself, he disgraces his wife, and he disgraces his friend. And his wife, who used to honor him, now stands and scoffs at him. When his friend hears of it [Rashi: because his wife, who empathizes with him, quarrels with the friend's wife—her former confidante, who then shares her discomfiture with her husband] and says: "Woe unto me! Sharp words between himself and me he went and told his wife!" And thus such a person disgraces himself, his wife, and his friend (*Avot de-Rabbi Natan* A:7).

The question that persists according to R. Hirsch, and to a lesser extent according to Me'iri, is that since *sichah* is looked askance at with regard to men no less than with regard to women, why does the Mishnah formulate the restriction in terms of a man talking to his wife, rather than in terms of human interactions independent of the gender of the participants? Apparently, even according to the more liberal approaches, one cannot deny the role of sexual attraction when males and females engage each other, and even if such high level interaction is permitted, one must always be wary in non-marital contexts, lest it degenerate to forbidden flirtation.

HOMOSEXUALITY

The Torah forbids sexual relations between men, as it says in *Acharei Mot*: "You may not lie with a man as with a woman; it is an abomination" (Lev. 18:22). The biblical punishment (if seen by two male witnesses) is described in the next portion, *Kedoshim*: "And a man who lies with a man as with a woman, they have both committed an abomination: they will be put to death; their blood is upon them" (Lev. 20:13). The Torah does not explicitly mention lesbianism; however, the previously cited Midrash (Sifra 8:12:8) includes "women marrying women" among the prohibited Canaanite and Egyptian practices.

Rambam takes this exegesis literally, as a Torah-level law prohibiting homosexual acts between women, but he admits that it is not one of the 613 *mitzvot* and therefore not punishable, although the rabbis may institute lashing, since they have behaved in a forbidden manner (*Hilchot Issurei Bi'ah* 21:8). The *Prisha* (*Even ha-Ezer* 20:11) believes that *Tur Even ha-Ezer* 20:11 considers the prohibition to be rabbinic in origin.

It should be noted that the previously described prohibitions relate to performing homosexual acts,[73] not to being homosexual, just as there is a prohibition to engage in an illegitimate marriage, but not to be the product of such. The Torah does not condemn people for being in a situation which is beyond their control.

Much has been made of the fact that this act is termed "an abomination [*to'evah*]" in two places (Lev. 18:22; 20:13), and it would seem that the term is reserved for major sins. It is used extensively in describing the corrupt behavior of the idol-

---

73. These acts would include caressing and kissing, just as is true regarding the other sexually forbidden relationships (*Aruch ha-Shulchan, Even ha-Ezer* 20:18).

worshipping nations who were the former occupants of the Land of Israel (Deut. 7:25; 7:26; 12:31; 13:15; 17:4; 18:9; 18:12; 20:18; 27:15). It is also used in connection with immoral business practices (Deut. 25:16), consuming non-kosher meat (Deut. 14:3), and of course the whole list of incestuous practices (Lev. 18:26-30).

Moral laws and statutes:
The laws of the Torah may be categorized as being either moral laws or statutes. Of those previously listed, clearly honesty in business represents a moral value, while the prohibition to eat non-kosher meat is a statute. As far as incestuous relations, different opinions are expressed in the sources. The Talmud states in two locations that even if those laws were not included in the Torah, man would have derived them on his own, for example by imitating the dove, who is loyal to its mate (BT *Yoma* 67b; BT *Eruvin* 100b). On the other hand, the Midrash (Sifra *Kedoshim* 10) says that one may admit to craving an incestuous relationship and rejecting it only because of the biblical prohibition, implying that these laws are statutes.

The same argument exists among biblical exegetes. Ramban says that if not for the biblical prohibition,

> what would it hurt if one would marry his daughter, as is permitted for the children of Noah (BT *Sanhedrin* 58b), or marry two sisters, as Jacob our father did; and a man cannot find a marriage as suitable as marrying his daughter to his older son, so that he could bequeath them his portion and they would be fruitful and multiply in his own house (Lev. 18:6).

Rambam in principle agrees with Ramban, saying that the Torah prohibited such marriages only because if they were permitted, then it would be forbidden for family members to spend time together in seclusion, just as is true for unrelated members of the opposite sex, and that would not be practical (*Guide for the Perplexed* 3:49). One might add that allowing the possibility of a father or older sibling marrying a young girl would deprive her of freedom of choice. How would she be able to withstand the pressure of a senior family member, one whom she is obligated to respect according to *halachah*?

The *Baal ha-Akedah* is astonished at the import of Ramban's words, and he writes the following:

> I am quite amazed at his words, for incestuous relationships such as [with a] mother, daughter, or sister, more than the Torah prohibited them, healthy human intuition distances them and holds them in disgust to a maximum of revulsion and loathing, to the extent that there is no nation or country where it is common (*Akedat Yitzchak, Vayikra* 64 – *Acharei Mot*).

Unfortunately, newspapers frequently report such incidents. If such behavior is abnormal in the view of the *Baal ha-Akedah*, how does this happen? He apparently foresaw this question, explaining that such acts are performed only by "people whose nature is corrupt and [they are] similar to animals who engage in pederasty and bestiality, for they are like those who eat coals or raw meat, or those who eat the flesh of their own sons and daughters." In short, such behavior is exhibited by those unpossessed of what he calls "healthy human intuition," i.e., mentally ill people.

R. Moshe Feinstein's view:

R. Feinstein was convinced that homosexuality is among the most serious sins recorded in the Torah. True, the Torah refers to the whole myriad of forbidden sexual relationships four times as *to'evah* (Lev. 18:26-30), but only homosexuality was singled out from all the others and called *to'evah* two additional times (Lev. 18:22; 20:13). According to R. Feinstein, the reason is that sins such as adultery are abominable because they are violations of Torah law, but not of human nature. Regarding homosexuality, however, he says:

> There is no natural desire, and all of the desire for this is only a deviation from nature to a different path which even wicked people—who are not deterred [from sinning] because it [some act] is a sin and a transgression—do not go there, because this evil drive is only because it is a forbidden act done in spite... and for the sin of homosexual activity the wicked person who transgresses this has no claim to justify himself, for it is not possible to crave to perform this sin... his entire craving is only because it is a forbidden thing and the evil inclination incites him to rebel against the will of the Almighty (*Orach Chayim* 4:115).

What the *Ba'al ha-Akedah* says of incest in general, R. Feinstein confines to homosexual activity, namely that it is an immoral, unnatural act. The *Ba'al ha-Akedah* speaks of the transgressors as mentally ill, while R. Feinstein calls them rebellious heretics. According to Rambam, rebellion against God implies negation of morality in general, as may be deduced from the following passage:

Our Sages declare it wherever opportunity is given, that the idea of God necessarily implies justice; that He will reward the most pious for all their pure and upright actions, although no direct commandment was given them through a prophet; and that He will punish all the evil deeds of men, although they have not been prohibited by a prophet, if common sense warns against them, as e.g. injustice and violence (*Guide for the Perplexed* 3:17).

On the other hand, one may take the approach of the previously cited Ramban, that the sexual prohibitions are in the category of statutes, rather than moral sins. In the view of R. Shmuley Boteach, homosexuality should not be referred to as an aberration or sexual deviation, but rather "as a sin, something which the Torah designates as spiritually unsatisfactory and undesirable to God, much as the flesh of a pig is spiritually undesirable."[74] The prohibition to eat pig is, of course, a statute and not a morality-based law (Sifra *Kedoshim* 9:4).

Scientific findings:

It must be pointed out that R. Feinstein's responsum was written before the "homosexual revolution," i.e., before the subject became a topic of much discussion and research, and before the public was aware of the frequency of this phenomenon among all strata of society and all religious streams within Judaism. The changed perception occurred when more people felt free to reveal their formerly concealed sexual inclinations. The results of some modern surveys are summarized below:

---

74. Shmuley Boteach, *Moses of Oxford* (London: Andre Deutsch, 1994), vol. 1, p. 36.

1. The incidence of lesbianism was in the 1-2% range, while the incidence of male homosexuality was in the 2-4% range.[75] The percentages were a bit higher when bisexuality was included in each group.

2. In identical male twins, if one was homosexual, the second was homosexual 52% of the time, while for females the parallel figure was 48%.[76]

3. In fraternal male twins, if one was homosexual, the second was homosexual 22% of the time, while for females the parallel figure was 16%.[77]

4. In adoptive brothers, if one was homosexual, the second was homosexual 11% of the time, while for females the parallel figure was 6%.[78]

5. Scientific studies have shown that sexual orientation is highly resistant to explicit transformation attempts and that conversion therapies are either ineffective or damaging, a waste of time and money, and possibly even have the following harmful effects: decreased self-esteem, increased self-shame, increased depression and anxiety, decreased religiosity, worsening of family relationships, and increased suicidality.[79]

---

75. P. Gebhard, "Incidence of Overt Homosexuality in the United States and Western Europe," in National Institute of Mental Health Task Force on Homosexuality: Final Report and Background Papers (DHEW Publication No. HSM 72-9116, 1972, pp. 22-29); Gary J. Gates, "How Many People are Lesbian, Gay, Bisexual, and Transgender?" (The Williams Institute, 2011); Ann Oakley, Sex, Gender, and Society (Routledge, 2016).

76. J. Michael Bailey; Richard C. Pillard, "Genetics of Human Sexual Orientation," Annual Review of Sex Research 6,1 (1995) 126-150.

77. Ibid.

78. Ibid.

79. J.P. Dehlin et al., "Sexual Orientation Change Efforts among Current or Former LDS Church Members," Journal of Counseling Psychology (17 Mar 2014).

In fact, in the U.S., seven states and seventeen cities have outlawed conversion therapy of minors, and any psychologist who practices it is in danger of losing his license.[80]

On the other hand, a number of rabbis claim to have successfully converted as many as one-third of their patients from homosexuality to heterosexuality.[81] A prominent rabbi with much experience in the area feels that conversion therapy should be neither shunned nor imposed, but rather presented in a transparent manner with due emphasis on both its promise and its drawbacks. [82]

Discussion:

Two questions must be dealt with. First, how should religious homosexuals relate to themselves? Second, how should the religious community relate to them?

A. **Relating to oneself:**

R. Aharon Feldman[83] has noted the following points with respect to Jewish homosexuals:

1.   He/she is as beloved in God's eyes as any other person, and is as responsible as any Jew to fulfill the laws of the Torah. Regarding those who are loyal to the laws of the Torah, the prophet says:

> For so the Lord said: "As for the [childless] eunuchs who keep My Sabbaths, and have chosen what I

---

80. Wikipedia, list of U.S. jurisdictions banning conversion therapy for minors.
81. *Arele Harel at Kenes Torah u-Madah*, Jerusalem College of Technology, 2017.
82. Yuval Cherlow, "Al Tipulei Hamara" (2015).
83. Aharon Feldman, *Jewish Action* 58:3 (Spring 1998) 69-70.

desire, and observe My covenant, I will give them, in My House and within My walls, a monument and a name better than sons or daughters. I will give them an everlasting name which will never perish (Isa. 56:4-5).

2. He/she is obligated to achieve life's goals by directing his/her life towards spiritual growth, sanctity, and perfection of his/her character - no less than any other person.
3. He/she will merit the same share in the world to come that every person merits, which may be maximized by devoting his/her life to the service of God.

R. Yuval Cherlow[84] has stressed the importance of homosexuals being aware of the complexity of their predicament and the difficulty of finding a means of satisfying both their personal and religious needs. On the one hand, it is far from certain that conversion therapy will work; on the other hand, the religion demands of them not to engage in homosexual acts. Marriage may be attempted with a heterosexual partner, but it may not be easy or fair to do so. Somehow, homosexuals are expected to find a way to handle this situation without becoming desperate or lapsing into depression. No simple task!

R. Feldman has suggested a means for homosexuals to solve this conundrum by devoting themselves to the welfare of their people and community, who will then become, in a manner of speaking, their spouse and children. They may even find a niche where they outshine heterosexuals, such as bringing Judaism to communities too small to have facilities for Jewishly educating the

---

84. Yuval Cherlow, *Kavei Mit'ar le-Mifgash be-Olam ha-Nimshachim le-Bnei Minam* (2015).

young, which does not pose a problem for them but would be a serious obstacle for rabbis with young families. Alternatively, such people may serve as fundraisers for charitable institutions, which involves prolonged absences from home and spending much time in different cities, thereby vastly extending their communal family.

Short stays in various locales would make it easier for homosexuals to abide by the normative religious standard which requires them to live on their own. Although the Talmud says: "Israelites are not suspected of homosexuality" (BT *Kiddushin* 82a), R. Yosef Karo, in his code of law, adds: "In these generations, when libertinism has increased, one [meaning a male] should avoid seclusion (*yichud*) with a male [and the parallel would be true for women] (*Even ha-Ezer* 24:1). Bach disagrees with R. Karo, saying: "He wrote so for his country and generation, and the implication is that this is to be enforced as a law, but in our country, where it is unheard of that this law has been transgressed, one need not distance himself [from *yichud* with a man], but at any rate, he who distances himself is to be praised (*Bach, Even ha-Ezer* 24).

It must be remembered that the Talmud was not aware of, or at least did not discuss, the concept of homosexual inclination, just homosexual acts. Today, when scientific evidence of this distinction exists, it would be reasonable to posit according to the *Bach* with respect to homosexuals, and according to R. Yosef Karo for those with tendencies, who compose a vulnerable cohort, not to be secluded with single members of their own sex. At any rate, heterosexuals should be aware of the formidable task facing homosexuals who wish to abide by *halachah*, and should respectfully view those who attempt to do so as "His angels, mighty creatures who do His bidding" (Ps. 103:20).

B. **How the community relates:**

The following guidelines are partially based on a brochure promulgated by the Israeli Orthodox rabbinical organization called Beit Hillel:[85]

1. Single people living on their own should be embraced by the community, which must substitute for their lack of an on-site family.

2. Members of the same sex residing together should also be embraced by the community in which they live. As noted, the *Bach* permits this behavior, and it is the norm in the dormitories of the most religious schools, as well as among yeshiva and university graduates who have not found a spouse, and there is no reason to surmise that such people are not Torah-observant Jews. Some people have great difficulty in finding a mate, and may even never succeed. For such people, life is hard enough, and it is a great mitzvah to lighten their burden and create mutually-rewarding friendships.

3. Even if there is reason to suspect that flatmates may be homosexual, two factors should be taken into consideration. First, until it is known for sure that they are behaving in a manner which contradicts *halachah*, a Jew is enjoined to "judge all men meritoriously" (*Avot* 1:6). Second, Jewish communities number among their members people whose observance is lacking with regard to laws between man and his fellow man (*bein adam le-chaveiro*) as well as between man and God (*bein adam la-Makom*). The reason is obvious. Nobody is perfect, and the very acceptance of people with flaws by the community is perhaps the most powerful stimulus for them to overcome their deficiencies. If even on

85. Folder 11 at the website of Beit Hillel: www.beithillel.org.il.

Yom Kippur the community "declares it lawful to pray with sinners" (*Kol Nidrei* service), how much more so does it follow that during the year the community must project all of its influence and charisma to help those who have lost their way. With this in mind, sexual behavior which does not conform to *halachah* should be no different than other equally serious transgressions.

4. Although the default communal relationship to same-sex couples should be welcoming, an Orthodox congregation cannot sustain members who preach or campaign against the principles upon which that community is based. Since the Torah only recognizes traditional heterosexual marriage and relations, any attempt to normalize other options is considered heretical. While a community can thrive even when some of its members cannot contain their appetite for forbidden acts (*mumar le-teiʾavon*), it cannot tolerate those who publicly negate its mores (*mumar le-hachis*).

The reason for this distinction should be clear. It was previously pointed out that homosexuality is the result of two significant factors—genetic and environmental, which means that the sexual identity of young people, when it is in the process of being formulated, is susceptible to external influences. Those who, through no fault of their own, have to cope with the difficulties of homosexuality in the Orthodox world should certainly be able to understand the congregation's desire to minimize the occurence of this phenomenon.

CONCLUSION

Orthodox Judaism relates to people as spiritual beings possessed of God-given intellect which enables them to investigate and understand their environment for the purposes of improving their lot during their relatively short stay in this world and delving into the spiritual aspect of their existence and the God Who enabled it.

On the one hand, there exists a powerful sexual attraction between genders. On the other hand, all humans are possessed of the potential to grow intellectually and spiritually, and as such must respect each other's body and spirit. The Jewish laws regulating sexual interaction are designed to preserve and enhance every person's potential to grow in all areas, and this may involve controlling, but not repressing, the sexual drive, since cross-pollination between the sexes is beneficial and reproduction is essential. Restrictions which deprive people of their ability to self-actualize do not contribute to the achievement of the religion's goal, but those which maintain their security, flexibility, and freedom of action (within the realm of *halachah*) are to be welcomed.

KEDOSHIM

The Torah commands holiness in the second verse of the portion of *Kedoshim* (literally, "holy"), which states: "Speak to all of the congregation of the Children of Israel, and say to them: You should be holy, for I, the Lord your God, am holy" (Lev. 19:2). Although other verses (to be cited) also command sanctification leading to holiness, in those it is clearly stated in reference to a specific mitzvah. Here, an order to be holy is given without immediate elaboration as to what holiness involves. However, the verse does explain why one should be holy by adding "for I, the Lord your God, am holy." In order to have a close relationship with God, one must emulate Him by being as holy as possible, just like He is holy (*imitatio dei*). Israel is like the court of a king, whose sole function is to imitate the king.[86]

Understanding the meaning of holiness will be approached sequentially. First, verses which promise holiness as a result of abstaining from negative behavior will be examined. This level of holiness is a prerequisite for achieving the higher level, which involves fulfilling positive commands as well.

---

86. *Sifra Kedoshim*, portion A, introduction to ch. A.

Mitzvot Leading to Holiness
– the First Step

1. Lev. 11:44, which appears after the list of permissible foods, says "sanctify yourselves [through observing the dietary laws] and be holy."

2. Lev. 19:2 was quoted above as an independent command. However, since it appears after a list of illicit sexual relations (Lev. 18), it may be looked upon as resulting from proper sexual behavior (Rashi on this verse).

3. Lev. 20:7, which appears after an enumeration of various forms of idol worship (Lev. 20:1-6), says "sanctify yourselves [through distancing yourself from idolatry] and be holy."

4. Lev. 20:26, which once more follows a verse stressing the obligation to proscribe oneself from forbidden foods, says: "And you will be holy to Me; for I, the Lord, am holy."

5. In Deut. 14:2, the charge to be a holy nation is followed immediately by an enumeration of non-kosher creatures, after which the goal of attaining holiness is again recorded (Deut. 14:21).

6. The first mention of the dietary laws in Exodus already stipulated that their goal is to enable one to become holy, by stating: "And you will be holy men unto Me; therefore, you should not eat any flesh that is torn from beasts in the field; you should cast it to the dogs" (Exod. 22:30), whereupon Rashi comments: "If you are holy and abstain from carrion and the flesh of animals torn by wild beasts, then you will be Mine; otherwise, you will not be Mine."

In short, the observance of three sets of laws is designated as enabling the achievement of holiness—dietary laws, sexual laws, and theological laws. One might distinguish between the first, which may be looked upon as catalytic in nature, enabling the person (and the nation) to be isolated from bad influences and develop positive personality traits,[87] and the two others, which in themselves lead to moral and spiritual elevation. Nevertheless, these last two are concerned mainly with overcoming negative impulses, such as having forbidden sexual relations and idol worship in any of its variegated forms. These two sets of laws were considered so vital that one is required to refrain from transgressing them even if his life is at stake.[88]

Although overcoming one's evil inclination can be looked upon as being limited to the development of self-control, Rambam considers the possibility that it might involve a total transformation of one's basic drives. This view will now be examined.

Rambam's viewpoint of the righteous person:

In *Shemonah Perakim* (Rambam's introduction to *Avot*), ch. 6,[89] Rambam discusses the difference between the man of self-restraint (*moshel be-rucho*) and the saintly man (*chasid*). He defines the *moshel be-rucho* as follows:

> Although he performs good and important deeds, yet he does them [while] desiring [to do] bad [immoral] deeds, and he craves for them, but [he] subdues his evil

---

87. See the chapter on the portion of *Shemini*.
88. BT *Sanhedrin* 74a. The third set of laws mentioned in *Sanhedrin*, composed of those associated with murder, is perhaps so basic that although necessary, it is far from sufficient, for the achievement of holiness.
89. The quotes from Rambam in this section are all from this source.

inclination… and he suffers in doing them [when acting morally and fighting against his natural drives] and is hurt [weakened in the process].

On the other hand, he defines the *chasid* in the following manner: "He is guided in his actions [to do] that which his inclination and disposition stimulate him [to do], and he does the [morally] good which he longs for." In other words, the man of restraint has to struggle intensely with his evil inclination, but because of his self-control, he overcomes it and does the proper thing. The saintly person, on the other hand, is naturally righteous and has no craving to behave immorally.

Which of these two is superior? According to Rambam, philosophers are of the unanimous opinion that it is the saintly person, since he is so holy and pure that his spirit is totally free of evil desires. The man of restraint, on the other hand, although he successfully curbs his passion, still yearns to do evil, even if he does not succumb, and this represents a flaw in his soul.

Rambam believes that King Solomon was of the same opinion as the philosophers, based on the following verse from the book of Proverbs: "To do justly is joy to the righteous, but torment to the evil-doer" (Prov. 21:15). Rambam interprets this verse to be saying that the *chasid*, who experiences no internal resistance when acting morally, thoroughy enjoys doing so, while for others, even if they prevail over their evil inclination and succeed in acting morally, it is only after serious effort and travail.

At this point, Rambam raises a question on his own theory. He cites a number of traditional sources which contradict the thesis of the philosophers and express adulation for those people who have an active evil inclination which they have to struggle against. He quotes three rabbinic sources:

1. "He who is greater than his friend has a greater evil inclination" (BT *Sukkah* 52a). Rambam apparently interprets this phrase to mean that if one is born with powerfully lustful drives and nevertheless overcomes them, he has proven himself more than one whose drives were not that strong in the first place.

2. "In proportion to the pain [in accomplishing a worthy goal] is the reward" (*Avot* 5:23). The implication is that those with an active evil inclination, who experience more pain in overcoming it, are superior to those who have trained themselves to minimize their lust.

3. A previously quoted Midrash which says explicitly that one should rather maintain his evil cravings than neutralize them:

> R. Elazar b. Azariah stated: How does one know that he should not say... "eating pig meat is disgusting,"... but rather [he should say] "I would [probably] enjoy [eating] it. What should I do if my Father in heaven has decreed against doing so?" (*Sifra Kedoshim* 9:4).

Rambam answers his question decisively and says: "Both [the philosophers and the rabbis] are correct and not the least in disagreement." The philosophers who praise those who have no desire to perform evil are referring to acts which are universally condemned, "such as bloodshed, theft, robbery, fraud, unprovoked injury, ingratitude, shaming of father and mother, and the like. These are laws regarding which the Sages, of blessed memory, said 'If they had not already been written [in the Torah], it would be proper to write them' [based on BT *Yoma* 67b]." Rambam bases himself on his belief that there exist moral truths, independent of any written law, which are at the foundation of human behavior, and that these follow from a true understanding of the meaning of the existence of a unique Supreme Being. He goes on to say that one will be punished for transgressing laws of this type even if no prophet prohibited them. [90] Summarizing the stance of the philosophers, he concludes:

> There is no doubt that a soul which desires one of these [aforementioned misdeeds] and yearns for it, is lacking [imperfect], and that a worthy soul will not lust at all after any of these evil deeds, and will not be pained by refraining from them.

The rabbis, on the other hand, who laud the man of self-restraint who controls himself in spite of his desire to sin, refer to what Rambam [after Saadia Gaon] calls *mitzvot shimiyot*, meaning laws which were heard at Mt. Sinai, i.e., statutes and ceremonial laws which, had they not been given at Sinai, would not be considered to be incumbent on a Jew to observe. It was regarding such laws that the rabbis said: "man should permit his soul to love these things, and there should be nothing which prevents him [from doing such deeds] other than [the prohibitions of] the Torah."

Rambam substantiates this distinction by making the following observation:

> Ponder their [the Sages'] wisdom, of blessed memory, [as manifested] in the examples they adduce. They did not say, "A person should not say, 'I have no desire to kill a person,' 'I have no desire to steal,' 'I have no desire to lie,' but [he should say] 'I have a desire [to commit these

90. *Guide for the Perplexed* 3:17; see also Abba Engelberg, *The Ethics of Genesis* (2014), p. 226.

crimes], but what can I do - my Father in heaven decreed concerning me [not to allow them]!'" But they cited instances, all of which are *shimiyot* [arbitrary laws given at Sinai]: [partaking of] meat and milk together, wearing *shaatnez* [clothes made of wool and linen], and entering into consanguineous marriages [beyond those prohibited by the Noahide laws]. These and similar enactments are what God called *chukkim* [statutes] and our rabbis, of blessed memory, said: "Statutes which I [God] have enacted for you, you do not have permission to question, and the nations of the world challenge them, and Satan denounces them, as for instance, the statutes concerning the red heifer, the scapegoat, and so forth." And those [transgressions] which the later scholars [specifically Saadia Gaon] called *sichliyot* [rational laws] are termed *mitzvot* [commandments], as the Sages explained.

Wrapping it all up, Rambam concludes:

> It is now evident, from all that we have said, which sins are such that a man who has no desire to commit them is on a higher plane than he who has a longing to do so and controls his passion for them; and for which [sins] the opposite is true.

Rambam as a basis for relating positively to non-believers:

A question that arises frequently among religious people of all faiths is how to relate to those who do not accept the principles of their faith. There is a difference in approach between Judaism and other monotheistic religions. Apparently, both Christianity and Islam assume that every human being would be better off sharing their respective religions, and various means may be used to bring about that situation, ranging from benign missionizing to the utilization of physical force. Judaism, on the other hand, is not a proselytizing religion. It purports to be the appropriate religion for Jews, but not for others, who will hopefully observe the seven Noahide commandments, which lay the foundation for ethically-based legislation.

However, Orthodox Jews, who believe that God revealed Himself at Mt. Sinai, where He gave the Torah to the Jewish people, often wonder how to relate to Jews who do not accept this premise, or those who do accept it, but feel that the laws are obsolete, or that age-old rabbinical enactments are no longer binding. Rambam's distinction between arbitrary religious laws (*mitzvot shimiyot*) and ethically-based laws (*mitzvot sichliyot*), as well as his distinction between a man of self-restraint (*moshel be-rucho*) and a saintly man (*chasid*), provide guidance for the attitude which may be adopted in dealing with such phenomena.

According to Rambam, it is expected of all cultivated people to behave morally. He would certainly respect anyone who refines his personality to the extent that he finds unethical deeds to be repulsive, and thus becomes a *chasid*. Rambam would apparently classify him as such even if he did not observe the *mitzvot shimiyot*. In fact, one could conceivably reach this level even if he were not Jewish at all.

On the other hand, as far as statutory religious prohibitions are concerned, Rambam admits that even the most religious person feels them to be arbitrary, and must oppose his own natural drives in order to properly observe them. It is thus clear that someone who does not believe in their Divine origin is acting in a completely logical manner if he doesn't comply with them, and he should not be condemned.

THE SECOND STEP IN ACHIEVING HOLINESS

It is now possible to proceed to the second step, namely seeking the positive actions necessary to fulfill the command of being holy. Two sources will be utilized. The first is *Yad ha-Chazakah*, Rambam's code of law, where he proclaims that the Torah was given in order to perfect inter-personal and inter-communal deportment.[91] The second is from the writings of R. Eliezer Berkovits, who suggests that ritual laws serve the same purpose as war games, i.e., to prepare soldiers for a real war.[92] Using Rambam's terminology in *Shemonah Perakim*, ritual laws teach self-restraint, and mastering that trait is a prerequisite to attaining *kedushah*, holiness. The second step is to engage in the actual war—diurnal social interaction—and to emerge as a victor.

The portion of *Kedoshim* commences: "And the Lord spoke to Moses, saying: Speak to all of the congregation of the Children of Israel, and say to them: You must be holy; for I, the Lord your God, am holy" (Lev. 19:1-2). Unlike other instances where the command to be holy follows a well-defined set of laws, here the command appears at the beginning of a section, so if it is associated with any laws, it must be connected to those which follow, which in fact represent a very prestigious subset of the 613 *mitzvot*. It will be shown that the stress in this subset is on laws between man and his fellow man (*bein adam le-chaveiro*), and it emphasizes not only laws demanding self-restraint, but also those requiring positive acts of charity and benevolence, which can help flesh out the abstract concept of *kedushah*. Hillel considered the core of the Torah to be based on the moral laws (BT *Shabbat* 31a); Rashi, wondering why no mention was made of the ritual laws, answered

---

91. *Hilchot Megillah ve-Chanukkah* 4:14.
92. Eliezer Berkovits, *God, Man and History* (1965), p. 109.

that most *mitzvot* are ethical in nature and Hillel based his answer on the majority.

The Midrash (*Lev. Rabbah* 24:5) states:

R. Chiyya taught: This portion was said at a gathering [of all of the nation] because the majority of the essentials of the Torah are embodied in it [in the laws which compose this portion].

R. Levi said: [This portion was said at a gathering of all of the nation] because the Ten Commandments are included in it.

(1) I am the Lord your God (Exod. 20:2). And it says here: I am the Lord your God (Lev. 19:4).

(2) You should not have [any other gods before Me] (Exod. 20:2). And it says here: Do not make molten gods for yourselves (Lev. 19:4).

(3) You should not take [the name of the Lord your God in vain] (Exod. 20:6). And it says here: And you should not swear by My name [falsely] (Lev. 19:12).

(4) Remember the Sabbath day [to keep it holy] (Exod. 20:7). And it says here: And you should keep My Sabbaths (Lev. 19:3).

(5) Honor your father and your mother (Exod. 20:11). And it says here: A man should fear his mother and his father (Lev. 19:3).

(6) You must not murder (Exod. 20:12). And it says here: You should not stand by [idly] if your neighbor's blood is being spilled (Lev. 19:16).

(7) You must not commit adultery (Exod. 20:12). And it says here: And the man who commits adultery with another man's wife, [for example he] who commits

adultery with his neighbor's wife, both the adulterer and the adulteress must be put to death (Lev. 20:10).

(8) You must not steal (Exod. 20:12). And it says here: You must not steal (Lev. 19:11).

(9) You must not bear [false witness against your neighbor] (Exod. 20:12). And it says here: You must not circulate as a tale-bearer [among your people] (Lev. 19:16).

(10) You must not covet [your neighbor's house; you must not covet your neighbor's wife, nor his man-servant, nor his maid-servant, nor his ox, nor his ass, nor any thing that is your neighbor's] (Exod. 20:13). And it says here: [You must not take vengeance, nor bear a grudge against the children of your people;] and you should love your neighbor as yourself (Lev. 19:18).

Although, according to R. Levi, the Ten Commandments are paralleled in *Kedoshim*, the last five commandments, which are ethical in nature, are expanded upon in a way which involves not only restraint, but positive actions as well. For example, the sixth commandment simply prohibits murder, while the corresponding verse in the present portion requires one to make every effort to save another person's life, even if it involves a certain degree of danger. Similarly, the ninth commandment refers to a witness's appearance in court, while the corresponding verse prohibits maligning others in any possible milieu. Finally, the last commandment forbids coveting the belongings of one's neighbor, while the parallel verse requires one to actually love his neighbor and to make every effort to wipe out any negative feelings that he may have toward him.

While R. Levi singled out the verses in the portion which parallel the Ten Commandments, R. Chiyya did not specify which particular verses, in his opinion, contain the essentials of the Torah. However, Maharzo (*Lev. Rabbah* 24:5) did select a number of verses which it will be shown roughly outline the three principles of faith according to R. Joseph Albo,[93] namely:

1. There exists a God.
2. God is concerned with the fate of each individual human being, as manifested by His involvement in people's lives to the extent that He rewards them for their good deeds and punishes them for their sins.
3. There is a right way (advocated by God) to live, which is detailed in the written and oral law.

The five commands which Maharzo considers to contain the essentials of the faith are listed below:

1. **You should keep My Sabbaths (Lev. 19:3).**

    Although some look upon the Orthodox approach to the Sabbath as a list of prohibitions, it is in essence intended to be a day of both fellowship and contemplation about how to improve one's self, one's immediate surroundings, and the world in general. Fellowship takes place around the Sabbath table among family, friends, and the needy. Contemplation takes place in the synagogue, the home, and the study hall. Sabbath is more than a day of the week, it is a way of life. Not every day can, or should, be Sabbath, but its place at the end of the week, and the beginning of the next, places on a pedestal the higher values in life.

    The Sabbath is described in the first depiction of the Ten Commandments as the day on which the Lord rested after creating the world, as it says: "For in six days the Lord made

---

93. *Sefer ha-Ikkarim*, Introduction to the First Article.

heaven and earth, the sea, and all that is in them, and rested on the seventh day" (Exod. 20:11).

Alternatively, Sabbath is portrayed in the second account of the Ten Commandments as memorializing the exodus from Egypt, as it says:

> Observe the Sabbath day to keep it holy… that your man-servant and maid-servant may rest as well as you. And you should remember that you were a servant in the land of Egypt, and the Lord your God brought you out by a mighty hand and an outstretched arm; therefore, the Lord your God commanded you to keep the Sabbath day (Deut. 5:12-15).

Why does the Sabbath recall the exodus? Ibn Ezra explains that it is mentioned to explain why God ordered one's servants to rest on the Sabbath, since the Israelites were themselves once slaves, and they certainly could have used a day of rest. Now that they are free, they should especially appreciate the opportunity which has been afforded them, realize that it was not always so, and be considerate enough of their own slaves to allow them this benefit. The Midrash (*Exod. Rabbah* 5:18) says that from the time of the patriarchs there was a tradition not to work on the Sabbath, but rather to devote the day to spiritual pursuits. The Children of Israel studied various scrolls which were handed down through the generations and which told of how they would eventually be redeemed. When Pharaoh was perturbed by Moses' supplication on behalf of the Israelite slaves (Exod. 5:6), he cancelled their day of rest. When Israel was redeemed and once more able to celebrate the Sabbath, they recalled the dark period when its observance had been marred.

Both remembrances, that of creation and that of the redemption from slavery, are recorded in the *Kiddush* (sanctification over wine) prayer said before the Sabbath feast. One notes that the first remembrance corresponds to R. Albo's first principle—God's existence and omnipotence as the Creator. The second remembrance corresponds to R. Albo's second principle—God's involvement and intervention in the human drama. The Sabbath is thus seen to be a fitting choice for the first of the five essential commands.

2. **Every man should fear his mother and his father** (Lev. 19:3).

The fact that this command appears in both sets of the Ten Commandments (Exod. 20:12; Deut. 5:16) together with a promised reward of "length of life" only highlights its importance. *Sefer ha-Chinnuch* (*Yitro*, mitzvah 33) explains that this command flows from the basic moral value of gratitude. One's parents have given him life, and according to Ibn Ezra, that is the reason that one who honors his parents is promised long life. One's parents nurture him and support him in his youth, when he needs them, and it stands to reason that he would be expected to do the same when they need his help.

Sefer ha-Chinnuch points out that by training oneself to be grateful to his parents, one realizes how much he must be thankful to God. The Talmud accordingly states:

> It says: "Honor your father and your mother (Exod. 20:12), and it says: "Honor the Lord with your substance (Prov. 3:9). It compares honoring father and mother to honoring the Omnipresent (JT *Pe'ah* 1:1).[94]

94. See also *Sifra* A, until ch. A; BT *Kiddushin* 30.

THE ETHICS OF LEVITICUS

The Talmud strengthens the comparison by concluding: "And this follows logically, because the three of them (father, mother, and God) are partners in him [in his creation]."

R. Albo's third principle is that there is a right way to live—the moral way—and that is how God wants people to live. Being willing to live as God desires presupposes instinctual morality. Otherwise, even if one knows for a fact that God wishes him to behave in a given manner, why should he do so? Should it be out of gratitude for the fact that He created him and sustains him? But gratitude is itself a moral value. Should it be because he is afraid of the punishment that God might mete out to him, or of not having a good life? But certainly a person has the right to take a chance and suffer the consequences, if there are any, unless one acquiesces to the impropriety of harming a human being, including oneself—again a moral value. In Hebrew, the necessity of morality preceding the acceptance of God as the Supreme Commander is formulated as *derech eretz kadmah la-Torah*, which means that basic morality is a logical prerequisite to the proper observance of *mitzvot*.

R. Albo's three principles are actually symbiotic. An elementary sense of morality logically precedes belief in God, as described above, but belief in God also shapes the moral imperative, as described by Rambam:

> Our Sages declare it, wherever opportunity is given, that the idea of God necessarily implies justice; that He will reward the most pious for all their pure and upright actions, although no direct commandment was given them through a prophet; and that He will punish all the evil deeds of men, although they have not been prohibited by a prophet, if common sense warns against them, as, e.g., injustice and violence (*Guide for the Perplexed* 3:17).

Rambam believes that there exist basic moral truths, independent of any written law, which are meant to serve as the basis of human behavior. No matter how one looks at it, gratitude is the central value which allows one to go from the first two principles to the third, which is to observe the law, in particular the moral commandments, which compose the remaining essential commands according to R. Chiyya.

3. **You must not rob** (Lev. 19:13).

The difference between robbery and theft is that robbery includes physical confrontation, i.e., violence, while theft is done on the sly. Regarding the state of civilization before the great flood, the Bible states: "And God saw the earth, and, behold, it was corrupt; for all flesh had corrupted their way on the earth" (Gen. 6:12).

Rashi, based on a Midrash quoted in the Talmud (BT *Sanhedrin* 108a), explains that the corruption referred to is sexual in nature, and the implication is that the various species of animals, beasts, and even men, all copulated with each other. The verse states:

> And God said to Noah: "The end of all flesh is come before Me, for the earth is filled with *chamas* ["violence," or Rashi: "robbery" (Gen. 6:11)] through them; and, behold, I will destroy them with the earth (Gen. 6:13).

Why does the verse speak of the "end of all flesh?" The Midrash (quoted by Rashi) explains: "R. Simlai said: Any place where you find promiscuity, indiscriminate punishment comes to the world and kills the good together with the bad" (*Gen. Rabbah*

26:5). The Midrash is apparently presenting a justification for the fact that innocent people, especially youngsters, were among the victims of the flood.

The Talmud (BT *Sanhedrin* 108a, cited by Rashi on this verse) continues the analysis of the verse with the following statement:

> R. Johanan said: Come and see how great is the power of robbery, for although the generation of the flood transgressed every law, the decree that they be punished was sealed only because they stretched out their hands to rob, as it is written, "for the earth is filled with violence [robbery] through them and, behold, I will destroy them with the earth."

Maharal (*Gur Aryeh*, Gen. 6:13) points out a contradiction. The previously quoted Midrash implies that the flood was caused by sexual crimes, while the segment from the Talmud says that their fate was due to widespread robbery. The question is especially acute regarding Rashi, who quotes both sources without comment. Maharal answers that although promiscuity is a serious crime and certainly played a role in the severity of the punishment, God generally hesitates before actually carrying out an evil decree. When robbery is rife, however, it leads to the cessation of commerce and the eventual bankruptcy of the world, which provokes God to say: "If the robbers don't have pity on the world and have no misgivings about causing its destruction, why should I feel any compunction about doing the same?"

Divrei David (Gen. 6:13; *Divrei David* is the same author as the *Turei Zahav*) adopts the same view as Maharal, basing his opinion on the following Midrash (*Gen. Rabbah* 38:6):

> Rabbi says: Great is peace, for even if Israel worships idols and peace prevails among them, God, so to speak, says I cannot rule over them [stringently], since peace prevails among them, for it says: "Ephraim [Israel] is joined to [his] idols; leave him alone [rebuking him is useless. Alternatively, Judea should leave him alone and not follow in his footsteps. Midrashic explanation: If Ephraim worships idols, but is joined into a cohesive unit—absolve him from punishment]" (Hos. 4:17). But when they are split [from each other], what does he [Hosea] say: "Their heart is split [from God]; now they will bear their guilt [Midrashic explanation: If they are split by arguments among themselves, then they will be punished for their sins]" (Hos. 10:2).

In short, peace is supreme and dissension is despised.

Siftei Chachamim, taking a slightly different approach, answers Maharal's question by noting that robbery includes all forms of violently stealing from others, whether it be material goods or human beings – thus including robbing men of their wives and abusing them sexually.

According to all of the explanations presented, violent robbery is seen to be a cardinal sin and it is quite understandable that the Maharzo wold have included it among the essentials of the Torah.

4. **You should not take vengeance, nor bear a grudge** (Lev. 19:18).

The Talmud explains the difference between these two prohibitions:

> What is "revenge" and what is "bearing a grudge?" "Revenge" is [if] one said [to his friend]: "Lend me your sickle," [and] he replied: "No," [and] the next day, he [the friend] said [to the first]: "Lend me your ax," and he said: "I will not lend [it to] you, just as you would not lend it [your sickle] to me" — that is "revenge." And what is "bearing a grudge?" [If] one said [to his friend]: "Lend me your ax," [and] he replied "No," [and] the next day, he [the friend] said [to the first]: "Lend me your garment," [and] he said: "Here it is. I am not like you, who would not lend me [what I asked for]" — that is "bearing a grudge" (BT *Yoma* 23a).

The commentators ask a straightforward question: Why is there a prohibition to take revenge by refusing to lend the ax, but no law against the first one refusing to lend his sickle in the first place? *Chizkuni* answers that the first one refused to lend his sickle because of his stinginess, or because he's afraid the second will be negligent and destroy it, but not because of intrinsic hatred, and the Torah does not force people to lend out their belongings against their will. The second one, on the other hand, apparently would have been willing to lend out his ax if not for his desire to get even with the first, and the only reason he does not is because he has developed feelings of hatred toward him, and the Torah says: "Allow love to overcome your hate for him, and as a result, peace will prevail in the world." Ra'avad[95] adds that if in fact the first did not initially lend it out of spite, he transgresses the prohibition of: "You must not hate your brother in your heart" (Lev. 19:17).

The Ra'avad's association of revenge with the prohibition of hating others is generalized by R. Moshe Botschko (*Hegyonei Moshe* pp. 94-96), who sees it as the source of many interpersonal sins and stresses that the seed of aggression is planted at the first moment that people take a dislike to others. Once the hatred grows, it may overpower them to the extent that they cannot control the violent feelings it arouses. The Torah thus commands one to eradicate those emotions before they take root.

5. **You should love your neighbour as yourself** (Lev. 19:18).

The neighbor being referred to is any (and every) member of the Israelite nation.[96] *Sefer ha-Chinnuch* (mitzvah 243) explains that the rationale behind this command is quite obvious. If people treat each other cordially and lovingly, this will certainly lead to peaceful co-existence in this world, which—in the view of Rambam—is the purpose of creation (*Hilchot Megillah ve-Chanukkah* 4:14). A more extensive treatment of this law is to be found in APPENDIX V: LOVING ONE'S NEIGHBOR.

That this commandment is one of the essential laws seems quite reasonable, based on the following words of *Sefer ha-Chinnuch* (mitzvah 243):

> One who loves his friend as much as he loves himself will not steal his money, will not commit adultery with

---

95. On *Sifra Kedoshim* B, end of ch. 3.
96. *Hilchot De'ot* 6:3; *Ma'or ha-Aphelah*, as quoted in *Torah Shleimah*, Lev. 19:18.

his wife, will not deceive him in deed [financially] or word, will not remove his landmark, and will not damage him in any way. Many other commands also depend on this [his attitude toward his fellow man], which is known to every intelligent person.

The fact that this command is a catalyst to the fulfillment of many others, in particular most of the laws between man and his fellow-man, is sufficient to ensure its role as one of the primary *mitzvot* in the Torah.

Apparently the Talmud was of the same view, as may be noted from the following quote:

It was stated: R. Akiva says: "Love your neighbor as you love yourself" (Lev. 19:18, the so-called Golden Rule) is a fundamental principle of the Torah. Ben Azzai says: "This is the book of the generations of mankind. [On the day that God created man He made him in the likeness of God]" (Gen. 5:1) — an even more fundamental rule (JT *Nedarim* 9:4; *Sifra Kedoshim* 2:4).

Torah Temimah (Lev. 19:18) explains the argument between R. Akiva and Ben Azzai. R. Akiva requires one to love others as much as they love themselves, but some people unfortunately have an inferiority complex and don't love themselves as much as they should. So Ben Azzai explains that no matter what one thinks of himself, remember that everyone is created in the image of God and must be loved and respected.

Another possible answer is that R. Akiva's golden rule applies technically only to your brother in Torah and *mitzvot*

(*Hilchot Avel* 14:1). Ben Azzai extends the rule to all moral human beings, as long as they fulfill the seven Noahide commands. In other words, Jews must respect righteous Gentiles and extend to them the same acts of kindness that they do to their own brothers and sisters. See APPENDIX V: LOVING ONE'S NEIGHBOR for the source of these laws.

EXTENDING THE DEFINITION OF HOLINESS

A number of sequential steps have been suggested to achieve holiness. First, it was required to refrain from dietary and sexual behavior which leads to defilement. Second, it was noted that persistence in observing the various prohibitions might lead to an improved—even holier—personality. Finally, it was claimed that the moral behavior resulting from a series of ethical *mitzvot* listed in the present portion could lead to holiness. The only problem with this approach is that if holiness only entails meticulous observance of the aforementioned prohibitions and positive commands, what additional requirement is added by the command "you should be holy" which appears in the second verse of *Kedoshim*?

Holiness—first answer:
The first possible response to this question is: Who said that these words have to add anything? Maybe they are just exhortative in nature. In fact, Rashi apparently takes this approach. The Midrash (*Sifra*, Lev. 19:2) says that holiness implies abstinence. Rashi (Lev. 19:2), in an attempt to concretize this concept, relates it to the laws at the end of the previous portion and adds the following phrase to the words of the Midrash: "Separate yourselves *from sexual transgressions.*" *Siftei Chachamim* explains that since Rashi

accepted the Midrashic view that holiness involves a degree of distinctiveness, it must result from laws which are observed only by Jews, such as the dietary and sexual laws of *Acharei Mot*.

A problem with Rashi's view is that the portion opens with God asking Moses to gather the entire congregation, which would indicate that a new subject is being broached in *Kedoshim*. In addition, although Gentiles also accept the social legislation introduced in *Kedoshim*, that does not mean that they actually observe those laws, leaving plenty of room for Israel to distinguish themselves and thereby achieve holiness. Taking these objections into account, Rambam agrees with Rashi that new legislation is not being introduced, but he does not limit holiness to a single set of laws. Rather, he generalizes it to virtually the entire Torah, as is clear from the fourth principle (*shoresh arba*) in his *Sefer ha-Mitzvot*, where he writes:

> Many have erred[97] regarding this principle, to the extent that they counted "you should be holy" as a commandment among the positive *mitzvot*, and they did not know that "you should be holy," "sanctify yourselves and be holy" (Lev. 11:44) are commands to fulfill the entire Torah, as if to say: Be holy when you do everything that I have commanded, and guard yourself from everything that I have warned against. In the words of *Sifra* (Lev. 19:2): "You should be holy — be removed." In other words: Separate yourselves from all of the abominations that I warned you against.
>
> In *Mechilta* [they said]: "And you will be holy men unto me" (Exod. 22:30) - Isi b. Yehuda says: When the

---

97. According to Ramban (in *Sefer ha-Mitzvot*), Rambam is referring to Behag (*Ba'al Halachot Gedolot*). Actually, the latter does not count 19:2, but he does count 11:44, since he feels it adds a second prohibition against eating the reptiles and crawling creatures mentioned in that section.

Lord introduces a mitzvah to Israel, he adds to their holiness.

In other words, the command [to be holy] does not stand by itself, but rather is connected to a mitzvah that they were commanded, for anyone who fulfills that command is called holy. If so, there is no difference whether He says "be holy," or whether He says "do my *mitzvot*." Can you imagine we would say that this is an additional positive command relating to the *mitzvot* whose fulfillment He commanded? Similarly, we will not say with regard to "you should be holy" and the like that it indicates another mitzvah, for it does not command [one] to do anything beyond what we already knew [that we are required to do]. In the words of *Sifrei* (Num. 15:40), "and be holy — this is the holiness of *mitzvot*." Behold what we wished to convey has been explained.

Holiness—second answer:

The Midrashic approach is that the command to be holy adds a new dimension to the basic Torah law. *Sifrei* (Deut. 14:21) utilizes these words to indicate that meat which some accept as being kosher and others don't, must not be eaten in the presence of those who are more stringent. The Midrash coins a new phrase: "Sanctify yourself by refraining from what is actually permitted [by Torah law]," in Hebrew: "*Kadesh atzmecha ba-muttar lach*." The Talmud (BT *Yevamot* 20a) uses the same phrase with respect to certain rabbinically prohibited marriages. By observing certain rabbinically ordained stringencies, one may achieve holiness.

Holiness—third answer:

The weakness of the second answer is that the phrase "sanctify yourself by refraining from what is actually permitted" is in reality being used to refer to an act which is not permitted. Even if one will say that by Torah law it is permissible, just not by rabbinic law, the Torah demands the observance of rabinically ordained extensions when it says: "You should not waiver from the verdict which they [i.e., the later authorities] tell you, neither to the right, nor to the left" (Deut. 17:11). One may answer that the verse cited refers only to decisions made by the Sanhedrin on the Temple grounds, so that most rabbinic decisions are not considered to have the strength of Torah law.

Nevertheless, Ramban (Lev. 19:2) prefers to associate the concept of holiness with fully permitted behavior, which the Torah does not at all prohibit, but from which one who strives for holiness should distance himself. He makes the following points:

1. Holiness is an all-encompassing attribute, and is not related specifically to sexual morality. In his words:

   > [I]n my opinion, this abstinence does not refer only to restraint from acts of immorality, as the Rabbi [Rashi] said, but it is [rather] the self-control mentioned throughout the Talmud, whose possessors are called *perushim* (Pharisees).

2. Ramban feels one can observe the law, and yet be very "unholy." He explains:

   > The Torah has admonished regarding sexual immorality and forbidden foods, and permitted

intercourse between man and his wife, and the eating of meat and wine. If so, a man of desire could allow himself to be overcome by lust for his wife or many wives, and to be "among the wine imbibers, among gluttonous eaters of flesh" (Prov. 23:20), and speak at his will all forms of profanity, for this prohibition is not recorded in the Torah, and behold he will become a vile person within the confines of the Torah (*naval bi-reshut ha-Torah*).

3. How does one become holy? Ramban continues:

Therefore, after having listed the prohibitions which He forbade entirely, Scripture commanded in general that we abstain from luxuries, minimize sexual intercourse as they [the Rabbis] have said, "Scholars should not be found with their wives as often as hens" (BT *Berachot* 22a), and he should not engage in it [intercourse] except as required in fulfillment of the commandment, and he should also sanctify himself by minimizing [his intake of] wine, in harmony with Scripture calling a Nazirite "holy" (Num. 6:5), and he should recall the evil which the Torah records [from drinking wine] with respect to Noah (Gen. 9:21) and Lot (Gen. 19:33). He should also guard his mouth and tongue from being defiled by overeating and by lewd talk, similar to what Scripture states, "and every mouth speaks despicably" (Isa. 9:16), and he should sanctify himself in this respect until he reaches [the level called] "abstinence," as was said concerning R. Chiya, that he never in his life engaged in idle chatter.[98]

4. Ramban compares the comprehensive exhortation of "you should be holy," which references commands associated with personal behavior, to the all-inclusive mitzvah of doing what is right and good (Deut. 6:18), which references the laws regulating interpersonal conduct. He states:

> This is the way of the Torah, to present details and then to generalize. Thus, after warning with detailed laws regarding all business dealings between people—not to steal, and not to rob, and not to cheat, and the other prohibitions, He said in general: "And you should do that which is right and good" (Deut. 6:18), thus including as a positive commandment doing what is right, and compromising, and always acting "beyond" the line of justice [i.e., agreeing to waive one's rights as defined by the strict letter of the law] for the sake of pleasing one's fellow man.

Understanding Ramban:

Ramban has clearly associated holiness with observing additional limitations which are not formally required. What is the philosophical basis of his approach?

One way of understanding Ramban is to say that he is essentially in favor of asceticism. After all, in point 3 above he suggested abstaining from luxuries and minimizing sexual intercourse. He

---

98. *P'nei Yerushalayim* (a commentary on Ramban) points out that this panegyric was actually stated concerning R. Eliezer and R. Yochanan b. Zakkai (BT *Sukkah* 28a), as well as Rav (*Hilchot De'ot* 2:4 [*Kesef Mishneh* says the talmudic source for this is unknown]; *Perush Mishnayot, Avot* 1:16).

even lauded abjuring wine by calling a Nazirite "holy." But there are sources in rabbinic literature, including in the writings of Ramban himself, which would seem to contradict that approach.

As far as abstaining from worldly pleasures, consider the saying of R. Hizkiyah: "In the future, anyone who did not taste of a delicious fruit which he saw with his own eyes will be held culpable" (JT *Kiddushin* 4:12). This maxim may be extended to non-edibles. It then stresses the importance of enjoying all of the material fruits which this world makes available.

As far as enjoying sexuality, Ramban[99] in *Iggeret ha-Kodesh* says: "One should not imagine that in the sexual fulfillment of the appropriate intimate relationship there is shame or ugliness."

Finally, the following text, although it relates specifically to refraining from the drinking of wine or from food in general by voluntarily fasting, can certainly be extended to all worldly pleasures. The Talmud states:

> Samuel said: Whosoever fasts [for the purpose of self-affliction] is called a sinner. He agrees with the following Tanna. For it has been taught: R. Elazar ha-Kappar Berabbi said: "Why does the Scripture say [regarding a Nazirite], 'And make atonement for him, for he has sinned against his soul' (Num. 6:11)?[100] Against what 'soul' did he sin? But [it must be because] he denied himself wine." Using *a fortiori* logic [one may say] if this man who only denied himself wine is termed a sinner, how much more so is this true of one who denies himself everything [by fasting] (BT *Ta'anit* 11a)!

---

99. Alternatively, *Iggeret ha-Kodesh* has been ascribed to Joseph Gikatilla.
100. Although the verse refers to a Nazirite who defiled himself, the Talmud makes clear that the same is true of every Nazirite.

In the words of the Jerusalem Talmud (*Nedarim* 9:1): "Does it not suffice that which the Torah prohibited, that you must add additional items?"

One may thus say, with a reasonable degree of confidence, that the Torah does not preach asceticism. Apparently, the most critical words of Ramban are the exhortation to "recall the evil [from drinking wine] which the Torah records with respect to Noah and Lot." It is not the seeking of pleasure which detracts from holiness, but rather the potentially deleterious effects of going to extremes, as in the popular saying: "Too much of a good thing is not good."

It is interesting to note that the commandment to be holy in one's personal behavior appears at the beginning of *Kedoshim*, a portion which deals mainly with interpersonal behavior, while the command to be holy in one's interpersonal behavior appears in the portion of *Va'etchannan*, in a section dealing mainly with personal religious behavior. Perhaps the implication is that there is cross-pollination between these two areas, both for good and for bad. The additional restrictions one imposes on himself in one area may enable improved performance in the other. For example, one who drinks to excess will frequently be lax in his social behavior, so that imposing self-control will enrich his overall personality.

How does one know which extensions are beneficial? It probably helps to have an overview of the *mitzvot*, an idea of their overall goal, and an understanding of the purpose of each individual law. For example, it has been noted that Rambam felt that the purpose of the entire Torah was to engender peace, so that any actions which lead to that goal may be incorporated in the mitzvah of doing "that which is right and good" (Deut. 6:18). As far as individual laws are concerned, it is true that many are in the category of statutes whose reason is unknown, but it is also true that *Sefer ha-Chinnuch* lists the motivation for many *mitzvot*, and Rambam, in his *Guide for the Perplexed,* includes his conjectures even regarding outright statutes (such as sacrifices and the dietary laws), although he would never allow leniencies based on such speculation, as he makes quite clear in *Hilchot Me'ilah* 8:6-7. Another means of guidance is to understand R. Soloveitchik's distinction between the act of a mitzvah and its true fulfillment (*Al ha-Teshuvah,* p. 40). Addenda would tend to ensure that one fulfills the true meaning and intention of the given command.

Holiness—fourth answer:

The preceding two methods (i.e., the second and third answers) of achieving holiness are based on the Hebrew saying "*Kadesh atzmecha ba-muttar lach*" ("Sanctify yourself by refraining from what is actually permitted"). The second answer relates the Hebrew phrase to rabbinical enactments, which are not required on the Torah level. The third answer relates it to common sense behaviors, which are not even required on the rabbinical level. R. Eliezer Simcha Weiss[101] has re-interpreted the phrase in the opposite fashion. He says that real holiness does not derive from adding restrictions, but rather by sanctifying those objects and behaviors that are fully permitted.

It was noted that the Sages encouraged enjoying nature and all that it has to offer. How does such enjoyment lead to holiness? The answer is that holiness occurs when pleasure is coupled with the proper blessings of gratitude to the Almighty for making it available to mankind, when beneficence is shared with those who are less fortunate, and when love is celebrated with a partner who cherishes the moment.

---

101. Eliezer Simcha Weiss, "*Kadesh atzmecha ba-mutar lach*," (Internet) http://he.rabbiweisz.com/?page_id=240.

Concerning the holiday pilgrimage made by the Children of Israel thrice yearly, the Talmud states:

> R. Kattina said: Whenever Israel came up [to Jerusalem] for the festival, the curtain was rolled up for them and the Cherubim were shown to them, while their bodies were intertwined with one another [Rashi: stuck one to the other, hugging and embracing each other as a male embraces a female], and they [perhaps the Cherubim] would say to them [the Israelites]: "Look! You are beloved before God as the love between man and woman" (BT *Yoma* 54a).

Even more surprising is the Talmud's description (BT *Yoma* 54b) of the events that occurred at the time of the destruction of the Second Temple:

> Resh Lakish said: When the heathens entered the Temple, they saw the Cherubim whose bodies were intertwined with one another. They carried them out and said: These Israelites, whose blessing is a blessing, and whose curse is a curse, occupy themselves with such things! And immediately they despised them, as it is said: "All that honored her despised her, because they saw her nakedness" (Lam. 1:8).

Both stories contain an element which is foreign to many other faiths. An embrace which contains elements of love, emotion, and lust represents a concept which cannot be understood by those for whom the Jewish tradition is alien. Such people may realize that the world has both a physical and a spiritual dimension;

however, they consider these two elements to be incompatible. Some religions even prohibit their clergy from cultivating intimate sexual relationships, while others ban all alcoholic drinks.

Judaism differs with this approach. Some of the foundational slogans used in describing the religion are the biblical phrase: "It is not in heaven… neither is it on the other side of the sea" (Deut. 30:12) and the talmudic phrase: "The Torah was not given to ministering angels" (BT *Kiddushin* 54a).

The Song of Songs exalts the physical connection between a man and a woman. *Avot de-Rabbi Natan* (A:1) indicates it was initially withheld from the canon until the Sages of the Great Assembly canonized it, explaining that its content could be seen as a paradigm of the love between God and Israel. The message that emanates from the parable and the derived lesson, taken together, is one of sanctification of the physical and material realms, and it is this view which characterizes Judaism. It is thus no wonder that R. Akiva referred to the Song of Songs as *kodesh kodashim* ("holy of holies," Mishnah *Yadayim* 3:5), the same name which is given to the location of the Cherubim in the Temple, since the purpose of both is to demonstrate controlling, but not repressing. Nevertheless, there were apparently also those among the Sages who favored the ascetic approach. The Mishnah records the view of R. Yosi that some did not believe the Song of Songs to be on the same level as the rest of the Bible, and that of Shimon b. Azzai, who felt it should be, but differed with R. Akiva in that he did not see it as being superior (and the Mishnah accepts the viewpoint of Shimon b. Azzai as being final).

Eventually, it seems that R. Akiva's philosophy prevailed, and indeed the seal of approval given to the most physical possible relationship between a man and a woman is called *kiddushin* (marriage, lit., "sanctification"), while the future groom says to his beloved bride: "Behold you are *sanctified* to me."

Accordingly, on holidays, when the nation attempts to attain the highest levels of holiness and spirituality, the Torah requires one to be happy and to eat tasty dishes, in keeping with the rabbinical dictum that "it is not possible to fulfill the requirement to be joyful without [partaking of] meat and wine" (BT *Pesachim* 109a). R. Shneur Zalman of Liadi,[102] the Alter Rebbe, wrote that "Purim and Yom ha-Kippurim [the Day of Atonement] are similar; the meaning of Yom ha-Kippurim is [a day that is] like Purim." Examining his phraseology leads to the conclusion that he considered Purim to be on an even higher level than Yom ha-Kippurim, since he used Purim as his basis, and Yom ha-Kippurim was only said to be like—i.e. an imitation of, but not identical. This statement may be explained as follows. On the Day of Atonement, one achieves spirituality by means of prayer and fasting. On Purim, one achieves spirituality by partaking of a festive meal and being joyful, acts which are considered to be more typical of our existence in this world.

In short, Purim is greater than Yom Kippur, because on Yom Kippur the emphasis is on spirituality, and the material aspect— the mitzvah to eat on the day before—only strengthens one's ability to fast. On Purim the main focus is on the physical nature of this world, and the spiritual dimension—the mitzvah to fast on the day before—fortifies the observant Jew and enables him to cope with the physical world in which he lives. In this vein, the Midrash[103] states: "All of the holidays will be cancelled in the future, with the exception of Purim, for it says, 'and these days of Purim should not pass [out of existence] from among the Jews' (Esth. 9:28)."

---

102. Torah Or, *Megillat Esther* 95:4.
103. *Shocher Tov*, Prov. 9.

Summary

Four possible explanations of the meaning of holiness were proposed. I would suggest that true holiness encompasses all four of them. Holiness can be achieved by observing the Torah on four levels. First, one must obey Torah-legislated laws. Second, one must adhere to rabbinical extensions. Third, one must adhere to his own common sense morality, as formulated in the Torah itself, when it says: "And you should do that which is right and good" (Deut. 6:18) and by Rambam, when he wrote that God "will reward the most pious for all their pure and upright actions, although no direct commandment was given them through a prophet; and that He will punish all the evil deeds of men, although they have not been prohibited by a prophet, if common sense warns against them" (*Guide for the Perplexed* 3:17).

Finally, one sanctifies himself by achieving the first three levels in a state of happiness and fellowship, as concisely formulated by R. Nachman of Breslav: "It is a great mitzvah to be happy at all times" (*Likkutei Moharan* 2:24). Furthermore, happiness occurs when the *mitzvot* (including those which demand jubilation) are performed as part of a community.

It will be noted that the Midrash (*Lev. Rabbah* 24:5) stating that the portion of *Kedoshim* "was said at a gathering" was quoted in the first Rashi in *Kedoshim*. The chasidic author of the commentary *Ma'or ve-Shemesh* (Lev. 19:2) asks what this particular Midrash wishes to impart, since all of the laws were taught by Moses four times—first to Aaron, then to his children, then to the elders, and then to the entire congregation. Aaron, his sons, and the elders then repeated the lesson, so that everyone heard it four times (BT *Eruvin* 54b), and so all of the laws were taught when the congregation was gathered together. He answers that the Midrashic comment that these laws were said at a "gathering" is not meant to emphasize the method of teaching as much as to accentuate the fact that the command "you should be holy" can only be performed by one who is socially integrated into the larger community. He explains that the second Rashi in the portion, which interprets this command as "separate yourselves from sexual transgressions," was purposely placed in a secondary position (after noting that it contained may Torah principles) in order to dissuade the reader from thinking that holiness can be achieved by separation. Holiness only follows from integration, while separation is a specific tool to distance one from certain temptations, but it is not the final destination.

R. Mordechai Elon[104] explains that *Ma'or ve-Shemesh* means to say that this "gathering" differed in that Moses immediately taught the lesson to the congregation without prior transmission through intermediaries, in order to show Aaron that the mitzvah of sanctification can only be accomplished in conjunction with the entire congregation.

Ma'or ve-Shemesh quotes a Midrash on the verse "you should be holy, for I, the Lord your God, am holy" (Lev. 19:2), which states: "'You should be holy.' Perhaps like Me? The verse continues: 'for I, the Lord your God, am holy' — My holiness is superior to your holiness" (*Lev. Rabbah* 24:5). He explains the Midrash, based on his emphasis on group dynamics, to mean:

> Perhaps like Me? — that a person should wish to be isolated, and he will think that by such behavior he will achieve elevated holiness. The verse continues: "for I the Lord your God, am holy" — My holiness is superior to

104. Mordechai Elon, "Kadesh Atzmecha ba-Mutar Lach," (www2.sde.org.il/keren/shiur_hebrew_doc/achriemot61.doc)

your holiness — that [form of holiness] applies to the Creator alone, who is single and unique. But if a person wants to devolve upon himself God's holiness, it is only possible by gathering together a congregation to worship him jointly.

In summary, one may achieve holiness by observing the law, making logical and reasonable extensions which do not involve self-denial, enjoying the pleasures of life, and doing all of this in a communal context.

EMOR

The portion of *Emor* is composed of four chapters (21-24). The first two and the first half of the fourth present regulations concerning priests and the Sanctuary (hence the opening words, "speak to the priests"), while the second half of the fourth chapter deals with the case of the blasphemer, who received the death penalty, and lists a number of other serious offenses.

Chapter 23, which is the heart of the portion, comprises three of the traditional seven sections of the weekly portion and relates to the holy days throughout the year. It opens with the following verses:

> 1. And the Lord spoke to Moses, saying: 2 .Speak to the Children of Israel, and say to them: The appointed seasons of the Lord, which you will proclaim to be holy convocations, these are My appointed seasons.

Ramban (Lev. 23:2) notes that, unlike the opening section of the portion, Moses is commanded to speak to the Children of Israel (i.e., the entire congregation, priests as well as laymen), because not only do the holidays concern the people in the sense that they must be celebrated by the entire community, but the Israelites also determine the dates upon which they will take place, as stated in verse 2: "which you will proclaim to be holy convocations." The timing of the holidays depends on which day is chosen as the first day of the month, which occurs when the new moon is sighted by two witnesses who testify before the Sanhedrin (Supreme Court). Additionally, the Sanhedrin had to occasionally decide to declare a leap year, which had the effect of delaying the festivals by a month. The festivals could thus fall on any day of the week. The day of the Sabbath, on the other hand, has been fixed by God and no human intervention is involved. After thus introducing the holidays, Ramban is baffled by the verse which follows, as it relates to the Sabbath:

> 3. Six days may work be done, and on the seventh day is a Sabbath of solemn rest, a holy convocation; you should do no manner of work; it is a Sabbath for the Lord in all your dwellings.

Also perplexing is the next verse, which seems to be redundant, as it is another introductory verse, which is finally followed by a description of the festivals:

> 4. These are the appointed seasons of the Lord, holy convocations, which you will proclaim in their appointed season.

Ramban solves this conundrum by noting that the object of the proclamation differs between verse 2 and verse 4. In verse 2, it is being proclaimed that on the given day there will be "holy convocations", and the laws associated with such events will be observed. This proclamation is relevant to both Sabbaths and holidays, which are both holy convocations and the Lord's seasons. In verse 4, on the other hand, what is being proclaimed is "their [the holidays'] appointed season," i.e., exactly when holidays fall, whose dates follow from the court's proclamation of leap months (those having 30 days as opposed to 29) and leap years (those having thirteen months), and this is relevant only for festivals. Verse 2 is a comprehensive proclamation which relates to the laws of the holy days, including the Sabbath—all of which are called "appointed seasons *of the Lord*" which Israel proclaims "to be holy convocations," even if it doesn't determine the timing of the Sabbath—while verse 4 relates specifically to the holidays, whose timing is fixed by the congregation and concerning which it is stated "you will proclaim in their appointed season."

By contrast, in a second exegesis, Ramban says that the moniker "appointed seasons" refers exclusively to festivals, which are being introduced in verse 1, and the appellation is repeated in verse 3 only because the train of thought was broken by interjecting the exhortation concerning the Sabbath, which differs from the holidays in that a complete cessation from all forms of productive work is demanded.

After stressing the distinctions between the Sabbath and the festivals (in terms of the means of fixing their dates and the form of work which is prohibited), what remains to be dealt with is the very fact that they were grouped together at all. What is it that they have in common which, in spite of their differences, makes it natural to juxtapose them in the first place? In order to answer this question, it will be necessary to investigate the intrinsic character of the Jewish Sabbath.

WHY WERE SABBATH
AND FESTIVALS GROUPED TOGETHER?

Although there are distinctions between Sabbath and holidays as to the forms of work which are prohibited, in terms of the positive manners of honoring (*kavod*), delighting in (*oneg*), and rejoicing (*simchah*) on these days, they have much in common. *Kavod* refers to acts which a person does in deference to the Sabbath, such as bathing oneself, wearing special clothes, setting the table decorously, refraining from eating a large meal on Friday afternoon, and going out to greet the Sabbath—steps taken to welcome an important guest, here the Sabbath. *Oneg* refers to bodily pleasures, such as eating, sleeping, Torah learning, and even sexual relations—activities that a person does to pleasure himself (*Hilchot Shabbat* 30). The degree of pleasure demanded to fulfill the mitzvah of *simchah* is even greater than that required by *oneg*. For example, Rambam requires one to wear special clothes on the Sabbath that are clean and elegant (*Hilchot Shabbat* 30:3). However, on holidays, as part of the fulfillment of *simchah*, he suggests buying *new* clothing and even expensive jewelry (*Hilchot Yom Tov* 6:18).

The command to rejoice (*simchah*) on the holidays is clearly of biblical origin, being explicitly stated in the present portion: "And you should rejoice before the Lord your God seven days" (Lev. 23:40). *Torah Temimah* (Deut. 16:12) is of the opinion that this commandment applies to the Sabbath as well. As far as *kavod* and *oneg* are concerned, the commentators dispute whether they are Torah-level requirements.

With regard to the words "On the first day there will be a holy convocation," which relate to the first day of Sukkot, *Sifra* (on Lev.

23:35, in Malbim par. 186)[105] states: "How does one sanctify it? With food, drink, and clean clothes." Note that elements of both *kavod* and *oneg* are mentioned here, and the Midrash is elucidating a biblical verse, so that one may understand that *kavod* and *oneg* are required by the Torah on holidays as well as on the Sabbath. This is the view of Ramban as well (Lev. 23:2), although Rambam (*Hilchot Shabbat* 30:3) considers these laws to be rabbinical in origin.

In short, one may say that according to the opinions that honoring and delighting are Torah-level requirements both on the Sabbath and holidays, it is quite natural to group them together, as the Torah did in the first verses of chapter 23.

An Original Answer by the Gaon of Vilna

The Vilna Gaon (*Divrei Eliyahu*, *Emor*) suggests an ingenious justification for the inclusion of the verse describing the Sabbath in the list of holidays. He says that in reality the verse does not refer to the Sabbath, in spite of the fact that it mentions it twice and portrays it as the culmination of six days of work. After all, the verse states:

> Six days may work be done, and on the seventh day is a Sabbath of solemn rest, a holy convocation; you should do no manner of work; it is a Sabbath for the Lord in all your dwellings (Lev. 23:3).

How can the Gaon claim that the verse is not referring to the Sabbath? The Gaon proposes that the six days enumerated actually refer to the six holy days celebrated throughout the year, namely

---

105. Alternatively, *Sifra, Emor*, ch.14, *parshata* 12.

Rosh Hashanah (New Year), two days of Sukkot (Tabernacles, the last day of which is known as Shemini Atzeret), two days of Pesach (Passover), and Shavuot (Pentecost). But the verse states that work may be done on those days. Is work not proscribed on the holidays just as it is on the Sabbath? The answer is that although hard labor is prohibited on holidays, those forms of work associated with food preparation, such as cooking and baking, are permitted, so in that sense one may work on those days. The "seventh day" mentioned in the verse, called "a Sabbath for the Lord," does not refer to the weekly Sabbath but rather to Yom Kippur (the Day of Atonement), which is also termed a Sabbath, as in the verse:

> It will be a Sabbath of complete rest for you, and you will afflict your souls; on the ninth day of the month in the evening, from evening to evening, you should observe your Sabbath (Lev. 23:32).

On a "Sabbath of complete rest" it is accurate to say that "no manner of work" may be done, not even that associated with readying food (whose consumption is forbidden on Yom Kippur).

Two questions may be asked on the answer of the Gaon.

1. The lesson of this verse would seem to be redundant, since the permissibility of food preparation on the holidays is written explicitly in the verse: "No work should be done on them; only what is to be eaten by every person, that alone may be prepared for you" (Exod. 23:16).

    Furthermore, regarding each of the six holy days the Torah states "you should not perform any type of hard labor [*melechet avodah*]" (Lev. 23:7, 8, 21, 35, 36), and Ramban explains that: "The meaning of *melechet avodah* is any work which is not for the purpose of [preparing] a person's food" (Lev. 23:7). How many times is it necessary to reiterate the same principle?

2. Even if it was desirable to repeat the distinction between work prohibited on the holidays and the more inclusive edict with respect to the Sabbath, why was it necessary to camouflage the reference as if the text were referring to the six days of the week contrasted with the Sabbath, rather than explicitly stressing the disparity between the holidays and the Day of Atonement?

R. Mordechai Kornfeld (*Torah from the Internet*, pp. 146-154), answering on a Midrashic level, justifies the formulation in terms of the days of the week by finding parallels between each holiday and the corresponding day of the week.

The first day of creation – the first day of Pesach

The Midrash (*Gen. Rabbah* 3:8) cites a dispute as to whether angels were created on the second or fifth day of creation, but what is certain is that "everyone agrees that on the first day nothing at all [no being] was created." The Midrash proceeds to explain that it was necessary to emphasize this point in order to discredit any claim that God had partners in creating the world, as Isaiah cites in God's name: "It is I, the Lord, who made everything, Who stretched out the heavens by Myself [and] alone spread out the earth" (Isa. 44:24).

Rashi relates to this Midrash in his exegesis of the phrase that concludes His activities on the first day of creation, which states: "And it was evening and it was morning, one day" (Gen. 1:5). Rashi comments:

According to the regular mode of expression in this portion, He should have written [here] "first day," as it is written regarding the other days: "second," "third," "fourth." Why does Scripture write "one [day]?" Because the Holy One, blessed be He, was then the Sole Being in His universe, for the angels were not created until the second day.

In other words, the phrase accentuates God's omnipotence and exclusivity. The same idea is presented in the Haggadah's explication of the phrase "And the Lord took us out of Egypt" (Deut. 26:8), where the Haggadah states:

Not by means of an angel and not by means of a seraph and not by means of a messenger, but [directly by] the Holy One, blessed be He, Himself, as it says: "And I will pass through the land of Egypt on that night and I will smite every firstborn in the land of Egypt, both man and beast; and against all the gods of Egypt, I will execute judgments, I am the Lord" (Exod. 12:12).

In other words, the first day of Passover, like the first day of creation, stresses God's oneness and uniqueness.

The second day of creation – the seventh day of Pesach

On the second day of creation, the earth was made habitable when God "divided the waters which were under the firmament from the waters which were above the firmament" (Gen. 1:6), calling the firmament "heaven." Although man was not yet created, splitting the universe, which was initially one big ball of water, into heaven and earth represented a giant step in transforming the planet into a potential residence for human beings, which progressed even further the next day, when dry land and vegetation came into being (Gen. 1:9-12).

The seventh day of Passover traditionally represents a second splitting of waters, namely those of the Red Sea. The Israelites had left Egypt on the fifteenth of the month of Nisan, as stated in the book of Numbers: "They travelled from Rameses in the first month, on the fifteenth day of the first month" (Num. 33:3). The verse continues: "It was on the morrow [of the bringing] of the Passover offering that the Children of Israel left with a high hand, in the sight of all of the Egyptians."

Since the Paschal lamb was sacrificed on the fourteenth of the month (Exod. 12:6), they clearly departed on the fifteenth. But Pharaoh soon changed his mind, as the Bible states:

When the king of Egypt was told that the people had fled, Pharaoh and his servants had a change of heart regarding the nation and they said, "What is this we have done, for we have released Israel from serving us" (Exod. 14:5).

Rashi, based on the Midrash,[106] comments:

"When the king of Egypt was told" — he sent officers with them, and as soon as they had reached the three days' journey which he had fixed [for them] to go and return (Exod. 3:18, 5:3, 8:23), and they saw that they were not going back to Egypt, they came and told Pharaoh on the fourth day.

---

106. *Mechilta de-Rabbi Yishmael, Beshallach, Mesechta de-va-yehi, parsha A.*

Since the Talmud (BT *Sotah* 12b) says explicitly that the Song of the Sea (Exod. 15:1-19), sung by the Israelites immediately after traversing the Red Sea, was sung on the twenty-first of Nisan (which would be the seventh day of Passover[107]), Rashi (BT *Sotah* 12b, s.v. *shira*) proceeds to describe the order of events as follows:

> On the fifth and sixth they pursued them. On the night of the seventh day they [the Israelites] went down into the sea; in the morning they sang the Song of the Sea, and this was the seventh day of Passover. Therefore, we read the Song of the Sea on the seventh day.

Is there any hint in the biblical text itself that the crossing took place on the seventh day of Pesach? One might say that since in the present portion (Lev. 23:7-8) both the first and the seventh days of Passover are singled out as being days of holy convocation, it is reasonable to assume that just as the first day of Passover commemorates something very revered, namely the exodus from Egypt, similarly the last day does so, and it is logical that it would be the splitting of the sea. In fact, the following verse in Exodus relates only to the festive nature of the seventh day: "For seven days you should eat unleavened bread, and the seventh day is a festival of the Lord" (Exod. 13:6). It is reasonable that the crossing of the Red Sea and the concomitant drowning of the enemy would be celebrated even more than the day of the exodus, because only then was the nation assured that Pharaoh could not recapture them.

It is now possible to appreciate the parallel between the splitting of the waters at creation—making the word inhabitable, and of the Red Sea during the exodus—making the escape irreversible.

---

107. This explains why the Song of the Sea is read on the seventh day of Passover (BT *Megillah* 31a, and Rashi, s.v. *va-yehi*).

Both symbolize important steps on the way to a sacred goal. In the former, the final result was the creation of man, while in the latter, it was the receipt of the Torah.

The third day of creation – Shavuot

On the third day fruits and vegetables emerged from the earth. It is therefore especially appropriate that on the parallel festival, Shavuot (Pentecost), agricultural produce plays a very central role, both that which God had blessed the nation with in the past—for which He is thanked, and that which Israel prays for in the future.

The following identical phrase appears twice in the book of Exodus: "The choice first fruits of your land you should bring to the house of the Lord your God" (Exod. 23:19; 34:26). That this offering, called *bikkurim*, is brought on Shavuot is derived by the Mishnah (*Bikkurim* 1:3) from a preceding verse in the portion of *Mishpatim*, where Shavuot is referred to as "the feast of the harvesting of the first fruits of your work—of what you have sown in the field" (Exod. 23:16). Furthermore, in Numbers, Shavuot is even referred to as *yom ha-bikkurim* ("the day of the first-fruits," Num. 28:26).

The text of the thanksgiving prayer which accompanies the offering is explicated in Deuteronomy (26:1-11), where it is stated that the farmer takes "*from among* the first fruits," from which the Talmud (BT *Menachot* 84b) derives that he is required to bring *bikkurim* from only certain produce, namely the seven varieties with which the Land of Israel is blessed, namely wheat, barley, grapes, figs, pomegranates, olives, and dates (Deut. 8:8). The Jerusalem Talmud (*Bikkurim* 1:3) explains that these specific fruits were chosen based on the similarity of the terminology[108] used in

---

108. The Hebrew word *artzecha* (Deut. 26:2) is used in describing *bikkurim*, while the Hebrew word *eretz* (Deut. 8:8) is used in describing the seven species.

describing the obligation to bring *bikkurim* and the seven species. At any rate, the fruits selected are fairly representative, including those which grow on trees (figs, pomegranates, olives, and dates) on vines (grapes), and from the ground (wheat and barley).

What eventually happens to the first fruits brought as an offering? They are donated to the priests. *Bikkurim* is accordingly enumerated among the priestly gifts listed in the book of Numbers (18:13): "The first fruits of everything in their land, that they bring to the Lord [as described in Exodus and Deuteronomy], will be yours."

Pentecost is also a time when prayers are offered for a successful year agriculturally. The Mishnah (*Rosh Hashanah* 1:2) states: "At four times the world is judged: On Pesach, with respect to the crops. On Shavuot, with respect to the fruits of the tree...." The Talmud bases this dictum on the fact that the *shtei ha-lechem* offering, which was composed of two loaves baked from newly harvested wheat and given to the priests (Lev. 23:20), was brought on Pentecost as a means of supplication for a successful harvest, as the Talmud states:

Why did the Torah say: Bring the *omer* [barley offering] on [the second day of] Passover? Because Passover is the time [of the first harvest] of grain. The Holy One, blessed be He, said: Bring the *omer* before Me on Passover so that the grain in the fields will be blessed for you. And why did the Torah say: Bring the *shtei ha-lechem* on Shavuot? It is because Shavuot is the time of the [earliest ripening of the] fruits of the tree. The Holy One, blessed be He, said: Bring the *shtei ha-lechem* before Me on Shavuot so that the fruits of the tree will be blessed for you (BT *Rosh Hashanah* 16a).

The prayers for a bountiful year start on Pesach and culminate with the *shtei ha-lechem*, which is all-inclusive as it relates to both fruits and grains.

Additionally, in the Shavuot prayers, the holiday is termed *zman matan torateinu* (the time of the giving of the Torah). Ibn Ezra (Lev. 23:11) writes:

> On Shavuot the giving of the Torah took place, concerning which it says: "We will go with our young and with our old; we will go with our sons and our daughters, our flocks and herds; for we must observe the Lord's festival" (Exod. 10:9).

Tying together revelation with the agricultural celebration, R. Kornfeld points out that trees symbolize the spiritual as well as the physical, in that the Torah is likened to a tree in the verse: "It is a tree of life for those who obey its laws, and those who support it are happy" (Prov. 3:18). Just as a tree stands firm and upright, he who observes the law proceeds steadfastly and confidently through the labyrinth of life.

R. Kornfeld goes on to indicate that the third day of creation was the only one for which the phrase "And God saw that this was good" appears twice (Gen. 1:10, 12). Perhaps one was to underline the emergence of vegetation, and one the spiritual facet symbolized by it.

The fourth day of creation – Rosh Hashanah

On the fourth day, God created "the greater light to rule by day, and the lesser light to rule by night, and the stars" (Gen. 1:16). It is these heavenly bodies which enable man to keep track of time. Rosh Hashanah is the holiday which celebrates the beginning of each new year, i.e., the Jewish New Year. The months in each year are based on the lunar cycle, but the decision as to which years will be composed of twelve months and which will be leap years having thirteen months is based on the solar cycle, and it is thanks to the extra month added to the leap years that the Jewish holidays are synchronized with the yearly seasons.

The fifth day of creation – Sukkot

The theme of the fifth day of creation is water, as a life-producing substance. The Bible states: "And God said: 'Let the waters swarm with swarms of living creatures, and let fowl fly above the earth across the expanse of the sky'" (Gen. 1:20).

After splitting the waters on the second day of creation, thus creating the lakes, seas, and oceans—all enveloped by the atmosphere, it was now time to fill the waters with sea creatures and the air with flying creatures. Of course, a prerequisite was the availability of vegetation (created on the third day), whose continued existence required sunlight (created on the fourth day).

The Talmud (BT *Chullin* 27b) goes even further, stating that not only did the sea creatures fill the waters, but they (as well as the birds) actually emanated from the waters. In the previously cited verse, the Talmud replaces the phrase "swarm with swarms of living creatures" with "bring forth swarms of living creatures." According to the Talmud, the waters were not only populated, but also took part in the creative process.

The fifth festival on the list, Tabernacles, also focuses on the essentiality and centrality of water. A previously quoted Mishnah (*Rosh Hashanah* 1:2) spoke of the four times that the world is judged, and one of them is Sukkot, when the world is "judged with respect to water." The Mishnah apparently made this determination based on the fact that the water libation, which is considered to be a law transmitted to Moses orally on Mt. Sinai (BT *Sukkah* 44a), took place on Sukkot, as described below:

> And why did the Torah say: Pour water [onto the altar in the Temple] on the festival [of Sukkot]? The Holy One, blessed be He, said: Pour water before Me on the festival [as derived in BT *Ta'anit* 2b] so that the rains of the year [which begin to fall after Sukkot] will be blessed for you (BT *Rosh Hashanah* 16a).

Water as a stimulus to productivity is thus accentuated on the fifth day of creation, as well as on the fifth annual holiday.

The sixth day of creation – Shemini Atzeret

Regarding the sixth day of creation, the Bible states: "And God created man in His image; in the image of God He created him; male and female He created them" (Gen. 1:27). But what is the meaning of "in His image?" Is there any reason to believe that man resembles God physically any more than, say, a lion or a gorilla does? The Talmud was convinced that the reference is to the cognizance and intelligence with which man was endowed, which would enable him to be aware of God, to experience revelation, and occasionally to even communicate with Him.

The Talmud notes that the Torah sums up the creations of the fifth day (and similarly of the previous days) with the verse: "And it was evening and it was morning – *a* fifth day" (Gen. 1:23). However, after creating man, the parallel verse reads: "And it was evening and it was morning – *the* sixth day" (Gen. 1:23). The Talmud wonders why the indefinite artice "a" was replaced by the definite article "the." The answer given is:

It teaches that the Holy One, blessed be He, made a condition with the works of creation, and said to them: If Israel accepts the Torah, you will [continue to] exist; and if not, I will return you to [a state of] chaos and disorder (BT *Shabbat* 88a, *Avodah Zarah* 3a).

In other words, the definite article is used regarding the sixth day in order to stress that it was not just any day, but the day upon which a strict requirement was imposed. Rashi explains that the day being referred to is the sixth of the Hebrew month of Sivan, the day on which the Torah was to be given, as if to say that the fate of the universe depends on Israel's acceptance (or rejection) of the Torah, which is to be given on the sixth of Sivan. Rashi, on Genesis 1:31, adds that the word "the" is written in Hebrew as ה, which is the fifth letter of the Hebrew alphabet, and symbolizes in another way that the world would be destroyed unless Israel accepted the five books of Moses.

Just as the sixth day of creation is associated with the giving of the Torah, it will now be shown that the same may be said about Shemini Atzeret.

On the Sabbath and holidays, additional sacrifices, called *musafim*, are offered. In particular, on the seven days of Sukkot the number of young bulls offered is thirteen, twelve, eleven, ten, nine, eight, and seven, respectively (Num. 29:12-34), leading to a total of seventy. However, on Shemini Atzeret a lone bull is offered (Num. 29:36). The Talmud notes the striking disparity and has the following to say about it:

Rabbi Elazar said: These seventy bulls, to what do they correspond? They correspond to the seventy nations [of the world; Rashi: (They are brought) to atone for their sins so that it will rain in the entire world, because we are judged on Sukkot regarding water]. Why a single bull [Rashi: on the eighth (day, i.e., Shemini Atzeret)]? It corresponds to a unique nation [namely, Israel]. This is comparable to a human king who said to his servants: "Make me a great feast." On the last day, he said to his beloved: "Make me a small feast so that I can derive pleasure from you [Rashi: I do not have pleasure and satisfaction from these but (only) from you]. Rabbi Yochanan said: Woe unto the star worshippers, who have lost and do not know what they lost. When the Temple exists, the altar [i.e. the sacrifices brought on it] atones for them. And now, who atones for them (BT *Sukkah* 55b)?

This extract would seem to contain contradictory ideas. On the one hand, it sounds as if Israel considers itself to be God's favorite. On the other hand, Israel is said to pray for both the spiritual and physical well-being of the nations of the world by beseeching God to even absolve idol-worshippers of their sins, and to furthermore grant them a fruitful year.

One may resolve this incongruity by noting that according to the Midrash, the willingness of Israel to abide by the covenant was in fact the main reason for the Torah being given to the Jewish nation, and so they were the chosen people only in the sense that they were capable of being more attuned to learning and acting upon the lessons of the Torah than other nations. The sequence of events, in the view of the Midrash, was as follows:

When the Lord appeared to give the Torah to Israel, it was not to Israel alone that He appeared, but to all of the nations. First He went to the children of Esau. He said to them:

"Will you accept the Torah?" They said: "What is written in it?" He answered: "You must not kill" (Exod. 20:13). They said: "The entire essence of our father is murder, as it is written: 'And the hands are the hands of Esau,'" (Gen. 27:22), [and his father had told him:] "And by your sword you will live" (Gen. 27:40). He then went to the children of Ammon and Moab. He said to them: "Will you accept the Torah?" They said: "What is written in it?" He answered: "You must not commit adultery" (Exod. 20:13). They said: "Incest is our entire essence, as it is written (Gen. 19:36): 'And the two daughters of Lot conceived by their father.'" He then went to the children of Ishmael. He said to them: "Will you accept the Torah?" They asked: "What is written in it?" He answered: "You must not steal" (Exod. 20:13). They said to him: "Our father's entire essence is stealing, as it says: 'And he (Ishmael) will be a wild man, his hand [raised] against all'" (Gen. 16:12). And so with respect to every nation, he asked them if they would accept the Torah... And even the seven Noahide commands which they took upon themselves they could not abide by, until they divested themselves of them. When the Lord realized what the situation was, He ceded them [the Noahide laws] to Israel. An analogy: One sent his ass and his dog to the threshing floor, loading his ass with fifteen sa'ah and his dog with three sa'ah. The ass went and the dog panted. He took a sa'ah from it and put it on the ass; and so with the second [sa'ah] and so with the third. Here, too, Israel accepted the Torah with all of its explanations and inferences; but the sons of Noah could not even abide by the seven commands that they did take upon themselves, and Israel came and accepted them upon themselves (*Sifrei Deut.* 343).

In summary, both the sixth day of creation and the sixth holiday are intimately related to the acceptance of the Torah.

The seventh day of creation (the Sabbath) –Yom Kippur

At first blush, it is hard to see the likeness between the Sabbath and Yom Kippur. The latter is a day of fasting and affliction of the soul. The former, on the other hand, is a day on which there is an obligation of *oneg Shabbat*, which includes eating, drinking, sleeping, and even sexual realtions, most of which are prohibited on the Day of Atonement.

However, there is one characteristic common to both the Sabbath and Yom Kippur, namely, that both may be portrayed as days devoted to repentance. Note the following points which have been compiled from the sources:

Rosh Hashanah behavior

One eats, drinks, and is happy, and does not fast, on Rosh Hashanah, and not on the intervening Sabbath of Repentance (*Orach Chaim* 597:1).

Repentance on Yom Kippur

1. Yom Kippur is an appropriate time for repentance for the individual and the congregation (*Hilchot Teshuvah* 2:7).
2. For sins between man and God, Yom Kippur atones. For sins between man and his fellow man, Yom Kippur does not atone until he appeases his fellow man (Mishnah *Yoma* 8:9).

From these sources, it is seen that on Yom Kippur a person repents for his sins against God. With regard to sins between man and his fellow-man, one must repent at an earlier stage, perhaps on Rosh Hashanah, when one eats, drinks, and is merry.

Repentance on the Sabbath

God initiated a conversation with Adam in order to create an opportunity for him to repent for the sin of eating the forbidden fruit, but Adam failed to take advantage of the opportunity (Tanchuma *Tazria* 9). Another Midrash (*Gen. Rabbah* 22:13) states:

> When Cain said "My sin [i.e. its punishment] is greater than I can bear" (Gen. 4:13), he intended to say that his sin [the murder of Abel] was in reality greater than that of Adam, and accordingly he does not deserve to be absolved. God considered his words to signify remorse, and as a result cancelled half of his punishment, influencing Adam to compose the psalm: "A Psalm: a song for the Sabbath day. It is good to thank the Lord" (Ps. 92:1-2).

The Hebrew word for Sabbath (*Shabbat*) contains the root of the Hebrew word for repentance (*la-shuv*), while the Hebrew word for thanking (*le-hodot*) also means to confess (*Yefei Toar, in situ*).

It may be suggested that the commonality between Sabbath and the Day of Atonement is that on both one engages in repentance. But Sabbath differs from Yom Kippur—for on the latter day one repents for sins between man and God, while the former parallels Rosh Hashanah, when one repents for interpersonal sins by means of joyous social interaction among friends.

The sins of Adam and Cain were between man and his fellow man. Adam indeed disobeyed God's command, but he also sinned against his wife when he blamed her for enticing him to eat from the tree of knowledge by saying: "The woman whom You gave to be with me—she gave me of the tree, and I ate [of it]" (Gen. 3:12). The sin of Cain was also between man and his compatriot, but there was no-one left from whom to beg forgiveness.

In summary, the Sabbath is designated for repentance—both for sins between man and God (by saying "it is good to thank [confess before] God"—where the intention is for sins of the type that Adam transgressed, and even for a sin like that of Cain, where there is no one to beseech other than God), but mainly for sins between man and his fellow man, which is a form of repentance which transpires by means of merriment, pleasure, friendship, and social relations. The main characteristic of Yom Kippur as well is as a day devoted to repentance, and that is the basis of its comparison to *Shabbat*.

SUMMARY

This chapter dealt with the juxtaposition of the Sabbath and the holidays in the portion of *Emor*, when the title of the section seemed to relate only to the latter. Two approaches were taken. In the first, the details of Sabbath and festival observance were examined, and it was noted that there is sufficient overlap to group them together when the intention is to emphasize their similarity. In the second approach, that of the Vilna Gaon, it was shown that the verse which seems to refer to the six work days culminating in the Sabbath actually relates to the six holidays which climax in Yom Kippur. Each of the seven holidays was seen to be parallel to the corresponding day of creation.

Behar

In the previous portion of *Emor*, the Torah lists the sacred days of the year. R. Joseph Hertz points out that the number seven plays a central role in the dates of these special days, the Sabbath being the seventh day of the week, Shavuot coming after counting seven weeks, and a number of holidays occurring in the seventh Hebrew month, Tishrei. The portion of *Behar* adds more seven-oriented sacred seasons, dealing with the laws of *shemittah*, the Sabbatical year, and *yovel*, the Jubilee year which comes after seven Sabbatical cycles.[109] During these years, the land was to lay fallow and its produce was freely available for public consumption. In addition, in the Sabbatical year loans were to be cancelled, while in the Jubilee year land which had been sold was to be returned to its original owner and slaves were to be freed. The point being made is that God is the true owner of the land, He may do what he wishes with it, and one of his priorities is to ensure that the poor are provided for, and that their assets (including their own bodies) are returned to them so that they can escape the cycle of poverty.

On the other hand, there are Midrashic sources (to be examined in detail in the next portion, *Bechukkotai*) which imply that the discussion of the Sabbatical year initiates a new section, thematically attached to what follows rather than what precedes

109. Joseph Hertz, *Pentateuch* (1938), p. 531.

it. The Bible itself would seem to indicate that this is the case, by writing the following introductory verses:

1. And the Lord spoke to Moses on Mount Sinai, saying:
2. Speak to the Children of Israel, and say to them: When you come to the land which I am giving you, then the land will keep a Sabbath for the Lord (Lev. 25).

Recording Mt. Sinai as the source of the law at this point implies the beginning of a new section. Furthermore, the reference to their arrival in the Land of Israel in verse 2 indicates that these laws would not be applicable for many years, as opposed to the festival-related laws of the portion of *Emor*, which were to go into effect immediately.

THE SABBATICAL YEAR

The Mishnah states: "Torah, together with an occupation, is an excellent thing, for the pursuit of both of these keeps sinful thoughts from arising" (*Avot* 2:2). In other words, a Jew's time should be divided between Torah and work. But what is actually meant by Torah? Obviously, it must include both studying the Torah and observing its laws, as stated in another Mishnah: "Study is not the most important thing, but rather the deed" (*Avot* 1:17).

Rambam's explanation of a third Mishnah provides a more comprehensive definition of what is actually meant by Torah: "The world stands on three things: on Torah, Divine worship, and acts of loving-kindness" (*Avot* 1:2). Rambam (*Perush ha-Mishnayot*) explains that "Torah" refers to the intellectual exercise involved in understanding the laws; "Divine worship" refers to obeying the commands associated with worshipping God, such as prayer, sacrifices, holidays, and the various statutes; and "acts of loving-kindness" refers to perfecting one's personality traits so that he is considerate of others and sensitive to their needs.

The word "Torah" mentioned in the first Mishnah is thus seen to be composed of three elements. The Hebrew words for "work" used in the Mishnah are *derech eretz*. R. Samson Raphael Hirsch, in his exegesis of the Mishnah, sees these words as being inclusive of more than pure work. He states:

> Accordingly, the term *derech eretz* is used primarily to refer to ways of earning a living, to the social order that prevails on earth, as well as the mores and considerations of courtesy and propriety arising from social living and also to things pertinent to good breeding and general education.

The Torah does more than indicate the various activities that a Jew should engage in. It also suggests a schedule for when they should be performed. The Torah has already divided the week into two sections, one for working ("Six days you should work, and do all your work," Exod. 20:9) and one for resting and indulging in Torah-oriented intellectual activity ("but the seventh day is a Sabbath for the Lord your God, on it you should not do any manner of work," Exod. 20:10). The Torah apportions time on a yearly basis as well, with six years allocated for agricultural work, and the seventh, the *shemittah* year (as well as *yovel*), for resting on the part of the land-owners and the land itself, and resetting the economy.

Shemittah is mentioned in passing in two locations (Exod. 23:10-11; Exod. 34:21), and dealt with extensively from an agricultural point of view in *Behar* (Lev. 25:1-16) and from a monetary point of view (cancellation of loans) in the portion of *Re'eh* (Deut. 16:1-3). In his *Hilchot Shemittah ve-Yovel* (ch. 1), Rambam counts nine positive commands and thirteen negative commands. One may thus say that it plays a central role in the civilization envisioned by the Torah.

REASONS FOR *SHEMITTAH*

Communal and ethical reasons:
The Torah presents the justification for the laws of *shemittah* the very first time the concept is introduced in the portion of *Mishpatim*, where it states:

> And the seventh year you should release it [Ramban: from being planted] and abandon it [Ramban: from being harvested], so that the poor of your people may eat; and what they leave, the beast of the field may eat (Exod. 23:11).

Not only is one to sustain the poor, but the verse also hints at being considerate of beasts, which points to a possible command not to cause pain even to animals.[110] The Midrash (*Mechilta, Mishpatim* 216, quoted by Rashi on this verse) says that animals are mentioned in order to indicate that just as an animal eats without being expected to separate offerings for priests and Levites, so the poor person who benefits from the fruits of the *shemittah* year need not do so; rather, he gets to keep them in their entirety.

The purpose of the law is not only to satisfy the needs of the poor, but to nurture the proper attitude of the well-to-do toward those who are less fortunate. In the words of R. Zvi Hirsch Kalisher:

---

110. The Talmud discusses whether such a command is Torah-based or just rabbinical in nature (BT *Bava Metzia* 32b-33a). Rif (BT *Bava Metzia* 51a) posits that it is in fact Torah-based. At the very least the verse's positive attitude would have stimulated the rabbis to legislate such a law.

... to learn from this [mitzvah] that the rich should not see himself as superior to the poor. Therefore, the Torah said that in the seventh year all are equal, together the wealthy and the pauper have permission to eat until satisfaction from the gardens and the fields (*Sefer ha-Brit, Behar*).

Finally, the laws of *yovel* include the return of land which was sold and thereby severed from the family inheritance. This approach ensures that poverty will not only be dealt with on an *ad hoc* basis, but rather in a manner which permanently removes the person from the ranks of the indigent. As Rambam explains, one of its purposes is:

... to secure for the people a permanent source of maintenance and support by providing that the land should remain the permanent property of its owners, and that it could not be sold: "And the land may not be sold forever" (Lev. 25:23). In this way, the property of a person remains intact for him and his heirs, and he [the purchaser] can only enjoy the produce thereof (*Guide for the Perplexed* 3:39).

Intellectual and spiritual renewal:

A simple explanation is proferred by the *Ba'al ha-Akeida* (*Akeidat Yitzchak, Vayikra* 69 [*Behar*]). He says both the weekly Sabbath and the Sabbatical year are meant to clarify that:

We were not sent here to be enslaved by the land, but rather for a more honorable and wonderful purpose... that their entry into the land is not to be subjugated by it and its work and to extract all of its benefits, and to store its fruits

- to gather them in order to become enriched, as is the intention of the other nations.... Rather, the intention is that they should evaluate themselves and seek their own perfection as their Maker desired... and to establish and strengthen this matter which is incumbent upon them, it was written and given over to them as a powerful signal that they should work six years and release [themselves] from work on the seventh, so that it will be known to them that not through the power of working the land will a man become strong, but that their work is something that one refrains from in God's name... that it should be known to you that what is intended for you from working it [the land] and all of your other employment is only what is needed for you to eat.

The *Ba'al ha-Akeidah* is simply stating that there is a spiritual side to life beyond the satisfaction of our physical needs. In addition to emphasizing the fact that this is indeed the case, the Sabbatical year provides the time to actually do something about it. Even in secular society, professionals in many areas today are entitled to a sabbatical year, during which they are exempted from their routine functions, and instead are free to devote themselves to researching new topics, studying new areas, or experiencing new techniques. Building on the spirit of democracy, which was referred to as one of the communal reasons, the Sabbatical year allows every Jew, even those employed in intensive agricultural work, to become an academic once every seven years, during which he can indulge in intensive Torah study as well as expand his horizons in other disciplines. In R. Kalisher's words:

Not always will they be burdened with working the land for their material needs. Just one year [out of seven] will he be free, and when he dispenses with the yolk of work, he will engage in Torah and [general] wisdom (*Sefer ha-Brit, Behar*).

To the academic facet, R. Kook (Introduction to *Shabbat ha-Aretz*) adds a spiritual aspect. He explains that the weekly Sabbath, by breaking the everyday routine, allows the individual's soul to free itself from mundane worries and depression, and to unite with the higher spheres in praise of God. In the words of the psalmist in the classical Sabbath hymn: "It is good to thank the Lord and to sing [praises] to Your great name, to declare Your lovingkindness in the morning and Your faithfulness at night" (Ps. 92:2-3). R. Kook proceeds to state that the same effect that the Sabbath has on the individual, the Sabbatical year has on the nation. By suspending the normative social order, society as a whole allows itself to internalize the most sublime attributes of morality and spirituality.

Religious reasons:
The sanctification over wine on the eve of the Sabbath emphasizes two communal memories, the remembrance of the creation and that of the exodus from Egypt. The first is intended to strengthen a Jew's belief in God as the Creator of the universe, and the second stresses His concern for the welfare of the nation and its destiny as the chosen people. What connection is there between these two concepts?

The answer is that looking upon oneself as God's gift to mankind quite naturally leads to pomposity and smugness. It is thus incumbent on the nation as a whole, and every individual in particular, to realize that it is God who created the world, every person is null and void in comparison with his Maker, and any special mission which God entrusts him with is not necessarily because he has outshone everyone else, but rather because this is the function which God has allocated to him—or more accurately "burdened him with." As the Talmud states concerning two students of R. Gamliel who declined his job offer out of modesty: "Do you imagine that I offer you rulership? It is servitude that I offer you [so accepting the job will not generate hubris]" (BT *Horayot* 10a).

By desisting from work on the Sabbath, the Jew accentuates that his creativity during the week is possible only because God, Who created the world, has endowed man with that ability.

Abarbanel (*Nachalat Avot* 5:8) compares the Sabbatical year to the weekly Sabbath, as does the following verse from the portion of *Behar*: "There will be a Sabbath of solemn rest for the land, a Sabbath to the Lord" (Lev. 25:4). Just as the weekly Sabbath highlights chosenness and the Lord's omnipotence, so does the Sabbatical year. The mission of the Jews is to inculcate God's ways to all of the nations of the world by setting up a political entity which functions in an ideal manner; in short, a paradise on earth. This entity is to be located in the Land of Israel, whose chosenness parallels that of the nation itself. Accordingly, the Midrash states that when God "formed man from the dust of the ground" (Gen. 2:7), He took holy dust from the future location of the Temple (*Matnot Kehuna, Gen. Rabbah* 14:8). Similarly, in order to fulfill his mission, Abraham is told to emigrate to the Land of Israel (Gen. 12:1), the only location where that mission could be accomplished.

The superiority of the land is attested to by the Bible when it describes it as "a land which the Lord your God supervises; the eyes of the Lord your God are always upon it, from the beginning of the year until the very end of the year" (Deut. 11:12). Similarly, God tells King Solomon, with respect to the First Temple, "and My eyes and My heart will be there perpetually" (1 Kings 9:3). Finally, when the Kingdom of Israel was exiled by Shalmaneser, King of Assyria, the Bible states:

> And the king of Assyria brought men from Babylon... and placed them in the cities of Samaria instead of the Children of Israel... they did not fear the Lord; therefore, the Lord sent lions among them, which killed some of them (2 Kings 17:24-25).

In short, because of its holiness, the Land of Israel itself cannot tolerate idol worship. In the words of Abarbanel: "One sees that the Land of Israel is chosen and desirable to He Who is blessed among all of the other lands, just as the nation of Israel is chosen among all other nations" (*Avot* 5:8, *Nachalat Avot*).

However, there exists a danger that this holiness will be misunderstood as reflecting intrinsic qualities of the land rather than the fact that the Lord has designated it as such in order for the nation to accomplish its mission. For that reason, an entire year is devoted to focusing on God and his plans by studying Torah and practicing beneficence.

Furthermore, one allows the land to remain idle during this period "in order that man might remember that the land which brings forth fruit every year does so not by its own strength and capability, for there is a Master over it and over its masters" (*Sefer ha-Chinnuch* 84). In the words of the Talmud: "Plant six [years] and desist [from doing so] on the seventh, so that you know that the earth is Mine" (BT *Sanhedrin* 39a). On the basis of this passage, which equates between observing the Sabbatical year and belief in God, *Torah Temimah* (on Lev. 25:13) explains why the punishment for neglecting *shemittah* both on a communal (Lev. 26:33) and an individual (BT *Kiddushin* 20a) level is very harsh.

Self-improvement:

Additional reasons proposed by *Sefer ha-Chinnuch* (84) are:

> To acquire the trait of altruism, for no one is as generous
> as he who gives with no expectation of compensation...
> To increase a person's trust in God, for anyone who finds
> [the willingness] in his heart to give and to freely abandon
> to the world all of the crops of his lands... will not suffer
> from a great degree of stinginess, nor from a small amount
> of trust [in God].

As R. Kalisher (*Sefer ha-Brit, Behar*) explains, it is not mere trust
which *shemittah* teaches, but the ability to withstand the most
challenging ordeal of relying on the Divine promise of adequate
sustenance with no relief in sight.

Ecological reasons:

Rambam proposes that the Sabbatical year allows the land to
be revitalized, a concept akin to "rotation of crops," a technique
apparently known already in prehistorical times. He explains: "the
land will also increase its produce and improve when it remains
fallow for some time" (*Guide for the Perplexed* 3:39).

Abarbanel (Lev. 25:1) expresses two objections to Rambam's
reasoning. First, he cites the verse: "Then I will command My
blessing on you in the sixth year, and it will bring forth produce
for the three years" (Lev. 25:21). Rashi (s.v. *le-shalosh ha-shanim*)
explains this verse as follows:

> For part of the sixth—from Nisan [when the crops are
> harvested] until Rosh Hashanah, and for the seventh,
> and for the eighth, for they will plant in the eighth in
> Cheshvan, but will only harvest in Nisan [forcing one to

rely on the sixth year's produce during the entire winter of the eighth year].

Abarbanel asks that if the land grew progressively weaker during the seven-year cycle, by the time of the sixth year it would already be quite weak, so how would it be able to produce enough for three years? Furthermore, neglecting to observe the Sabbatical year is punishable by exile, as stated in the next portion (Lev. 26):

> 33. And I will scatter you among the nations, and I will draw the sword [out of the sheath of those who chase] after you; and your land will become desolate, and your cities will become a wasteland. 34. Then will the land be compensated for her Sabbaths [which were not observed], as long as it lies desolate, while you are in your enemies' land; then the land will rest and repay her Sabbaths. 35. As long as it lies desolate it will rest; the rest which it did not have during your Sabbatical years, when you dwelled upon it.

Abarbanel's second objection is that if the land grows progressively weaker, punishment by exile would be superfluous, since by default the land would become unproductive and eventually sterile.

One might answer that Rambam works simultaneously on both the natural and the supernatural level. On the natural level, it is beneficial to allow the land to rest. The mitzvah was given in order to increase a Jew's awareness of the importance of preserving the earth's pristine potential in agriculture as well as in other areas. On the other hand, during a period when miracles were prevalent, in spite of its weakness, the land's yield would increase in order to prevent starvation. Not observing the Sabbatical laws represents calling God's plan for the proper functioning of the Land of Israel into question, and is accordingly punishable in the most severe manner.

THE JUBILEE YEAR

Unlike the secular calendar, which is divided into years, decades, and centuries, the Jewish calendar is divided into years, Sabbaticals, and units of fifty years, each of which is called a *yovel* (Jubilee). The Bible states (Lev. 25):

> 8. And you should number for yourselves seven sabbaths [units of seven] of years, seven times seven years; and there will be for you the days of seven sabbaths of years, forty-nine years. 9. And you should proclaim [the Jubilee] with the blast of the horn on the tenth day of the seventh month; on Yom Kippur [the Day of Atonement] you should proclaim with the horn throughout your land. 10. And you should sanctify the fiftieth year, and proclaim liberty throughout the land to all of its inhabitants; it will be a Jubilee for you, and every man will return to his possession, and every man will return to his family. 11. The fiftieth year will be a Jubilee for you; you may not plant, nor reap that which grows on its own, nor gather the grapes which were reserved [for private use].

The fifty-year cycle:
After counting seven sets of seven years, verse 10 indicates that the fiftieth year is celebrated as the Jubilee year, making a fifty-year cycle. Just as the last year in each set is holy (Lev. 25:4), so is the fiftieth year at the end of the seven sets. As Rashi (Lev. 25:11) says: "There are thus two adjacent holy years—the forty-ninth year (*shemittah*) and the fiftieth year (*yovel*)."

That the Jubilee year was thus implemented in practice would seem to follow from its description by Josephus, who states:

> He gave then rest to the land from ploughing and planting every seventh year, as he had prescribed to them to rest from working every seventh day, and ordered that then what grew of its own accord out of the earth should in common belong to all that pleased to use it, making no distinction in that respect between their own countrymen and foreigners, and he ordained that they should do the same after seven times seven years, which in all are fifty years (*Antiquities of the Jews*, 3:12:3).

Although this is the simple interpretation of the text, R. Judah in the Talmud (BT *Arachin* 33a) holds that the Jubilee cycle is actually only forty-nine years long. How is this possible if verse 10 refers explicitly to the fiftieth year? The answer is, in the words of R. Judah: "The fiftieth year counts for here [the previous cycle] and here [the next cycle]." In other words, the fiftieth year of the previous Jubilee is also the first year of the first Sabbatical cycle in the next Jubilee. It follows that in the first Sabbatical cycle of each Jubilee, both its first and seventh years are holy, while in the remaining six Sabbatical cycles, only the seventh year is holy.

According to R. Judah's approach, the first Sabbatical cycle is structurally different from the following six. Yet, nowhere does the text hint at this distinction. Furthermore, one still remains with two consecutive years of no agricultural activity (the last year of the previous cycle and the first year of the next cycle), with only five years to recuperate. Perhaps it would have been preferable to let the seventh Sabbatical year overlap the Jubilee year. However, that would conflict with verse 10, and even a Tanna cannot propose an interpretation which contradicts Scripture.

As problematic as R. Judah's view is, Rambam does cite the view of the Geonim (*Hilchot Shemittah ve-Yovel* 10:5), who felt that in the period of exile between the two Temples, and after the destruction of the Second Temple, when the Jubilee would not be celebrated (to be discussed later), the entire cycle would contract from fifty years to forty-nine, since there would be no functionality associated with the fiftieth year. According to *Kesef Mishneh* (*in situ*), even the Sages who argued with R. Judah during the period when the rules of the Jubilee were in force, would agree with him when they became obsolete.

Laws pertaining to the Jubilee year:
Verse 11 repeats the restrictions on planting and harvesting which were in effect during the Sabbatical year (Lev. 25:4-5). Verse 10, which speaks of proclaiming liberty and of men returning to their families, is referring to two types of slaves:

1. Those who have been sold by the court for six years in order to make restitution for a theft which they have committed are freed. If a slave prefers not to be released after six years, he undergoes the ear-piercing ceremony, and is then permitted to prolong his servitude (Exod. 21:2-7). Jubilee frees court-ordered slaves whether they are within the first six years of their sentence or whether they had requested an extension (Rashi, Lev. 25:10).
2. Those who have sold themselves into slavery because of poverty are freed (Lev. 25:40).

The phrase in verse 10 "and every man will return to his possession" refers, according to Rashi, to the land returning to its original owner in the Jubilee year. Note the unusual language: instead of the land returning to its owner, the owner returns to his land. The implication is that the land is eternally designated for a specific person, whose indigence compelled him to temporarily separate from it, as described later in the chapter, in verses 25-28. This person doesn't even have to wait for the Jubilee year; if he or a relative is able to redeem it at an earlier stage, they are encouraged to do so.

One aspect of *shemittah* is not reflected in *yovel*, and that is cancellation of debts (*Sifrei* Deut. 112, on Deut. 15:2). Even before Hillel enacted the *prozbol* (a legal means of maintaining loans during the Sabbatical year), which resolved the difficulty of having one year during which debts were to be cancelled, it was clear that two such years would be too much to expect of even the most righteous individuals.

The aim of the Jubilee was to emancipate the individual from the shackles of poverty and allow him to start anew financially, as a free man with his own plot of land to work on. How appropriate that the Jubilee was welcomed with a blast of the *shofar* specifically on Yom Kippur, the holy day which allows each individual to start anew spiritually.[111]

The Jubilee year represented much more than the return of a person's land and his independence, if the latter had been forfeited. It symbolized the entire social system which functioned in the Land of Israel and was the *raison d'etre* of the Jewish nation. In the words of R. Zalman Sorotzkin, Israel was to be "a nation composed entirely of priests, which is required to set an example for all nations of its pure belief in God, its just laws, its righteous statutes which treat citizens and sojourners equally, and its inherent goodness" (*Oznayim la-Torah*, on Exod. 19:6). When the Jubilee was not in effect, the entire corpus of legislation regarding

111. Joseph Hertz, *Pentateuch* (1938), p. 532.

Hebrew servitude, inherited lands and dwelling places in walled cities, and even social obligations to the Gentile residents of the Holy Land was in abeyance (BT *Arachin* 29a).

Historical scope of the Jubilee:

The Talmud states that observance of the Jubilee year became inoperative with the waning of the first commonwealth. It is important to note that the Kingdom of Israel was destroyed, and its inhabitants exiled, in three stages:

1. Exile of two and a half tribes (1 Chron. 5:25 -26):

   And they rebelled against the God of their fathers, and went astray after the gods of the peoples of the land, whom God had destroyed for them. And the God of Israel awakened the spirit of Pul, king of Assyria, and the spirit of Tillegath-pilneser, king of Assyria, and he exiled the Reubenites, and the Gadites, and the half-tribe of Manasseh, and brought them to Halah, and Habor, and Hara, and to the river of Gozan, [where they remain] to this day.

2. Exile of the northern tribe of Naftali (2 Kings 15:29):

   In the days of Pekah, king of Israel, came Tiglath-pileser, king of Assyria, and took Ijon, and Abel-beth-maacah, and Janoah, and Kedesh, and Hazor, and Gilead, and Galilee, all the land of Naphtali; and he exiled them to Assyria.

3. Exile of the remainder of the ten tribes (2 Kings 17:6):

   In the ninth year of Hoshea, the king of Assyria captured Samaria, and exiled Israel to Assyria, and he settled them in Halah, and in Habor, on the river of Gozan, and in the cities of the Medes.

The following extract from the Talmud describes the cessation of the observance of *yovel*:

It is written: "And all those exiled who returned from captivity made *sukkot*, and they dwelt in the *sukkot*; for since the days of Joshua the son of Nun the Children of Israel had not done so. And there was very great joy" (Neh. 8:17). Is it possible that when David came, they made no *sukkot*, when Solomon came, they did not make *sukkot*, until Ezra came? [It is not referring to the construction of *sukkot*, but] rather he compares their arrival in the days of Ezra to their arrival in the days of Joshua: just as at their arrival in the days of Joshua they counted the years of *shemittah* and *yovel*, and consecrated cities encompassed by walls, thus also at their arrival in the days of Ezra they counted the years of *shemittah* and *yovel* and consecrated walled cities.... But did they count the years of *shemittah* and *yovel* [after the return from Babylon]? If even after the exile of the tribe of Reuben, the tribe of Gad, and the half-tribe of Manasseh, the Jubilees were abolished, would Ezra—in regard to whom it says: "The whole congregation together was forty two thousand three hundred sixty" (Ezra 2:64)—have counted them [since the majority of the tribes and of the nation were missing]? For it was taught: From the time of the exile of the tribe of Reuben, the tribe of Gad, and the half-tribe of Manasseh, the Jubilees were abolished, as it says: "and proclaim liberty throughout the land to all of its inhabitants" (Lev. 25:10), i.e., [only] at the time when all of its inhabitants are on it, but not when some of them are exiled. One might have assumed that if they were there, but intermingled, the tribe of Benjamin with that of Judah, and the tribe of Judah with that of Benjamin, then the [laws of the] Jubilee would apply [when a majority of each tribe is in Israel], therefore it says "to all of its inhabitants," which means, only at the time when its inhabitants are there in the proper manner [separated into tribes], but not when they are intermingled! R. Nahman b. Isaac said: They counted the Jubilees to keep the *shemittah* years holy (BT *Arachin* 32b).

Rashi comments:

Definitely, *yovel* was no longer in effect, which would have implied that slaves would be freed because of *yovel*, and sold fields were not returned, but *shemittah* was in effect to release money [which had been loaned] and to prohibit planting and harvesting, for they needed to count the year of *yovel* in order for *shemittah* to occur at the right time, for at the end of seven Sabbatical cycles they reserved a fiftieth year, which they did not count toward the next *shemittah*, as it was designated for the [potential] year of *yovel*, and [only] the year after would the count [toward the next *shemittah*] start. For if they wouldn't count Jubilee years, they would have counted that year as part of the *shemittah* cycle, and the *shemittah* years would be displaced.

The Talmud explains that for *yovel* to be in effect one needs the majority of the nation to be situated in the Land of Israel, and therefore during the period of the Second Temple, since only a minority of the people had returned with Ezra (R. Gershom records a tradition that the Jewish population of the world would never be less than 600,000, so 46,360 is less than a tenth of the nation), *yovel* was not in effect. Furthermore, one may derive from the talmudic extract that even if the majority of the nation resides in Israel, if the majority of each tribe does not, or if at least some identifiable representation of each tribe does not, then once more *yovel* does not apply, and for that reason from the time of the exile of the two and a half tribes, *yovel* and all of the associated legislation was cancelled. The Talmud does say, however, that a year would be reserved for *yovel* so that the *shemittah* cycle would not get out of sync.

One would assume that a year would always be set aside for *yovel*, whether or not the associated practice would be in effect. It is thus surpirising that Rambam (*Hilchot Shemittah ve-Yovel* 10:3) says:

> From the time the Temple was destroyed, this counting [of *yovel*] was cancelled... and in the seventh year after it [the Second Temple] was built, Ezra immigrated, and this is the second coming [to Israel], and from this year they started another counting [i.e. from year 1].

Rambam states here that the count was cancelled at the time of the destruction of the First Temple, and renewed when Ezra returned at the beginning of the Second Temple period. Why was the count cancelled in its entirety? R. Chaim Kanievsky (*Derech Emunah, in situ*) explains that once *yovel* was cancelled, *shemittah* was also not required on the Torah level,[112] because the two are linked. Not until the time of Ezra was *shemittah* legislated as a rabbinical enactment. However, according to R. Kanievsky, one may ask why the count was not already cancelled from the time of the exile of

112. The topic will be discussed later.

the two and a half tribes. Kesef Mishneh (*Hilchot Shemittah ve-Yovel* 10:5) answers that until the destruction of the First Temple, there was still hope that the tribes would return and *yovel* would resume, so the count continued intact.

In the following section, the Talmud (BT *Arachin* 33a) finds verses which indicate that *yovel* was being practiced even after the two and a half tribes were exiled:

But did they not count years of *shemittah* and *yovel* [after the exile of the two and a half tribes]? Does it not say [Rashi: regarding Zedekiah (the last Judean king)]: "At the end of seven years every man must free his brother who is a Hebrew who has been sold to you" (Jer. 34:14), and we asked: Why [does it say] "at the end of seven years"? Is it not written: "He [a Hebrew servant] must serve you six years" (Deut. 15:12), and to this R. Nahman b. Isaac replied: "Six for one who had been sold and seven for one who had his ear pierced" [indicating he wished to remain a slave. Rashi: implying that in the time of Zedekiah *yovel* was practiced]. This is as reproof [for past misdeeds], for the prophet said: "Did you set them free [Rashi: in those years when you should have done so (i.e. when the Jubilee was still being observed)]? But it says: "They listened and released them" (Jer. 34:10). Rather, said R. Johanan: Jeremiah brought them back, and Josiah b. Amon ruled over them.

In other words, *yovel* ceased to be in effect when the two and a half tribes were exiled, but was re-instituted over a hundred years later, when Jeremiah left Israel to seek out the remnants of the ten tribes and return them to Israel. However, soon after the First Temple was destroyed and the remnants of the nation were scattered throughout the world, *yovel* was once more cancelled. When the Talmud (BT *Arachin* 32b) states: "They counted the Jubilees to keep the *shemittah* years holy," it is in reference to the Second Temple period, when *yovel* was important only to determine the proper Sabbatical years (Ramban, BT *Gittin* 36a).

Surprisingly, Rabbeinu Tam (Tosafot *Gittin* 36a, s.v. *bi-zman*) is of the opinion that the Torah required *yovel* to be observed during the Second Temple period as well. His proof is from a Mishnah (*Arachin* 9:4) which discusses a rabbinical enactment that Hillel made regarding the subject of selling homes within walled cities, whose laws appear in the portion of *Behar* (Lev. 25:29-34) and are in effect exclusively when *yovel* is functional (BT *Arachin* 29a). Even though the Talmud itself (BT *Arachin* 32b) had said that during the Second Temple period "they counted the Jubilees to keep the *shemittah* years holy," i.e., that it was not for the purpose of obeying the laws of *yovel,* Rabbeinu Tam explains that at that stage of talmudic development, the assumption was that the exiled ten tribes were lost forever. As soon as the Talmud stated that Jeremiah had actually redeemed representatives of every tribe from exile, it became possible to permanently re-establish *yovel.* Ramban (BT *Gittin* 36a) vociferously debates this point by noting that although Jeremiah did bring back members of the ten tribes, at the destruction of the Temple they returned to their former places of residence (Halah, Habor, Hara, Gozan), and hence did not participate in Ezra's contingent.

Chatam Sofer (BT *Gittin* 36a) sees the argument between Ramban and Rabbeinu Tam as being synchronized with the Tannaitic dispute in the following Mishnah:

The ten tribes will not return [to Israel. Rashi: from their place of exile, and regarding that which it says in the Talmud that Jeremiah retrieved them, (it does) not (mean) that he returned all of them, but (rather, that) he only returned some of them], for it says: "And He cast them into another land as it is this day [when the curse was realized]" (Deut. 29:27). Just as the day goes and does not return, so they too went and will not return. These are the words of R. Akiva. R. Eliezer says: Just as the day darkens [at night] and becomes light [in the morning], so regarding the ten tribes, for whom it is [presently] dark, it will become light for them in the future (*Sanhedrin* 10:3).

Chatam Sofer explains that Rabbeinu Tam agrees with R. Akiva that those members of the ten tribes who were exiled by Sennacherib will never return. Consequently, those returned by Jeremiah before the destruction constituted the majority of each tribe, and after the destruction they too returned with Ezra. The Mishnah discussing the laws of walled cities, which implies that *yovel* was in effect during the Second Temple, was in accordance with R. Akiva, but the *psak* (ruling) is not according to him. Ramban's view is in accordance with R. Eliezer, who holds that in the future, at the time of *techiyat ha-meitim* (the revival of the dead), the ten tribes will return in their entirety, implying that Jeremiah brought back only a small percentage—certainly not enough to permit *yovel* to be re-instated.

SUMMARY

The laws of *shemittah* and *yovel* compose the last large code of laws in the book of Leviticus. Previous groups of laws were those which pertained to sacrifices, purity and impurity, and kosher and non-kosher foods. With regard to those sets, an effort was made to show how they improve a Jew's moral standard, in keeping with Hillel's statement that the core of the Torah (Rashi: the majority of its laws, BT *Shabbat* 31a) is ethical in nature and with Rambam's view in *Yad ha-Chazakah* that the Torah was given in order to perfect inter-personal and inter-communal deportment.[113] Although they are also classified as *chukkim* (statutes), it is a lot easier to verify that claim with regard to the laws associated with the Sabbatical year, mainly because the text says so explicitly in verses such as:

> And the [produce of] the resting of the land will be yours to eat - for you and your servant and your maid, and for your hired worker, and for the settler who lives in your midst (Lev. 25:6).

Furthermore, the remainder of the portion proceeds to list numerous inter-personal laws either directly or indirectly related to the Sabbatical year, such as not to taunt or cheat one's fellow man (Lev. 25:14-18), to help the poor redeem an heirloom which they sold (Lev. 25:25-28), to provide non-interest loans to the needy (Lev. 25:35-38), and not to overwork a slave (Lev. 25:39-46).

These morally-transparent statutes may serve as a reminder that many of the seemingly arbitrary laws have ethical facets and ramifications.

---

113. *Hilchot Megillah ve-Chanukah* 4:14.

BECHUKKOTAI

Bechukkotai, the last portion in the book of Leviticus, differs in essence from the previous nine portions. Most of its predecessors are of a sacerdotal nature, dealing with the priestly service and the details of the sacrifices which were administered. The portions of *Kedoshim* and *Behar* legislate ethical behavior for the individual and the community. *Bechukkotai*, on the other hand, speaks of the benefits of observing the law, but more extensively of the suffering which will accompany wholesale transgression of the law. Its admonitions, called the *tochachah*, remind one of the latter prophets. The parallel should not be surprising, since Moses was the father of prophecy. The content of the portion may be looked upon as a covenant between God and the Jewish nation.

The question that arises is whether *Bechukkotai* appears in chronological sequence. In other words, was this covenant presented after the laws contained in the previous portions were transmitted to the nation, or was it introduced at a much earlier stage, maybe even before the Torah was given, and presented here for didactic reasons, whatever they may be?

One may mobilize reasons to support either possibility. Ramban generally makes concerted efforts to synchronize between the sequential and chronological order of biblical events (see his comments on Lev. 8:2). If the text appears in a particular location, the default must be that it reflects the sequence of events.

On the other hand, wouldn't it be more logical to present the covenant before revelation? Why would God transmit His law to a nation which had not undertaken the obligation to fulfill it? One might answer that the Torah played to emotion rather than logic. The fragile state of the Israelites soon after escaping from Egypt would not have enabled them to deal with the threat of such dire consequences. Furthermore, why deal with punishment for disobedience of a law which has not yet been transmitted?

It was previously noted that the Torah's method of inculcation is a gradual one. Just as God started with only seven commands and gradually enlarged the number, so He started with small dosages of exhortations (e.g. Exod. 20:20; 34:10-16), and only after the Israelites achieved a sufficient level of intellectual maturity did He expand on them. Continuing in this manner, the *tochachah* of this portion is considerably less intense than that which appears in the portion of *Ki Tavo* (Deut. 28:15-68). Rashi (Deut. 29:12), based on *Midrash Tanchuma* (*Nitzavim* 1), notes that the *tochachah* in *Bechukkotai* contains only forty-nine curses, while that in *Ki Tavo* contains ninety-eight, twice as many. Furthermore, the curses in *Bechukkotai* are formulated in the plural form, so that no individual feels personally responsible. The guilt is shared among all members of the congregation, and each person can convince himself that it was mainly the others who sinned. Finally, the set of curses ends on a positive note (Lev. 26:44-45). The curses in *Ki Tavo*, on the other hand, are much more focused. They appear in singular second person form, as if to say that each individual has sinned and punishment is directed at him specifically. Unlike the curses recorded in *Bechukkotai*, they do not include a happy ending. In short, as in the case of the laws, the admonitions were transmitted first in a simple form, and only eventually did they become more comprehensive and intensive.

Because of the frightening nature of the *tochachah*, it is generally read in a soft voice. As is well known, when reading each weekly Torah portion, the reading is apportioned to seven people who are honored by being called to the Torah for an *aliya*. Since the curses in the *tochacha* could be construed as relating specifically to the person chosen, the custom is to allocate the blessings over this section to the *ba'al kri'ah* (Torah reader) so as not to dishearten any member of the congregation (*Mishnah Berurah* 428:17).

Another custom is edifying as to the proper way of viewing the *tochacha*: the entire section may not be split among more than one person (*Orach Chaim* 428:6), and the reason given is that it would appear as if the person given the *aliya* is spurning God's criticism (*Mishnah Berurah* 428:15). But the purpose is not to demoralize or upset people; rather, it is to stimulate them to self-examination and repentance.

The positive aspect of the *tochacha* is brought out in the following Midrash (*Tanchuma, Nitzavim* 1):

> Why were the [Gentile] idol-worshippers deserving of destruction, while we still exist? Because when they suffer affliction they vent their fury because of it and do not mention the name of the Lord, as it says: "Pour out Your anger on the nations that do not know You, and upon the kingdoms that do not call upon Your name" (Ps. 79:6). But Israel, when affliction devolves upon them, submit [to God's decree] and pray, as it says: "I will lift up the cup of salvation, and call upon the name of the Lord" (Ps. 116:13) [and also] "The cords of death surrounded me, and the straits of the nether-world found me; I found trouble and

sorrow. But I called upon the name of the Lord: 'Please, O Lord, deliver my soul'" (Ps. 116:3-4). Therefore, the Almighty said to them, even though these curses will devolve upon you, they will give you permanence, and so it says: "Who fed you manna in the wilderness, which your fathers did not know, so that He might afflict you, and that He might test you, [in order] to do you good in the end" (Deut. 8:16). And so Moses said to Israel: "Even though these curses will devolve upon you, you will have permanence," therefore it says [immediately following the admonitions in the portion of *Ki Tavo*]: "You are all standing here today" (Deut. 29:9).

The last Lubavitcher Rebbe, R. Menachem Mendel Schneerson, noted (*Likutei Sichot* 2, p. 392) that each of the admonitory portions is read before a Jewish holiday. The *tochachah* in *Bechukkotai* is read before Shavuot (Pentecost), which commemorates the giving of the Torah. The *tochachah* in *Ki Tavo* is read before Rosh Hashanah (New Year's Day), which is when each Jew repents for his sins and begs forgiveness from the Almighty. On both occasions, one is in need of purification. The Jewish nation started with a clean slate, so on Shavuot the preparation to receive the Torah was relatively less intense (forty-nine curses), as opposed to that of Yom Kippur, when each Jew is sullied by the sins he has performed during the year, and a greater amount of purification (ninety-eight curses) is needed in order to nullify the transgressions which he has committed. Both sets of curses contain the threat of exile which, along with its concomitant suffering, is considered to be an outstanding catalyst for atonement and eventual cleansing.[114]

---

114. *Shulchan Shabbat, Ki Tavo*, pp. 219-220, based on *Likutei Torah Vayikra* 48:1.

Once more, it is seen that the emphasis is on building for the future, rather than destruction on the basis of the past.

THE TIMING OF THE *TOCHACHAH* – THE MIDRASHIC VIEW

If one adopts the approach that *Bechukkotai* is out of place, when did the covenant described therein actually occur, and what is the source for saying so? It turns out that the basis for this view is found back in the portion of *Mishpatim* in the book of Exodus. After Moses was privately summoned by God at the beginning of ch. 24 in Exodus, the following verses appear:

> 3. And Moses came and told the people all the words of the Lord, and all the ordinances; and all the people answered with one voice, and said: "All the words which the Lord has spoken we will do." 4. And Moses wrote all the words of the Lord, and he woke up in the morning and built an altar at the foot of the mountain, and twelve monuments for the twelve tribes of Israel. 5. And he sent the lads of the Children of Israel [to make sacrifices], and they offered burnt offerings, and sacrificed peace offerings of oxen to the Lord. 6. And Moses took half of the blood and put it in basins, and half of the blood he sprinkled on the altar. 7. And he took the book of the covenant and read it in [hearing distance of] the ears of the people, and they said: "All that the Lord has spoken we will do, and we will hear." 8. And Moses took the blood, and sprinkled it on the people, and said: "Here is the blood of the covenant, which the Lord has made with you concerning all these words."

This passage may be outlined as follows:

- Verse 3: Moses told the nation of God's words and ordinances (which ordinances will be discussed later).
- Verse 3: The nation agreed to fulfill God's words.
- Verse 4: Moses committed God's words to writing.
- Verse 4: The next morning Moses built an altar and twelve monuments to show that each tribe agreed to, and had a part in, the covenant about to be made (Rashbam on Exod. 24:4).
- Verse 5: The young men of Israel ("the first-born" — Rashi on Exod. 24:5) brought sacrifices.
- Verse 6: Moses sprinkled half of the blood on the altar (which served as the representative of God; Sforno on Exod. 24:6), and the other half was placed in basins, one for the blood of the burnt offerings, another for the blood of the peace offerings—to be sprinkled on the nation after they underwent ritual immersion, a prerequisite for conversion (Rashi on Exod. 24:6).
- Verse 7: Moses read the Book of the Covenant to the people, so that they would know what they were committing themselves to (Sforno on Exod. 24:7).
- Verse 7: The people said: "All that the Lord has spoken we will do, and we will hear."
- Verse 8: Moses sprinkled the blood from the basins on the people (the elders — Ibn Ezra on Exod. 24:7) to seal the covenant.

Note that the integration of the covenant with the bringing of animal sacrifices is reminiscent of the Covenant of the Pieces (Gen. 15:9-21). In addition, the text describes the transmission of verbal information to the Children of Israel in three locations. In verse 3,

Moses told the people the words of the Lord and His ordinances; in verse 4, he transcribed the words of the Lord; and in verse 7, he read the Book of the Covenant to the people. Two questions will be dealt with:

1. When did the events described occur? It will be shown that the time of their occurrence has a direct effect on when the portions of *Behar* and *Bechukkotai* took place.
2. What were the contents of each of these transmissions and, in particular, are they all referring to the same material?

Not unexpectedly, the answers to these questions are dependent on differing views which appear in the Midrash.[115]

Answering the First Question:

According to R. Yosi b. Yehudah, verses 3-4 took place on the same day as revelation (but afterwards), and the acts described in verses 5-8 took place on the next day. According to R. Yishmael, on the other hand, everything described in verses 3–8 occurred on the days preceding revelation.

Hence, according to R. Yosi, the text at the end of *Mishpatim* is in chronological order, while R. Yishmael holds that the end of *Mishpatim*, as well as *Behar* and *Bechukkotai* (see further), are out of chronological order and—taken together—describe what happened before the giving of the Ten Commandments. If the Torah were in chronological order, those sections would have appeared at the beginning of the portion of *Yitro*.

Note that verse 7 contains the famous words: "All that the Lord has spoken we will do, and we will hear." This phrase, according to tradition, indicates absolute obedience, symbolized by the people's

---

115. *Mechilta de-Rabbi Yishmael, Yitro, Mesechta de-ba-chodesh, parashah* 3.

commitment to act before even hearing the commandments, implying that they would not weigh each law and only then decide whether to fulfill it, but rather that they were willing to accept them all upon themselves sight unseen. According to R. Yishmael, they had not yet heard "what the Lord has spoken" because they made the pronouncement before revelation. They had not even heard "that the Lord has spoken," because He had not yet spoken. According to R. Yosi, on the other hand, the Lord had already spoken and revelation had occurred, but most of the commandments had not yet been given to Moses (since he would spend thirty-nine more days on Sinai) and certainly not to the Children of Israel, who would be taught by Moses only afterward.

Answering the Second Question:
Concerning the contents of the verbal information which was transmitted to the nation, R. Yosi certainly has more options available than R. Yishmael. Since he believes that ch. 24 occurred after revelation, both the laws given before revelation and the material given at the time of revelation, such as the Ten Commandments and the laws in the portions of *Yitro* and *Mishpatim*, could have been handed down at that stage.

In the previously cited Midrash, there exists a second difference of opinion, with R. Yosi himself saying that Moses read to the Children of Israel from the beginning of the book of Genesis until the giving of the Torah. This approach fits nicely with the talmudic view that the Torah was given in parts, with each section written on a scroll at the appropriate time (BT *Gittin* 60a). If this was indeed the case, it is perfectly reasonable to assume that the material referred to in verse 4 was the book of Genesis and the first half of Exodus—until the point that the Torah was given. However, according to the view that no part of the Torah was written until the very end of the journey through the desert, how can one say that Moses had already written the book of Genesis? Tosafot[116] answers this question by saying that according to both opinions, parts of the Torah were put in writing during their travels. The argument is only whether every part was written immediately. According to the alternative view, those sections which actually occurred earlier, but were to appear in the Torah after a later event, were not committed to writing until the later event transpired. That approach would allow Genesis to have already been written down, immediately after revelation, according to both viewpoints.

A second view cited in the Midrash is that of Rebbi, who says that what was written were "the laws commanded to Adam, and the laws commanded to the children of Noah, and the laws commanded [to the Israelites] in Egypt [this might have been Rambam's source when he mentioned laws given to Amram in *Hilchot Melachim* 9:1] and in Marah, and all of the remaining *mitzvot*." The last phrase is especially baffling, since according to all opinions, before revelation or even until the day after, not all of the 613 commandments had been received. Chaim Shaul Horovitz, who edited *Mechilta de-Rabbi Yishmael*, proposes three possible explanations:

1. The phrase is an error in transcription.
2. The phrase simply means that additional *mitzvot* were written.
3. The laws referred to are those given in connection with the manna.

Finally, R. Yishmael, who places verses 3-8 before revelation, holds that God revealed to the Children of Israel through Moses the contents of the portion of *Behar*, which starts with the phrase:

116. BT *Gittin* 60a, Tosafot, s.v. *Torah chatumah nitnah*.

"And the Lord spoke to Moses on Mt. Sinai" (Lev. 25:1), and the blessings and curses in the immediately following portion of *Bechukkotai*, which concludes with the verse: "These are the commandments which the Lord commanded to Moses for the Children of Israel on Mt. Sinai" (Lev. 27:34). This set of blessings and curses is termed the covenant, and this is what Moses told the Children of Israel in verse 3: "And Moses came and told the people all the words of the Lord, and all the ordinances." After acquiescing to this covenant, Moses sprinkled the blood on them to seal it, saying (according to the Midrash): "You are now tied, bound, and committed. Come tomorrow and accept upon yourselves all of the *mitzvot*." Apparently, according to R. Yishmael, a covenant must be composed of a series of blessings which would occur if it is fulfilled, and a series of curses to take effect in the opposite case. For this reason, he says that Moses must have informed them of the blessings and curses enumerated in *Bechukkotai*. (The portion of *Behar* was presented to the Israelites in the same session as *Bechukkotai*. At the beginning of *Behar*, as well as at the end of *Bechukkotai*, it says that the entire section was said at Mt. Sinai.) One may assume that the covenant, as so defined, was what Moses told them in verse 3, put in writing in verse 4, and repeated in verse 7 after bringing the sacrifices so that he could sprinkle blood on them (in verse 8), which was part of the covenantal ceremony.

The opinion of R. Yishmael contains a new idea, namely that the frequently joined portions of *Behar* and *Bechukkotai* were said at Sinai before the Ten Commandments were given. According to R. Yishmael, then, the texts at the end of *Mishpatim* and at the end of Leviticus are indeed out of chronological order and, taken together, describe what happened before the giving of the Ten Commandments. If the Torah were in chronological order, they would have appeared at the beginning of the portion of *Yitro*.

THE TIMING OF THE *TOCHACHA* — CLASSICAL COMMENTATORS

Ibn Ezra:

It was noted that Scripture in Exodus refers to three transmissions of information by Moses to the congregation, first orally (Exod. 24:3), then in writing (Exod. 24:4), and finally as the Book of the Covenant (Exod. 24:7). Ibn Ezra makes it clear that the content in each case was identical. He explains that "all the words of the Lord" (Exod. 24:3) refers to the exhortations and laws at the end of the portion of *Yitro* and the entire portion of *Mishpatim* until ch. 24, i.e., all of the legislation which was given to Moses on Mt. Sinai (see Rashi, Exod. 21:1) immediately after the Ten Commandments. On the next verse (Exod. 24:4), Ibn Ezra comments: "After he told them all of the words of God—the commandments and the ordinances—he wrote them. And this is the Book of the Covenant" (referred to in Exod. 24:7).

Ibn Ezra has adopted the previously cited view of R. Yosi b. Yehuda in the *Mechilta* that these events took place immediately following revelation. As far as the content, his view differs from all of the three opinions cited in the Midrash (R. Yosi, Rebbi, and R. Yishmael). Nevertheless, his opinion is quite reasonable, since it allows a completely sequential interpretation of events, with the Ten Commandments being given in *Yitro*, followed by a series of laws appearing right after and continuing through most of the portion of *Mishpatim*, with a covenant based on these very laws at the end of *Mishpatim*.

The only weakness of Ibn Ezra's exegesis is that a covenant is generally expected to include, in addition to a description of required behavior, an indication of the repercussions of acting or not acting accordingly. This shortcoming is mended by Ibn Ezra at the end of Leviticus, where he states (Lev. 25:1):

> There is no earlier or later [i.e., order] in the Torah, and this section comes before [the portion of] *Vayikra* and all of the portions which follow it [until this point], for this message was at Mt. Sinai [which is where the laws at the end of *Yitro* and *Mishpatim* were given, unlike those in Leviticus, which were given from the Tent of Meeting (Lev. 1:1)]. And now [see Lev. 26:15] he made the covenant which is written in the portion of *Mishpatim*. And he mentioned it in this location [rather than when it occurred, just after revelation, where this covenant is described at the end of *Mishpatim*] in order to juxtapose [it to] conditions for remaining in Israel. And as it says with regard to incestuous relations that because of them the land will vomit them out (Lev. 18:25; 20:22), similarly it says in the portion of *Bechukkotai* with regard to [ignoring] the land's Sabbaticals [Lev. 26:34-43], and first it mentions [in ch. 25] the laws regarding Sabbaticals.

Although Ibn Ezra's definition in Exodus of the text of the covenant relates only to legislation, in Leviticus he extends it to the contents of the last two portions, *Behar* and *Bechukkotai*, adopting the view of R. Yishmael in the Midrash (in spite of his rejection of the second opinion of R. Yishmael, namely that the covenant was made before revelation). He now has a solid reason for the fact that Mt. Sinai is specifically mentioned in connection with the Sabbatical laws and the *tochacha*, because that is exactly where they were stated and written, together with the other texts which composed the covenant.

Ramban:

Clearly, Ramban would have a hard time accepting the view of Ibn Ezra, since he generally makes every effort to interpret the biblical text in chronological sequence. It is thus no surprise that Ramban feels that *Bechukkotai* is written exactly where it belongs. But certainly the admonitions of this portion are a form of covenant, as is the text in Exodus at the end of *Mishpatim*. Could there be two covenants? Ramban answers that indeed there are. The first was made right after revelation. The basis of that covenant was exactly that ascribed to it by Ibn Ezra in Exodus, namely the laws given on the day of revelation (Exod. 20:19-23:33). It was sanctified as a covenant by the sacrifices which accompanied it (Exod. 24:5). With the breaking of the tablets by Moses, the first covenant was annulled, and a second was called for. It materialized here in the portion of *Bechukkotai*, with the blessings and curses of the *tochacha* indicating that the congregation was accepting upon itself a second covenant, which was essentially a renewal of the original one, whose sacrifices thus validated and became linked to it as well. The contents of this covenant included the laws of the Sabbatical year, whose maintenance was essential for keeping a foothold on the Land of Israel (as stressed by Ibn Ezra as well). These laws were taught to Moses at Mt. Sinai when he received the second tablets but, since the Tabernacle was now standing, the actual covenant was administered from the Tent of Meeting (Lev. 1:1), as were all of the communications in the book of Leviticus. In the words of Ramban (Lev. 25:1):

> In my opinion, it [this section] is written here in its proper order, because [the expression] "at Mt. Sinai" means [it was told to Moses] when he went up there to receive the second tablets [and not immediately after revelation as Ibn Ezra

says], and the interpretation of the matter is [as follows]: At the beginning of the first forty days of the first tablets, Moses wrote in the Book of the Covenant all the words of the Lord (Exod. 24:4) and all the ordinances stated there (Exod. 20:19-23:33), and he sprinkled the blood of the covenant on the people (Exod. 24:8). But when the people sinned with the [golden] calf and the tablets were broken, it was as if the covenant with the Almighty was cancelled, and when the Almighty became reconciled with Moses by giving him the second tablets, He commanded him concerning a new covenant, as it says: "Behold, I am making a covenant" (Exod. 34:10), and He repeated there the stringent commandments that had been said in the portion of *Mishpatim* (Exod. 21:1) at the first covenant, and He [now] stated:] "Write these words, for on the basis of these words I have made a covenant [the first time] with you and with Israel" (Exod. 34:27). And the Lord wanted to be stricter with them in regard to this second covenant, that it should impose on them oaths and curses, and that it should be like the first one regarding all the original commandments and all of the ordinances, as it says of the first covenant: ["And Moses came and told the people] all the words of the Lord, and all the ordinances" (Exod. 24:3). Therefore, it states here at the end of the exhortations: "These are the statutes and ordinances and laws, which the Lord gave [concerning the relationship] between Him and the Children of Israel on Mt. Sinai by the hand of Moses" (Lev. 26:46), this being an allusion to all the commandments and ordinances which had been said at the first covenant, in the portion of *Mishpatim*, for they were all [embodied] in this [second] covenant.

Ramban goes on to make a comparison between the Sabbatical laws and the building of the Tabernacle. Both were given in outline form initially (the Sabbatical year in Exod. 23:11; the Tabernacle in the portions of *Terumah*, *Tetzaveh*, and *Ki Tissa*) and in a more thorough manner during the forty days during which the second tablets were transmitted, when God already planned the second covenant, which came to fruition in the portions of *Behar* and *Bechukkotai*.

There was in fact a third covenant, that of *Ki Tavo*. It was made on the plains of Moab at the end of the forty-year trek in the desert, after the death of most of those who had been present at the second covenant, and so it too was a re-affirmation of the original covenant (eliminating the need to bring new sacrifices), as is clear from the following verse:

> These are the words of the covenant which the Lord commanded Moses to make with the Children of Israel in the land of Moab, besides the covenant which He made with them in Horeb (Deut. 28:69).

RELATIONSHIP BETWEEN
THE TWO SETS OF ADMONITIONS

Ramban distinguishes between the two sets of admonitions as follows:

> Know and understand that these oaths allude to the first exile [the Babylonian exile after the destruction of the First Temple], for in the First Temple all of the words of this covenant, concerning the exile and the redemption from

it, took place…. However, the covenant in Deuteronomy alludes to our present exile, and to the redemption by which we will be redeemed from it [eventually] (Lev. 26:16).

Ramban buttresses his theory by citing verses from the *tochacha* in *Bechukkotai* which point specifically to the period of the First Temple.

1. As noted in APPENDIX VI: SOME BASICS OF JEWISH HISTORY, the Talmud relates the destruction of the First Temple, but not the second, to idol worship. Accordingly, the following verse, found in *Bechukkotai*, must refer to the First Temple: "And I will destroy your high places, and cut down your sun-pillars, and cast your carcasses upon the remnants of your idols" (Lev. 26:30).

2. The *tochachah* in *Bechukkotai* records Jewish suffering in the following verses:
   Sword: "and I will bring a sword upon you" (Lev. 26:25).
   Plague: "and I will send the pestilence among you" (Lev. 26:25).
   Hunger: "and you will eat, and not be satisfied" (Lev. 26:26).
   Exile: "and I will scatter you among the nations" (Lev. 26:33).

Note the fulfillment of these curses in Jeremiah's description of the destruction of the First Temple:

I will consume them by the sword, and by the famine, and by the pestilence (Jer. 14:12).

Therefore will I cast you out of this land into a land that you have not known (Jer. 16:13).

I will scatter them as if blown by an east wind [which is very strong] before the enemy (Jer. 18:17).

> Behold the mounds [for scaling the walls] have come to
> the city to capture it; and the city is given into the
> hand of the Chaldeans who fight against it, [and defeat
> the Jews] because of the sword, and the famine, and
> the pestilence; and what You have spoken [in Lev.] is
> come to pass; and, behold, You see it (Jer. 32:24).

At this stage, Ramban moves away from the description of the
punishments, which were seen to fit the prophetic portrayal
of events surrounding the destruction of the First Temple, and
proceeds to the nature of the return from exile, which corresponds
to the return from the Babylonian exile after the First Temple's
destruction, and not to the eventual hopeful return from the
second exile.

The relevant verse from the *tochacha* is: "And I will remember
My covenant with Jacob, and also My covenant with Isaac, and also
My covenant with Abraham will I remember; and I will remember
the land" (Lev. 26:42). The verse is saying that God will return the
Jews because He has no choice—He made a covenant with the
patriarchs, and also with the land, saying that it will not be inhabited
by anyone other than the tribes of Israel. Ramban indicates what
the present promise of return does not contain, namely:

1. that He will forgive them for the serious sins which they
   committed during the First Temple period,
2. that He will love them as much as He did before they sinned,
3. that He will gather them all from the Diaspora.

In fact, the lack of these positive elements of redemption
characterized the return from the first exile. Since the ten tribes
were exiled many years before the Temple was destroyed (see

APPENDIX VI: SOME BASICS OF JEWISH HISTORY) and only Judah, Benjamin, and a small group of Levites were exiled to Babylonia, the assumption is that only those tribes returned to Israel. Instead of total redemption, they were still in a state of poverty and servitude, as indicated by the following verse from the book of Ezra:

> For we are slaves, yet our God has not forsaken us in our bondage, but has extended mercy unto us in the sight of the kings of Persia, to give us a reviving, to set up the house of our God, and to repair the ruins thereof, and to give us a fence [to protect us from predators] in Judah and in Jerusalem (Ezra 9:9).

In addition, since the return from the first exile did not require the achievement of a spiritual goal, its length could be predetermined to be seventy years.

According to Ramban, the portion of *Ki Tavo* refers to the destruction of the Second Temple and the exile which followed, while the next chapter in Deuteronomy (ch. 30) describes the final return from that exile, when all of the twelve tribes (as opposed to only two which returned from the first exile) will be redeemed and cleansed as a result of true repentance for their previous transgressions. Ramban then cites verses from the admonitions of *Ki Tavo* which, in his opinion, relate to the Second Temple:

1. The duration of the exile was not predetermined, but rather conditioned on full repentance, as may be understood from the following verses:

   > And it will come to pass, when all these things have occurred... and you will return God to your heart

> when you are among all the nations, where the Lord
> your God has driven you... and hearken to His voice
> according to all that I command you this day... then
> the Lord your God will return you from captivity,
> and have compassion upon you, and will return and
> gather you (Deut. 30:1-3).

2. Idol worship was not mentioned, only a general rebuke
   for not fulfilling all of the commands, as it says:

   > And if you do not listen to the voice of the Lord your
   > God, to observe [and] to do all of His commandments
   > and His statutes which I command you this day, then
   > all of these curses will come upon you and overtake
   > you (Deut. 28:15).

   The verse may be referring to groundless hatred and the
   associated Torah laws, whose transgression was widespread in
   the Second Temple era (BT *Yoma* 9b; Appendix VI - Some
   Basics of Jewish History).

3. The enemy at the time of the Second Temple was Rome, as
   it says: "The Lord will bring a nation against you from far"
   (Deut. 28:49).

4. The enemy will speak a foreign tongue (Latin), as opposed to
   the enemy at the time of the First Temple, who spoke Aramaic,
   a language known to the educated Judean classes (2 Kings
   18:26), and so the verse states: "a nation whose tongue you
   will not understand" (Deut. 28:49).

5. The first exile was localized to Babylonia, while the second
   was spread throughout the world, as it says: "And the Lord
   will scatter you among all the nations, from one end of the
   earth to the other end of the earth" (Deut. 28:64).

6. A source available to Ramban, *Yossipon*[117] (ch. 91), tells of Titus sending many of the priests and influential people to Goshen in the land of Egypt, where the Jews had resided in the days of Joseph, which fits the verse: "And the Lord will return you to Egypt in ships" (Deut. 28:68).

7. *Yossipon* (ch. 64) relates that King Agrippa II went to Rome to tell Emperor Nero about the Jewish rebellion, and as a result he sent an army to the Land of Israel which eventually destroyed the Temple. Ramban sees a prediction of this calamity in the verse: "The Lord will bring you, and the king whom you will set over you, to a nation that you did not know, neither you nor your fathers" (Deut. 28:36). Ramban notes that the verse speaks of "the king whom you will set over you" rather than "the king who will reign over you." He explains that the verse is referring to Agrippa II, who was king during the destruction, and who the people set over themselves even though he was not a legitimate king, being descended from a slave (Tosafot BT *Sotah* 41b).

Ramban ends on a positive tone, as noted by the Midrash (and quoted by Rashi). With respect to the verse: "And I will make the land desolate; and your enemies that dwell on it will be discontented" (Lev. 26:32), the Midrash states:

This is a beneficial measure, that Israel will not have to

---

117. *Yossipon* is a Hebrew history book attributed to Josephus, but probably compiled in the early 10th century by a Greek-speaking Jew from Southern Italy, who based himself on the writings of Josephus. The author tried to harmonize between Josephus and rabbinic sources when conflicts were discovered. The Oraita edition (1999) has been used. Yossipon tells of Titus sending a contingent of Jews to the Egyptian mines, based on Josephus's *Wars of the Jews* 6:9:2.

say: "Since we were exiled from our land, now the enemy has come and found contentment," for it says: "and your enemies that dwell on it will be discontented." Even the enemies who come afterwards will not find contentment on it (*Torat Kohanim, Bechukkotai* 6:5).

Ramban, at the end of his commentary on Lev. 26:16, embellishes this idea with the following words:

In the whole inhabited world one cannot find such a good and large land [based on Exod. 3:8] which was always lived in and yet is as ruined as it is, for since we left it, it has not accepted any nation or language, and they all try to settle it, but are unable to.

Of course, since the time of Ramban, the State of Israel has been established and the land is no longer desolate. Nevertheless, the ten tribes have not yet been identified, and it may be assumed that they have not yet returned to the land, and certainly the Jews of the world have not yet repented and perfected themselves, so there is still some way to go before one can say that there has been a complete redemption.

Abarbanel:

Abarbanel does not relate the first set of admonitions to the destruction of the First Temple and its subsequent exile, and the second set of admonitions to the destruction of the Second Temple and its concomitant exile. He does agree with Ramban that after returning from the first exile, the Jews had not fully expiated their sins. Specifically for that reason, he looks upon the Second Temple period as a continuation of the period of repentance, and the second exile as merely a continuation of the first exile. In his words (on Lev. 26:27):

> For it is all one exile, and indeed the gathering [to build] the Second Temple was not a redemption but rather the order of Cyrus, king of Persia, and they were always subjugated there, either to Persia, or to Greece, or to Rome.... And with respect to disregarding the Sabbatical years and Jubilees, because it was insulting to the land, [the victim of] theft [of the produce] that was stolen from it, the Almighty wanted it to be repaid first in those seventy years that they spent in Babylon, during which time the land rested, and it was not cultivated by Israel or their enemies in those years, in correspondence to the number of Sabbatical years and Jubilees that they didn't observe. And regarding the remaining sins that they did, among them idol worship and incest and murder and desecration of the Sabbath and other sins, the Roman exile came [upon them], and the exile because of them continues to this day... after those seventy years God wished to remember his nation and bring it to Jerusalem. And this was for a praiseworthy purpose, namely, so that they would have a place [to live] and much preparation when they were there, to repent and pray to Him, and through their prayer and repentance, God would forgive their sins and return his Presence [to dwell] among them... However, the children of Judea did not do so, but rather continued to sin during the tenure of the Second Temple, for they held onto the sins of their fathers... and although they didn't worship idols, the Saduccee and Epicurean cults took root among them, and the Karaites and followers of Jesus the Christian are more dangerous than all of them.

Abarbanel proceeds to quote verses from each set of admonitons which refer to both exiles in order to demonstrate that Ramban's distinction is not valid. Some examples appear below:

1. The words "and I will scatter you among the nations" (Lev. 26:33) refer to the second exile, when the Jews were not transferred as a unit, but rather in smaller groups to many destinations, where they were to atone for most of the cardinal sins which led to the destruction of the First Temple, other than the neglect of the Sabbatical and Jubilee years, which was expiated during the seventy years in Babylon.

2. Abarbanel considers the following verse from Leviticus (26:39) to refer to the second exile: "And those who are left of you will pine away in your enemies' lands because of their iniquities; and they will also pine away because of the iniquities of their fathers." He sees "those who are left" as referring to those who were in the Land of Israel even after the first exile. Both in the partial exile of Jehoiachin and the final exile of Nebuchadnezzar, the most indigent were allowed to remain (2 Kings 24:11, 25:12). Furthermore, 42,360 returned with Zerubavel (Ezra 2:62, Neh. 7:67) from Babylon as a result of the decree of Cyrus inviting the Jews to return to the Holy Land for the express purpose of rebuilding the Temple, and more came together with Ezra (Ezra 7:6-7; see *Metzudat David* thereon).

   The verse then speaks of "pining away"—indicating a long exile, ever since the destruction of the Second Temple. This occurred because instead of repenting, the Israelites continued to sin, and they certainly did not expiate "the iniquities of their fathers."

3. In the book of Deuteronomy, Abarbanel attempts to show that some of the verses refer to the First Temple period. It will be recalled that Ramban said that the verse: "The Lord will bring you, and the king whom you will set over you, to a nation that you did not know" (Deut. 28:36) refers to Agrippa II going to Rome to tell Emperor Nero about the Jewish rebellion, while the phrase "the Lord will bring a nation against you from far" (Deut. 28:49) refers to the arrival of the Romans in the Land of Israel. The verses are actually in order, since first Agrippa II informed Rome, and then they sent their armies. Abarbanel apparently understood Ramban to be saying that verse 36 was referring to Agrippa being taken to Rome as a prisoner of war,[118] and he therefore claimed that according to Ramban's interpretation, verse 49 should have preceded verse 36. At any rate, Abarbanel interprets verse 36 to be referring to King Zedekiah (see APPENDIX VI - SOME BASICS OF JEWISH HISTORY), who was taken by force to Babylonia (2 Kings 25:7). Abarbanel then interprets the words "the king whom you will set over you" to refer to the fact that Zedekiah was not really appropriate to serve as king, since he was not chosen by the people, but rather by Nebuchadnezzar (2 Kings 24:17). Once more, Ramban is easily defended, since the verse says "you," meaning the Nation of Israel, not the king of Babylonia. On the other hand, Abarbanel is supported by the Talmud (BT *Yoma* 52b), which states that King Josiah was upset when he found the Torah scroll (2 Kings 24:11) specifically because it was rolled to verse 36, indicating that indeed the verse refers to King Zedekiah.

---

118. Abarbanel may have based himself on the phrase "the Lord will bring you," which would imply that it was by force and not voluntary.

4. Regarding the verse "and the Lord will return you to Egypt in ships" (Deut. 28:68), Ramban had said that it referred to Titus deporting Jews to Egypt, as described in *Yossipon*. Abarbanel found two entire chapters in the book of Jeremiah which speak of returning to Egypt after the destruction of the First Temple (chs. 42-43), so he assigns the given verse to that occurrence. However, Ramban may be justified by noting that the verse says "the Lord will return you." The chapters in Jeremiah, on the other hand, speak of God being strongly opposed to the return to Egypt, which was engineered by the wicked pair, Johanan and Jezeniah.

The difference between Ramban and Abarbanel:

As noted, the difference between Ramban and Abarbanel is whether the first set of admonitions relates only to the First Temple and the second to the Second Temple, or whether they each relate to both. More intrinsically, Ramban would say that the Second Temple was destroyed exclusively because of groundless hatred, which concurs with the Talmud (BT *Yoma* 9b), while Abarbanel sees its destruction as being the result of the sins which occurred during the tenure of both Temples. In addition to his view being supported by the Babylonian Tamud, Ramban's opinion stresses the overriding importance of the laws between man and his fellow-man (*bein adam le-chaveiro*) as opposed to those between man and God (*bein adam la-Makom*). Although both sets of laws are incumbent and vital, and they enhance each other, in the long run it is the perfection of interpersonal behavior which is the final goal of the Torah, as has been previously indicated by numerous citations (e.g. *Hilchot Megilllah ve-Chanukkah* 4:14), including the Jerusalem Talmud's (*Yoma* 1:1) justification for the destruction of the Second Temple.

Appendix I:
The Different
Types of Sacrifices

Burnt Offerings

Obligatory individual burnt offerings:

As noted, although burnt offerings are frequently voluntary, they are also obligatory in numerous situations:

1. Pilgrimage offering (*olat re'iyah*), based on the verse:

    > Three times in a year all of your males should appear before the Lord your God in the place which He will choose; on the feast of unleavened bread, and on the feast of weeks, and on the feast of Tabernacles; and they should not appear before the Lord empty-handed (Deut. 16:16).

    "Empty-handed" is understood to mean without bringing the pilgrimage sacrifice, which is to be sacrificed on the first day of the holiday, but can be offered throughout the holiday of Passover or Tabernacles (BT *Chagigah* 9a) and throughout the next week in the case of Pentecost (BT *Chagigah* 17a). Women are exempted, as they are from all time-bound commandments, and so are infants, the lame, the blind, the sickly, and the aged (Mishnah *Chagigah* 1:1), because of their potential walking difficulties. The Babylonian Talmud (*Chagigah* 7a) restricts this sacrifice to cattle or sheep, while the Midrash (*Mechilta de-Rashbi, Mishpatim, Mesechta de-Kaspa* 20) allows birds as well.

2. Four persons whose purification is not complete until they bring a burnt offering (*mechussarei kapparah*):

   a. A woman who gives birth must bring a young sheep, or a pair of birds if she is indigent (Lev. 12:6-8).

   b. A recovering leper must bring a young sheep, or a pair of birds if he is indigent (Lev. 14:10, 14:21).

   c. A man (Lev. 15:14-15) or woman (Lev. 15:29-30) who has aberrant bodily issues brings a single bird as a burnt offering.

3. The ram brought by the high priest as a personal burnt offering on Yom Kippur (Lev. 16:3).

4. One of the two birds brought by a poor person who unintentionally eats sacrificial meat or enters the Temple while impure (Rashi Lev. 5:2), or inadvertently transgresses an oath that he has made (Lev. 5:7). Wealthier people bring a more expensive animal guilt offering (Lev. 5:6).

5. Burnt offering of a convert: On Mt. Sinai, the Children of Israel were converted after undergoing circumcision (see Joshua 5:5) and immersion (based on Exod. 24:8, which says that holy blood was sprinkled on them, implying they had previously undergone immersion), and after bringing a sacrifice (based on Exod. 24:5; see BT *Keritot* 8b).

6. A Nazirite who became impure during the period of his vow brings a bird as a burnt offering (Num. 6:10). At the successful culmination of the period, he brings a sheep as a burnt offering (Num. 6:14).

Obligatory communal burnt offerings:

1. The daily sacrifices in the Temple consisted of a young sheep brought in the morning and evening (Num. 28:3-4).

2. On Sabbath and holidays, extra burnt offerings were brought in addition to the daily burnt offerings (*musafim*), as described in the following table:

Occasion	Additional Burnt Offering	Source (book of Numbers)
Sabbath	2 sheep	28:9
New Moon, Passover, Shavuot	2 bulls, 1 ram, 7 sheep	28:12, 19, 27
Rosh Hashanah, Yom Kippur, Shemini Atzeret	1 bull, 1 ram, 7 sheep	29:2, 8, 36
Sukkot (Day x, where x varies from 1-7)	2 rams, 14 sheep, 14–x bulls	29:13, 17, 20, 23, 26, 29, 32

3. Burnt offering brought with the wave offering: The wave offering (*minchat ha-omer*) was taken from the newly grown barley and sacrificed unbaked on the altar on the second day of Passover (BT *Menachot* 66a) as a prerequisite to the community being enabled to eat barley from the latest crop. A young sheep was brought with it as a burnt offering (Lev. 23:12).

4. Burnt offering brought with the two wave-loaves (*shtei ha-lechem*): The two wave-loaves were baked in an oven from the newly grown wheat and were not offered on the altar, because they were *chametz* (leavened), but were rather eaten by the priests on the holiday of Pentecost (Lev. 23:17; *Hilchot Temidin u-Musafin* 8:11). In addition to the *musafim* for Pentecost, the two wave-loaves were accompanied by a burnt offering of seven sheep, a bull, and two rams (Lev. 23:18).

5. Yom Kippur: A communal burnt offering of a ram is mentioned in Lev. 16:5 and Num. 29:8. The Talmud (BT *Yoma* 70b) discusses whether they refer to the same sacrifice. This entry is included according to the view of R. Elazar b. Shimon, who says they are distinct sacrifices, while according to Rebbi this sacrifice has already been included in the additional offerings for Yom Kippur.

6. Bull brought for unwitting idol worship: If the Sanhedrin erred and allowed idolatry, a bull was brought as a burnt offering (Num. 15:24). There is an argument among the Tannaim (Mishnah *Horayot* 1:5) if only the High Court brought this sacrifice, or if each tribe must do so (i.e. twelve are brought), or whether both the tribes and the court did so (i.e., thirteen are brought).

7. Dessert for the altar: The Talmud (BT *Shavuot* 12a-12b) notes that when sacrifices were disqualified, they would be held until they developed a blemish and then sold. The proceeds would be used to buy animals which were brought as voluntary communal burnt offerings, which were sacrificed at slack times, when the altar was idle. These offerings were called "dessert for the altar" and they represented the only instance of voluntary communal offerings. Rashi derives this option from the use of the plural form in the phrase: "from the cattle or the flock you may bring your [plural form] offering" (Lev. 1:2), thus indicating that at times the entire community may donate an animal as a burnt offering.

SIN OFFERINGS

External, individual sin offerings

There are six external, individual sin offerings.

1. Individual's sin offering: a female sheep or goat brought by one who unintentionally transgressed a negative command liable to excision (Lev. 4:27-35).

2. Ruler's offering: parallel to an individual offering, just that the sin was performed by a ruler, and the offering must be a male goat (Lev. 4:22-26).

3. Individual's offering for idol worship: specifically for inadvertently indulging in idolatry. The offering must be a female goat (Num. 15:27). This law applies to a ruler or high priest as well (Mishnah *Horayot* 2:6).[119]

4. Ascending and descending (*oleh ve-yored*) offering: a sacrifice whose expenditure is proportionate to the economic status of the sinner, varying from a female sheep or goat to a pair of birds to a meal offering. The sacrifice is specified for three transgressions: one who falsely swears that he is ignorant of a particular matter, thus winning exemption from testifying; one who inadvertently eats holy foods or enters the Tabernacle in a state of impurity; and one who forgot that he made an oath and subsequently transgressed it (Lev. 5:1-14 and Rashi thereon).

5. Sin offering for *mechussarei kapparah*: there are four persons whose purification is not complete (*mechussarei kapparah*)

---

119. Ra'avad (*Hilchot Ma'aseh Korbanot* 1:16) quotes Rabbeinu Nissim, who says that this offering is actually an internal sin offering. Ra'avad believes this to be the view of Rambam, but *Kesef Mishneh*, *Lechem Mishneh*, and Radbaz say that Rambam also considers this to be an external sin offering.

until they bring a sin offering, as specified in the Mishnah (*Kereitot* 2:1): a man (Lev. 15:14-15) or woman (Lev. 15:29-30) who has aberrant bodily issues, a woman who gives birth (Lev. 12:6), and a recovering leper (Lev. 14:10; 14:22). In the first three cases, a single bird is brought as a sin offering, while in the fourth, a bird is offered only if the person affected cannot afford a young female sheep.

Sin offerings atone for iniquity. Abarbanel (Lev. 15:1) presciently looks upon bodily issues as being caused by adulterous relationships. The Talmud relates leprosy to seven moral sins (BT *Arachin* 16a). Regarding a woman giving birth, the Talmud states that "when she kneels in bearing, she swears impetuously that she will have no further intercourse with her husband" (BT *Niddah* 31b). According to R. Zalman Sorotzkin (*Oznayim la-Torah*, Lev. 12:6), the reason a single dove is brought is to remind the woman who gave birth that a dove mourns for its partner if it disappears, and it does not mate with another bird for the remainder of its life; although giving birth is painful and the woman may swear that she will never again fulfill her marital duty, she should learn loyalty to her husband from the dove, who provides a shining example of fidelity.

6. Nazirite sin offering: elucidated in the portion of *Tzav*. A Nazirite who became defiled during the period of his consecration is required to purify himself and bring a bird as a sin offering in order to renew his vows (Num. 6:10-11). At the successful conclusion of the consecrated period, he brings a young female sheep as a sin offering (Num. 6:10-14), for he who deprives himself of wine is called a sinner (BT *Nedarim* 10a), as it says in the Jerusalem Talmud (*Nedarim* 9:1): "Is it not sufficient what the Torah has prohibited? Rather, you seek to forbid yourself from [consuming] additional items."

External, public sin offerings:

These consist of a male goat, which was part of the additional sacrifices on New Moons and holidays (Num. 28-29), and was also brought with the two loaves on Pentecost (Lev. 23:19). These were intended to atone for defiling the Sanctuary or its holy objects (*tum'at Mikdash ve-kodshav*) by entering the Sanctuary or eating consecrated food in a state of uncleanness. If one knew that he was impure before entering, forgot, and remembered only afterwards, then he had to bring an *oleh ve-yored* sacrifice (no. 4 of the individual sin offerings). If he initially knew he was unclean, but permanently forgot before entering, then the internal goat sin offering on Yom Kippur atoned (Lev. 16:15; Mishnah *Shavuot* 1:2). If he did not know he was unclean before entering, perhaps because of a lack of basic knowledge, and realized he had been so only after entering or eating, the male goat brought externally as part of the additional service on Yom Kippur atoned (Num. 29:11; Mishnah *Shavuot* 1:3). Finally, if he was totally unaware of being unclean, both before entering and afterwards, then the male goat offered in the additional service of holidays and New Moons atoned (Mishnah *Shavuot* 1:4).

Internal, individual sin offerings:

1. Anointed priest's bull (Lev. 4:3): a sacrifice brought by a high priest who erred and performed an act punishable by excision if done on purpose, but requiring a sin offering if done unintentionally (Mishnah *Horayot* 2:6). A layman who made the same error would have brought a female goat or sheep. The higher level sacrifice demanded was indicative of the special standing of the high priest as a decisor of *halachah*.

2. High priest's bull on Yom Kippur (Lev. 16:3): the high priest made a confession (*viddui*) with regard to every sin which he

may have committed during the year in order for him to be worthy of asking for atonement throughout the day for all of Israel's sins.

3. Individual's offering for idol worship: as previously noted (see "External, individual sin offerings"), this is an internal offering only according to Rabbeinu Nissim. His logic is that since the anointed priest brings an internal sin offering when accidentally transgressing any excision level prohibition, one would at the very least expect the same for idolatry.

Internal, public sin offerings:

1. Bull brought for erroneous public decisions (Lev. 4:14): a sacrifice brought if the Sanhedrin erred by permitting an act punishable by excision if done on purpose and requiring a sin offering if done unintentionally (Mishnah *Horayot* 2:6). There is an argument (Mishnah *Horayot* 1:5) concerning whether the Sanhedrin brings this sacrifice, or each tribe, or both (leading to thirteen bulls).

2. Goat brought for inadvertently indulging in idol worship (Num. 15:24): the same situation as that requiring the bull brought for erroneous public decisions, just that the specific mistake relates to idol worship. Instead of sacrificing a bull as a sin offering, as in the previous case, a goat is sacrificed (Num. 15:27-31). The question regarding how many sacrifices to bring, mentioned with respect to the bull, is relevant here as well, i.e. the number of goats offered may be one, twelve, or even thirteen.

3. Goat brought on Yom Kippur (Lev. 16:9): a goat sacrifice intended to atone for the sins of the entire nation.

Note that except for the public sin offering for idol worship and Yom Kippur, all internal sin offerings were of a bull.

GUILT OFFERINGS

Listed below are the five types of guilt offerings. For the first three, a ram (adult male sheep) is sacrificed, while for the last two a young male sheep is brought.

1. Guilt offering for thievery: brought by one who swore that he did not steal or withhold wages, and later admits that he in fact did do so (Lev. 5:21-26).

2. Guilt offering for trespassing: brought by one who unintentionally benefits from consecrated property belonging to the Tabernacle or Temple (Lev. 5:16-17).

3. Guilt offering of a *shifchah necherefet*: brought by an Israelite who has relations with a *shifchah necherefet* (Lev. 19:20). Every Gentile woman sold as a slave to a Jew goes through a form of conversion which involves immersion and a commitment to observe the laws. She is allowed to form a union with a Canaanite or a Jewish slave, but such marriages have no legal status. Only upon obtaining complete freedom does she attain the status of a full-fledged Jewess. The portion of *Kedoshim* (Lev. 19:20-22) describes the case of a Canaanite female slave who was purchased by two partners, and freed by one of them, leaving her half-Jewess and half-slave (BT *Kereitot* 11a), and she is referred to as a *shifchah necherefet*. As a half-Jewess, she is prohibited to live with a Canaanite servant, while as a half-slave, she may not marry an Israelite. She is permitted only to a Hebrew slave, who is allowed to marry the side of her that is half-Jewish, but as a Hebrew slave he is also permitted to marry a female Canaanite slave. If a normative Israelite had relations with a *shifchah necherefet* who had been set aside for a Hebrew

slave, he is required to bring a guilt offering, as opposed to if he has relations with a fully Jewish engaged woman, in which case he is liable to the death penalty.

Ibn Ezra was apparently bothered by the unusual situation described by Rashi and Ramban, which is not hinted at by the text in *Kedoshim*. He therefore says that the reference is to a young Jewish woman who has been sold into slavery by her father, as described in Exod. 21:7, and is designated to marry her master, but has not yet done so. One who has relations with such a woman must bring this guilt offering.

The word *necherefet*, according to Rashi (Lev. 19:20), means engaged or designated, and according to Ramban means young. Ibn Ezra, who describes the situation differently, derives the word *necherefet* from the Hebrew word for shame, *cherpah*, since she is embarrassed by having been sold as a slave and by being under the control of a master who is not her husband.

4. Guilt offering of a Nazirite: elucidated in the portion of *Tzav*. A Nazirite accepts upon himself three restrictions: not to shave, not to drink wine, and not to be defiled by coming in contact with a dead person. If during the period which he has accepted upon himself he inadvertently breaks his vows, then he must bring two birds as a burnt offering and a sin offering, as well as a guilt offering of a lamb (Num. 6:11-12), and then restart the period of abstention.

5. Guilt offering of a leper: on the eighth day of the purification ceremony of a leper, he brings a sin offering and a burnt offering, as well as a young lamb as a guilt offering (Lev. 14:10-32).

PEACE OFFERINGS

Types of peace offerings[120]:

1. Individual offering: an animal (cattle, sheep, or goat of either sex) offering as described in Lev. 3

2. Festal (*chagigah*) offering

3. Peace offerings of jubilation

4. Peace offering of the fourteenth (of Nisan)

5. *Bikkurim* peace offering

6. Thanksgiving offering

7. Nazirite's ram: on the day of the successful completion of his vow, a Nazirite brings a ram as a peace offering, together with a burnt offering and a sin offering, as well as ten unleavened loaves and ten wafers (Num. 6:14-15; BT *Menachot* 77b).

8. Pentecostal communal peace offering—on Pentecost, two loaves of bread were brought as an offering, after which the nation was permitted to consume the newly grown wheat. Together with the wheat offering, in addition to burnt offerings and a sin offering, two lambs were brought as peace offerings (Lev. 23:18-19; *Hilchot Ma'aseh ha-Korbanot* 1:17), and this was the only case in which a peace offering was communal, and as such was considered to be most holy (*kodshei kodashim*), as opposed to individual peace offerings, which were classified as less holy (*kodshim kalim*).

---

120. Types 2–6 are in the portion of *Tzav*.

THREE ADDITIONAL ANIMAL SACRIFICES: PESACH, BECHOR, AND MA'ASER BEHEMAH

1. *Pesach*: the Passover offering is described as being "without blemish, a one-year-old male... you should take it from the sheep or from the goats" (Exod. 12:5). Although similar to a peace offering, it differs with respect to a number of details, such as:

    a. It was to be eaten together with matzah and bitter herbs (Exod. 12:8).

    b. It was to be roasted, not cooked or eaten raw (Exod. 12:9).

    c. It was to be eaten by one household exclusively (Exod. 12:46).

    d. It was prohibited to break its bones, since this is the way of the poor (Exod. 12:46; *Sefer ha-Chinnuch*, mitzvah 16).

    e. Unlike normative peace offerings, which could be eaten for two days and a night (Lev. 7:16), or thanksgiving offerings (Lev. 7:15), which could be eaten for a day and a night, it could be eaten for only one night (Exod. 12:8; BT *Pesachim* 120b).

    f. Rabbinically, it was not permitted to eat anything after partaking of the Passover offering (*Pesachim* 1:8, according to Shmuel).

2. *Bechor* (first-born): the Torah states: "You should transfer that which [first] opens the womb to the Lord; and every [first] opening ejected by an animal, if it is a male, should be for the Lord" (Exod. 13:12).

    The questions which arise are threefold:

    a. Which animals are being referred to?

    b. What does "being for the Lord" mean in practice?

    c. If the answer to b is that it is to be sacrificed, to what existing offering may it be compared in terms of procedures, rules, and beneficiaries?

310

The answers to these questions may be derived from the second mention of the sanctity of the first-born, where the twenty-four gifts rendered to the priests are enumerated. Merely being mentioned in that list implies that the main benefactors of this ritual (in answer to the third question) are the priests. The Torah states:

> But the first-born of an ox, or the first-born of a sheep, or the first-born of a goat you may not redeem; they are holy: you must dash their blood against the altar, and burn their fat as an offering made by fire, for a sweet savor for the Lord (Num. 18:17).

This verse answers the first question by specifying the animals referred to, and the second question by clarifying that "being for the Lord" refers to a sacrifice. The phrase "you may not redeem" is added because first-born male Israelites and first-born donkeys are also among the priestly gifts, but the humans are redeemed from the priest's ownership for five *shekalim* (Num. 18:16) and the donkeys by switching them for a lamb, which is given to a priest (Exod. 13:13).

In addition to the priestly families receiving all of the meat of the sacrifice, other restrictions distinguish the first-born offering from a typical peace offering, such as:

a. It is forbidden to work or shear the wool of the first-born before it is sacrificed, base on the phrase: "You should do no work with the first-born of your ox, nor shear the first-born of your flock" (Deut. 15:19).

b. It must be sacrificed in its first year (Mishnah *Bechorot* 4:1), as it says: "You must eat it before the Lord your God, year by year" (Deut. 15:20).

311

3. *Ma'aser Behemah* (animal tithe): one of every ten animals born to their owner must be sacrificed at the Temple and eaten there. The source of this mitzvah is found at the end of the portion of *Bechukkotai*: "And all the tithe of the herd or the flock, whatever passes under the rod, the tenth will be holy to the Lord" (Lev. 27:32).

As the verse states, the requirement relates to the herd (cattle) and the flock (sheep and goats) exclusively. Two items must be explained:

a. What is the meaning of "passing under the rod?"
b. What is the meaning in practice of being "holy to the Lord?"

The Mishnah provides the answer to the first question:

How does one tithe them [animals]? He brings them to a shed and makes a small opening for them so that two cannot go out at the same time, and he counts with the rod – one, two, three, four, five, six, seven, eight, nine; and the tenth that goes out he marks with a red marker and says: "This is the tithe" (Mishnah *Bechorot* 9:7).

As far as being "holy to the Lord," the following verses fill in the details:

5. Rather to the place which the Lord your God chooses from all of your tribes to put His name there, you should seek His habitation and come there; 6. and you will bring there your burnt offerings, and your sacrifices [Rashi: required peace offerings], and your tithes, and the offering of your hand [Rashi: *bikkurim*

(first-fruits)], and your vows, and your free-will offerings, and the first-borns of your herd and of your flock; 7. and you will eat there before the Lord your God (Deut. 12).

With regard to the the words "your tithes," R. Akiva states: "Scripture speaks of two kinds of tithes, one the animal tithe, and the other the grain tithe" (BT *Bechorot* 53a).

Accordingly, the verses cited indicate that the animal tithe must be brought to the Temple, sacrificed like the other animal offerings mentioned in the verse, and consumed in the vicinity. In fact, the Mishnah (*Zevachim* 5:8) states that the animal tithe is of lesser holiness (*kodshim kalim*), slaughtered anywhere in the Temple court, and eaten anywhere in Jerusalem for two days and one night, in accordance with the rules for a peace offering (*Zevachim* 5:7). It differs only in one respect, namely that the priests have no share in its meat, since it is not mentioned as being among the priestly gifts in Numbers 18 (Rashi, Lev. 27:32).

Sefer ha-Chinnuch sees the importance of this mitzvah in that it requires animal owners to frequent Jerusalem and come in contact with Torah scholars.

MEAL OFFERINGS

Types of meal offerings:

Three types of meal offerings may be distinguished: those with drink offerings; public meal offerings (obligatory); and private meal offerings, four of which are obligatory in certain situations, while one is voluntary. The latter is the preferred voluntary sacrifice of a poor person, who does not own animals (Rashi, Lev. 2:1).

Meal offerings with drink offerings:

This meal offering, together with a drink offering of wine, is brought with burnt offerings, peace offerings, and the sin and guilt offerings of a *Metzora*, as summarized by the Mishnah:

> All public and private sacrifices require drink offerings, except for first-born, animal tithe, Passover, sin, and guilt offerings; but the sin and guilt offerings of a leper do require drink offerings (*Menachot* 9:6).

The source of the laws concerning meal and drink offerings is Num. 15:1-16. The Talmud (BT *Menachot* 90b-91a) establishes the general rule that only voluntary offerings are accompanied by a meal and drink offering, since Scripture mentions them in connection with "a burnt offering, or a sacrifice [brought] in fulfillment of a vow or as a freewill offering or [one brought] in your appointed seasons" (Num. 15:3). The only sacrifices brought voluntarily, i.e. "in fulfillment of a vow or as a freewill offering," are the burnt and peace offerings. Although public holiday offerings are obligatory, since the verse explicitly mentions "your appointed seasons," it is clear that they too require a meal and drink offering, although the public sin offerings on those occasions do not. The rationale is that the meal and drink offering elevates a sacrifice and is thus appropriate for those offered voluntarily as well as those offered in honor of the public, but not those that relate to the sins of the public. In a similar vein, the Nazirite's sacrifices are not accompanied by meal and drink offerings because he is compared to a sinner, as R. Elazar ha-Kappar (BT *Nazir* 19a) derives from the words: "for the guilt that he incurred through the corpse" (Num. 6:11). The leper, on the other hand, was stricken randomly,[121] and is thus compensated by bringing a more prestigious sacrifice (Bartenura, *Menachot* 9:6).

---

121. Of course, on the Midrashic level, the leper has in fact sinned (BT *Arachin* 16a).

Public meal offerings:

1. *Omer* meal offering (Lev. 2:14-16; 23:10-14): offered from barley on the sixteenth of Nisan, brought together with the *omer* burnt offering—an unblemished one-year-old lamb. It allows the populace to consume the barley from the new crop. A small amount is burned on the altar (Mishnah *Menachot* 6:1), and the remainder belongs to the priest.

2. Two bread loaves (Lev. 23:16-20): the sacrifice which permits eating the wheat of the new season. It is brought on the holiday of Pentecost, seven weeks after the second day of Passover, as the Bible states:

> And you should count for yourself from the morrow of the day of rest [the first day of Passover], from the day that you brought the sheaf of the waving [the *omer* meal offering], seven weeks… until the morrow of the seventh week you should count fifty days, and [then] you will present a new meal offering to the Lord (Lev. 23:15-16).

Because the loaves were baked with a leavening agent (Lev. 23:17), they were not allowed on the altar, as it says: "You may not make any leaven or honey into smoke as a fire offering to the Lord" (Lev. 2:11).

The two loaves were offered together with seven lambs, a bull, and two rams as a burnt offering, a male goat as a sin offering, and two lambs as a peace offering (Lev. 23:18-19),[122] and eaten in their entirety by the priests (Mishnah *Menachot* 6:2).

---

122. This is the only instance of a communal peace offering, and it is accordingly treated as *kodshei kodashim* (most holy) and brought in the appropriate manner (Mishnah *Zevachim* 5:5).

3. Showbread: the Torah states:

> And you should bake twelve cakes…. and set them in
> two columns, six in a column… and you should put
> pure frankincense on each column… Every Sabbath
> day he should set it up. And it will be for Aaron and his
> sons, and they must eat it in a holy place (Lev. 24:5-9).

The oral law has expanded these verses in the following
manner: twelve loaves of bread were to be arranged in two
sets of six on the table in the Tabernacle and Temple every
Sabbath, with a small bowl of frankincense on top of (or next
to, according to Abba Shaul) each stack (Mishnah *Menachot*
11:5). A new set of loaves was brought each Sabbath (Mishnah
Menachot 4:4). After offering the additional Sabbath sacrifices,
the frankincense was burnt on the altar (Mishnah *Menachot*
11:7), the new weekly priestly shift replaced the old, and each
shift would receive six of the previous week's loaves (Mishnah
Sukkah 5:8) and give half of them to the high priest.[123]

Private meal offerings:
There exist six private meal offerings, five of which are obligatory,
and one of which is voluntary, although it can assume four different
forms.

1. Sinner's meal offering: a person who transgressed one of three
   serious sins (suppressing testimony; entering the Temple or
   partaking in sacrificial meat, having forgotten his being impure;
   or inadvertently breaching a vow) must bring an ascending and
   descending (*oleh ve-yored*) offering, which by definition allows
   a pauper to bring a meal offering (Lev. 5:11-13).

---

123. BT *Yoma* 17b, according to Rebbi. See *Hilchot Temidin u-Musafin* 4:14.

2. Meal offering of a suspected adulteress (*sotah*): a meal offering brought by the husband for her, as part of the procedure for investigating the innocence of the *sotah*, as it says:

    > And the man will bring his wife to the priest, and he will bring her offering for her, the tenth part of an *ephah* of barley meal; he will not pour oil on it [Rashi: so that her sacrifice will not be elegant, (and also) because oil is called light and she acted in darkness], nor put frankincense on it [Rashi: for the matriarchs are called (figuratively) frankincense, and she deviated from their ways]; for it is a meal offering of jealousy, a memorial meal offering, a reminder of iniquity (Num. 5:15).

3. Meal offering of initiation (Lev. 6:12-15): on the day of their inauguration, the high priest, as well as the regular priests, must bring a special meal offering which is burnt in its totality on the altar (as is any voluntary meal offering brought by a priest – Lev. 6:16). These requirements are derived from the verse:

    > This is the offering which Aaron and his sons will bring to the Lord on the day when he is anointed: the tenth part of an *ephah* of fine flour for a meal offering perpetually, half of it in the morning and half of it in the evening (Lev. 6:13).

The Talmud (BT *Menachot* 51b) understands this verse to mean that both Aaron, as the high priest, and his sons, as regular priests, bring the aforementioned meal offering (since the word for bring – *yakrivu* – is in the plural form in Hebrew).

A second verse states: "And the anointed priest that will be in his stead, from among his sons, will offer it. It is an eternal decree of the Lord" (Lev. 6:15). The Talmud understands this verse to be referring to high priests that will replace Aaron in future generations, and the assumption is that also regular priests of future generations will continue to bring the initiation sacrifice on the day of their inauguration. The Talmud (BT *Menachot* 50b) notes that this is the only meal offering which is both baked and then fried.

4. High priest's griddle cakes, called *minchat chavitin* (derived from the Hebrew word for frying pan: *machavat*) is a meal offering identical to that brought upon the initiation of a new priest, just that the high priest brought it not only on his first day, but every day, in the morning and evening, at his own expense, in honor of the entire priesthood (BT *Menachot* 51b). According to Siftei Chachamim, the derivation is from verse 6:13 quoted above, which seems to have an internal contradiction. On the one hand, the verse states that it is brought "on the day when he is anointed" but, on the other hand, the verse states "perpetually," i.e., daily. The resolution of the contradiction is that the former phrase refers to regular priests, as well as the high priest, while the latter word refers only to the high priest, and this is reinforced (although not absolutely proven) by referencing the priest's offering as an "eternal decree" in verse 6:15: "The meal offering of initiation and the high priest's griddle cakes were identical and consisted of twelve loaves" (Mishnah *Menachot* 6:5).

5. Nazirite meal offering: at the completion of his vow, the Nazirite brought four of the five types of sacrifice: a burnt offering, a sin offering, a peace offering, and a meal offering, the fifth—a

guilt offering—having been brought if he inadvertently transgressed his vow (Num. 6:12-15). The meal offering consisted of ten loaves of unleavened bread mixed with oil and ten unleavened wafers spread with oil. One of each type was given to the priest, and the rest to the terminating Nazirite (Mishnah *Menachot* 7:2).

6. Voluntary meal offering (a less expensive version of the animal burnt offering): may be brought in one of five varieties:

   a. Flour meal offering (Lev. 2:1-3): a meal offering which is not baked or fried, but rather mixed with oil.

   b. Oven-baked meal offering (Lev. 2:4): baked meal offering which is either unleavened bread mixed with oil or unleavened wafers spread with oil (BT *Menachot* 63b).

   c. Shallow-pan-baked meal offering (Lev. 2:5-6): a meal offering which is baked in a shallow pan with a minimum of oil, causing it to be hard (Mishnah *Menachot* 5:8 and Rashi *in situ*).

   d. Deep-pan-baked meal offering (Lev. 2:7): a meal offering which is baked in a deep pan which allows the oil to accumulate, causing it to be soft and to creep (Hebrew: *marcheshet*) when pressed with a finger (Mishnah *Menachot* 5:8).

   e. Thanksgiving meal offering (Lev. 7:12-13): Together with the animal sacrifice, one brought ten loaves of unleavened bread mixed with oil, ten unleavened wafers spread with oil, ten loaves of scalded flour mixed with oil (before being baked), and ten loaves of leavened bread. One loaf of each species was given to the priest, with the rest belonging to the offering's donor (Mishnah *Menachot* 7:2).

Appendix II:
Making Decisions in the
Presence of One's Teacher

The following talmudic statements are relevant:

1. It was decreed that a disciple must not make decisions unless he was granted permission by his teacher (BT *Sanhedrin* 5b).

2. A disciple should not make a halachic decision in the place where his teacher resides, unless there is a distance of three parasangs [equivalent to 12 mil or 3.84 kilometers] — the space occupied by the camp of Israel —- between them (BT *Sanhedrin* 5b). Rashi explains that within the camp, people would bring their questions to Moses, even if they were at the most distant point, so this is taken as the distance one is expected to walk in order to get an answer to a halachic question. Rashi bases his exegesis on the verse in Exodus which describes the procedure for consulting with Moses: "And Moses would take the tent and pitch it outside of the camp, far from the camp; and he called it the Tent of Meeting. And every one that sought the Lord went out to the Tent of Meeting, which was outside of the camp" (Exod. 33:7).

3. Rava said: A young scholar may examine his own knife [Rashi: if he is using it himself for his own beast, he need not submit it (for examination) to his teacher] (BT *Eruvin* 63a).

4. Rava ruled: In the presence of one's master it is forbidden [to make a legal decision] under the penalty of death [Rashi: in the heavenly court]; in his absence, this is forbidden, but the penalty of death is not incurred (BT *Eruvin* 63a).

Basing himself on the view of Rambam (*Hilchot Talmud Torah* 5:2-3), R. Yosef Karo's *Shulchan Aruch* states:

A person is forbidden to make halachic decisions in the presence of his teacher, and he who does so is liable to the death penalty [in the heavenly court]. Rama: And having permission does not help within three parasangs (*Yoreh De'ah* 242:4).

Shach points out that Rambam, Yosef Karo, and Rama all adopt the view of Tosafot regarding the apparent contradiction between the first two sources. Source 1 implies that permission always allows the student to make decisions, while source 2 implies that he can never make decisions within three parasangs. Tosafot (BT *Sanhedrin* 5b, s.v. *ella im ken*) assumes that source 2 is speaking about when he received permission, and he is still forbidden when the teacher is near. Ra'avad, Rashbah, and Rivash, on the other hand, hold that the second source is referring to the case when permission was not given, and only then is he not permitted in close range, although he is permitted to answer ad hoc questions when far away. Source 4 then applies to forbidden behavior in both close and far range from his teacher's residence.

Why did the rabbis formulate their displeasure in such strong terms? R. Abraham Isaac Kook relates to this question (*Ein Ayah, Berachot* 31b, note 35). He explains that the Jewish religion strives for perfection in two areas: intellectual and moral. If the intellect is subservient to morality, all will work out well. But when the intellect is allowed to overtake morality, degeneration sets in. Respecting one's mentor by deferring halachic decisions to him highlights the superiority of the moral over the intellectual. Being that this is one of the mainstays of the religion, it was necessary to decree a serious penalty for anyone who did not internalize its centrality in the Jewish outlook on life.

Tosafot (BT *Eruvin* 62b, s.v. Rav Chisda) says that the laws prohibiting a student from making a halachic decision are relevant when a new situation arises, but do not apply when dealing with basic matters, where even the one who asked knows that it is a routine question. Rosh (*Eruvin* ch. 6, par. b) and his son the Tur (*Yoreh De'ah* 242) agree, with the latter extending the leniency to any established ruling.

Rosh says that he is in doubt as to whether a young scholar may *always* decide for himself, as implied by point 3 above, where he was permitted to check the *kashrut* of a knife he wishes to use for slaughtering his own animal, or whether the Talmud permitted it *only* with regard to a knife, since the teacher does not wish to bother his student to come every time for such a routine and frequent problem. In other cases, perhaps a young scholar should not decide even for himself. Rosh tends to be stringent in this matter, and Tur follows in his footsteps. One may assume that Rosh is speaking with regard to advanced questions, since he had already permitted the young scholar to decide independently with regard to simple questions even for others, and certainly for himself.

Hagahot Maimoniyot (*Hilchot Talmud Torah* 5, note *gimel*) states in the name of Maharam mi-Rutenberg that any written decision which appears in the name of the Babylonian Geonim may be utilized by a student without consulting his teacher, as long as he checks it out before publicizing his answer, and makes certain not to extrapolate the decision to different situations. Perhaps this comment motivated R. Aharon ha-Kohen of Lunel (13th century, Provence) to posit in *Orchot Chayim* (*Hilchot Talmud Torah* 21) that these laws do not apply today when the majority of one's knowledge is from the printed book, while R. Yekutiel Yehuda Halberstam, the first Sanz Klausenberger Rebbe, says in *Divrei Yatziv* (*Yoreh De'ah* 131) that they do not apply today because they were said with regard to a *rebbe muvhak*, a teacher with an outstandingly significant relationship with his students, and such teachers do not exist today.

APPENDIX III: SPIRITUAL AND PHYSICAL IMPURITY

EXAMPLES OF SPIRITUAL IMPURITY

The Torah associates spiritual impurity with a number of cardinal sins which it wishes to rail against, such as murder, idol worship, and sexual immorality (*Guide for the Perplexed* 3:47), for example:

1. Murder: "Whoever kills a person... And you may not defile [make *tamei*] the land which you inhabit" (Num. 35:30, 34).
2. Adultery: "And you may not lie carnally with your neighbor's wife, to defile [make *tamei*] yourself with her" (Lev. 18:20).
3. Incest: In the portion of *Acharei Mot*, after listing prohibited marital partners, the following verses appear in Lev. 18:

> 24. Do not *defile* yourselves in any of these things; for in all these, the nations which I cast out from before you *defiled* themselves. 25. And the land was *defiled*, so I visited its iniquity upon it, and the land vomited out its inhabitants.

The Hebrew word used for "defiled" in each case is a conjugated form of *tum'ah*.

4. Necromancy: "Do not turn to ghosts or spirits; do not seek to be defiled by them" (Lev. 19:31).

5. Pagan rites: "And I will set My face against that man… because he has given of his seed to Molech, to defile [make *tamei*] My sanctuary" (Lev. 20:3).

6. Unclean animals do not technically contaminate one who touches them while they are still alive, but because of the prohibition to eat them, they may arouse revulsion, and accordingly the Torah, when speaking of the pig, says: "they are unclean to you" (Lev. 11:8).

How does one purify himself if he has become spiritually impure? He does so by praying for forgiveness, repenting, and changing one's ways. After sinning, King David asked of God: "Create for me a clean [*tahor*] heart, O God" (Ps. 51:12).

EXAMPLES OF PHYSICAL IMPURITY

The three main causes of physical impurity are (a) leprosy, (b) bodily secretions (from sexual organs), and (c) corpses and carcasses of certain animals.

Leprosy (biblical references are all from Leviticus, unless otherwise indicated):

The Hebrew word used in the Bible for this disease is *tzara'at*. Although the King James version translates it as leprosy, today leprosy is used to refer to Hansen's disease, which is characterized by the swelling of organs and the rotting of limbs, while the disease described in *Tazria* is a skin disease. According to tradition, the leprosy of the Bible is brought about by sin (BT *Arachin* 16a); it was deemed to be curable with the intervention of a *kohen* (priest), while Hansen's disease was considered incurable until modern times. In addition to affecting people (13:1-46), *tzara'at* could appear on wool, linen, or leather garments (13:47-59), or even on the walls of a house (14:33-53).

Without disputing the spiritual origin of the disease, R. Joseph Hertz found known diseases which fit the biblical description of *tzara'at*. A form of leprosy called elephantiasis, an illness which was once quite common in the Near East, is a near match to the human version of *tzara'at*,[124] while spots on clothing could be caused by mildew of a parasitic infection[125] and a building might be affected by a fungus caused by dry rot or parasitic insects of nitrous incrustation.[126]

R. Samson Raphael Hirsch (13:59) notes that if one considers *tzara'at* to be leprosy, he is inadvertently supporting the thesis of the great, but anti-Semitic, Roman historian Tacitus (late first-early second centuries). In *The Histories*,[127] he twice mentions leprosy in connection with the Jews. He uses it to explain why the Jews refrain from eating pig: "They abstain from swine's flesh, in consideration of what they suffered when they were infected by the leprosy to which this animal is liable." He also uses it as the reason for the expulsion of the Jews from Egypt. He writes:

> Most writers, however, agree in stating that once a disease,
> which horribly disfigured the body, broke out over Egypt;

---

124. Joseph Hertz, *Pentateuch* (1938), p. 461.
125. Ibid. p. 465.
126. Ibid. p. 473.
127. Tacitus, *The Histories*, Vol. 5, translated by Alfred John Church and William Jackson Brodribb.

that king Bocchoris, seeking a remedy, consulted the oracle of Hammon, and was bidden to cleanse his realm, and to convey into some foreign land this race detested by the gods.

R. Hirsch stresses that *tzara'at* could not be leprosy for the following reasons:

1. One of the manifestations of *tzara'at* is in the aftermath of leprosy, after it has been cured. He bases himself on the verse: "And when the flesh has in its skin a boil [considered by R. Hirsch to be leprosy], and it is healed" (13:18). R. Hirsch understands this verse to imply that during the period of being ill with leprosy, he doesn't have *tzara'at* and is not considered to be impure. Only after he is cured does he become susceptible.

2. The outbreak of *tzara'at* over the whole body actually leads to a state of purity, as it says: "If the *tzara'at* covers all his flesh, he will declare the blemish to be clean" (13:13).

3. In the previous situation, the skin is considered unclean when it is healthy, and it becomes clean upon discoloration, as it says: "On the day that fresh flesh will be seen in it, he will be unclean... if the blemish turns white, then the priest declares the blemish to be clean" (13:14, 17).

4. The priest is ordered to remove everything from the house before examining it for *tzara'at*, as it says: "And the priest will command that they empty the house before the priest enters to see the blemish, so that all that is in the house should not become unclean" (14:36). If the purpose of the entire procedure were to prevent the spread of infection, it would certainly be strange to spare some of the infected objects.

Bodily Secretions

1. Menstrual women (*niddah*): A woman is considered impure for seven days from the beginning of her period, after which she must immerse in a ritual bath (15:19).[128] Anyone who touches her (or even touches an object that she sat or leaned on—called *tum'at midras*) is impure for a day and must wash his clothes and immerse (15:20-23). If a man has relations with her during this period, he himself becomes *tamei* for seven days, and contaminates all items in the same way as the *niddah* (15:24).

2. Gonorrhoeists: A man (*zav*) who has a sickly penile emission (15:2-14) or a woman (*zavah*) who emits blood for three days straight[129] not during her monthly cycle (15:25-30). They are impure for seven days after the last emission, when they must immerse and wash their clothes, and on the eighth day they must bring one dove for a sin offering and another for a burnt offering. They transfer impurity to others according to the same rules as menstrual women. Touching liquid emissions of a gonorrhoeist or a *niddah* causes one to be *tamei* for the day (15:8).

3. A man or woman who cohabit, and a man who has a nocturnal emission, are *tamei* until the evening after immersion (15:15-18).

4. A woman who is unclean as if she were a menstruant, for seven days after giving birth to a male and fourteen after a female (12:2, 5). During the following 33 or 66 days, respectively, she

128. Although not explicit, Rambam (*Hilchot Mikvaot* 1:2) says it is learned from Lev. 11:32 that purification from all forms of *tum'ah* requires immersion. *Aruch ha-Shulchan* (*Yoreh De'ah* 183:3) brings additional proofs.

129. BT *Niddah* 73a explains that if the flow is one or two days, she may immerse on the following day and becomes clean at nightfall.

may not enter the Temple (12:4) nor touch the heave offering, if she is the wife or unmarried daughter of a priest (12:4; BT *Yevamot* 75a), after which she brings a lamb as a burnt offering and a dove as a sin offering (12:6).

Dead Bodies:

1. Carcasses of any animal except for properly slaughtered kosher animals cause one to be *tamei* until evening if he touches or carries them (11:24-28, 39-40).[130]

2. The carcass of an improperly slaughtered kosher bird causes one to be *tamei* only upon swallowing it (Rashi 17:15, based on BT *Zevachim* 69b).

3. Carcasses of the eight swarming creatures (weasel, mouse, great lizard, gecko, land-crocodile, lizard, sand-lizard, and chameleon) contaminate upon contact (11:29-30).

4. Corpses: One who touches a corpse becomes *tamei* for seven days (Num. 19:11), and is not allowed to enter the courtyard of the Temple, in which Israelites are normally permitted (from *ezrat yisrael* inward),[131] although the rabbis extend the prohibited area to the rampart (*chayil*, Mishnah *Kelim* 1:8). Not only a person who touches a corpse or a sword protruding from a corpse, but also clothing or any other vessel which touches the unclean person (who touched the corpse) are unclean for seven days, based on Num. 31:24, as noted in Mishnah *Ohalot* 1:3.

   In addition, even if there is no direct or indirect contact with the dead, just being under the same roof is enough to engender a seven-day period of impurity (19:14). Interestingly enough, carrying a corpse is not specifically mentioned, but

130. See Rashi on 11:26.
131. Rashi, Num. 5:2, based on BT *Pesachim* 67a, b.

Sifrei on Num. 19:17 explains that if carrying a carcass, which has less *tum'ah* associated with it, leads to the same period of impurity as touching a carcass (i.e., one day), similarly carrying a corpse should lead to the same period of impurity as touching a corpse, namely seven days. *Kesef Mishneh* explains that although punishment is never derived by *a fortiori* logic, in this case, as in the case of eating meat cooked with milk and having sexual relations with one's own daughter, both of which are not written explicitly in the Torah, logic is used merely to clarify Scripture's intent (*Hilchot Tum'at Met* 1:2). Rambam accordingly explains that the impurity associated with carrying a corpse is treated as if it were written explicitly.

5. Internal sin offerings: The meat of internal sin offerings[132] is burned, as described in the text: "And the whole bull should be taken out of the camp to a clean place, where the ashes [from the altar] are poured out, and burned on wood with fire" (Lev. 4:12).

Regarding the priest who burns the Yom Kippur sin offerings, the text states: "And he who burns them should wash his clothes, and bathe his flesh in water, and afterward he may come into the camp" (16:28). The Talmud extends the scope of this verse to all internal sin offerings (BT *Zevachim* 83a), and to everyone directly involved in the burning (BT *Yoma* 68b, *Zevachim* 106a), all of whom are unclean for the day.

Another person who became *tamei* was the person who accompanied the scapegoat to the desolate land, as it says: "And he who sends the scapegoat to Azazel must wash his clothes, and bathe his flesh in water, and afterward he may

---

132. I.e., the sin offerings of the anointed priest (4:3), of the entire congregation (4: 13), and of the entire congregation when it has accidentally engaged in idol worship (Num. 15:22).

come into the camp" (16:26). The Talmud generalizes this status to all those who lead sin offerings out of the Temple grounds to where they are to be burnt (BT *Zevachim* 105a, *Hilchot Parah Adumah* 5:4).

6. Red heifer: The rite described in Num. 19 is one of the strangest in the Torah. A pristine, unblemished red heifer was slaughtered outside of the camp (Num. 19:2-3). The carcass was burned, while cedar wood, hyssop, and scarlet-colored wool (Rashi, Lev. 14:4) were thrown onto the pyre (Num. 19:5-6).[133] The ashes were then gathered together and stored in a clean place (Num. 19:9).

When someone who was unclean as a result of exposure to a corpse wished to cleanse himself, the stored ashes were dissolved in water, and three stalks of hyssop (Mishnah *Parah* 11:9) were dipped in it and used to sprinkle the mixture on the contaminated person, on the third and seventh day after making the mixture (Num. 19:17-18).

One of the strangest aspects of the red heifer was, to use the characterization of Saadiah Gaon (*Emunot ve-De'ot* 3:10), that it "purifies the impure and defiles the pure." Although the contaminated person was purified, almost everyone else who had anything to do with the procedure became unclean— specifically, the one who burns it (Num. 19:7); the one who gathers the ashes, and his clothes (Num. 19:10); the one who carries the mixture, and his clothes;[134] and anyone who touches the mixture (Num. 19:21).

---

133. Similar ingredients were used in purifying a leper (Lev. 14:4).
134. The verse (19:21) actually mentions the one who sprinkles, but the Talmud (BT *Yoma* 14a) understands it to be referring to the one who carries the mixture.

The eleven biblical causes of impurity have thus been enumerated, namely:

General Category		Type of Impurity
Bodily Secretions	1	menstrual woman (*niddah*)
	2	male gonorrhoeist (*zav*)
	3	female gonorrhoeist (*zavah*)
	4	a man having a seminal emission
	5	a woman who gives birth
Dead Bodies	6	carcass of any animal except for a properly slaughtered kosher animal
	7	carcasses of the eight swarming creatures
	8	corpses
	9	one who burns internal sin offerings
	10	one who gathers, touches, or carries the ashes of a red heifer
	11	leprosy

Leprosy is included in the category of dead bodies based on the Talmudic statement (BT *Nedarim* 64b):

Four are accounted as dead: A poor man, a leper, a blind person, and one who is childless…. A leper, as it is written, ["Then Aaron turned to Miriam and behold, she was leprous. And Aaron said unto Moses . . .] let her not be as one who is dead" (Num. 12:10-12).

RABBINICAL EXTENSIONS

In addition to the biblical impurities, the Sages extended the concept of *tum'ah*. Interestingly, some of the practices which Malbim states lead to spiritual impurity, rabinically also lead to physical impurity. For example, the Talmud in *Shabbat* (83b) states: "an idol the size of an olive [defiles]," and Rambam (*Hilchot She'ar Avot ha-Tum'ot* 6:1) extends this prohibition to vessels, sacrifices, and wine used in connection with idolatrous service, basing it (loosely) on Jacob's words after despoiling Shechem, where his sons might have come into the possession of idolatrous statues: "Remove the strange gods that are among you, and purify yourselves" (Gen. 35:2, and Rashi thereon). The Mishnah (*Avodah Zarah* 3:6) actually suggests another verse on which the Sages might have based their enactment. Scripture (Deut. 7:2) describes idolatry as being detestable (*sheketz*), a word that sounds like *sheretz* (a swarming creature), which causes bodily impurity.

A second form of spiritual impurity was sexual impropriety, and to prevent non-Jews from being a bad influence, they were declared a source of bodily impurity by the Talmud, which states:

> "Speak to the Children of Israel" [the verse continues "when any man has an issue out of his flesh," i.e., becomes a *zav*] (Lev. 15:2), the Children of Israel defile through gonorrhoea, but heathens do not defile through gonorrhoea, but they [the rabbis] decreed concerning them that they are considered as a *zav* [or *zavah*] in all respects (BT *Niddah* 34a, *Shabbat* 83a).[135]

---

135. Rashi provides a sexual motivation for this ruling, which was adopted by Rambam, *Hilchot Metamm'ei Mishkav u-Moshav* 2:10).

A third rabbinical extension was to declare foreign land (out of the borders of Israel) to be unclean. The decree evolved gradually, as is apparent from the following talmudic segment:

(1) They [Yosi b. Yo'ezer and Yosi b. Johanan] came and decreed suspension [neither to burn nor to eat the heave offering] regarding a clod [of earth] and nothing at all with respect to the atmosphere; (2) then the rabbis of the eighty years came and decreed suspension in both cases; (3) then they came at Usha and decreed burning regarding a clod, and as to the atmosphere - they left it as is (BT *Shabbat* 15b).

EXPLANATION

Stage 1: Yosi b. Yo'ezer and Yosi b. Johanan lived in the second century BCE and were the first of five pairs (*zugot*), one of whom was the administrative head of Israel (*nasi*) and the second the head of the Jewish court (*av beit din*). Hillel and Shammai were the members of the fifth and last pair, and served at the end of the first century BCE, about 100 years before the destruction of the Second Temple. They decreed that if a piece of earth whose origin was outside of Israel touched a person or a heave offering, there is a possibility that they have become unclean, and therefore the heave offering is not eaten, as it might be unclean, but is also not burned, because it might be clean. It is merely held in abeyance.

Stage 2: Eighty years before the Temple's destruction (during the time of Hillel) it was decided that even if one were in a foreign land and did not actually touch the land, but was riding on a horse, for example, he was possibly unclean.

Stage 3: After the Bar Kochba revolt, the Sanhedrin was re-established in the Galilean town of Usha, where it was decided that contact with a clod of earth from outside of Israel causes *tum'ah* (impurity), implying that a heave offering which touches it be burnt, and this is affirmed by the Mishnah in *Ohalot* (3:2).

The reason for the rabbinical enactment with respect to a clod of earth is explained by Rambam (*Peirush ha-Mishnayot Ohalot* 2:3) as resulting from the carelessness of Gentiles with regard to the burial of their dead. Consequently, the rabbis feared that every clump of earth might contain bones of a dead person. Tosafot (*Nazir* 54b, s.v. *eretz ha-amim*) suggests that the stimulus for the decree might have been the large number of Jews who were killed there, or even the many non-Jews who were drowned in the great flood.

As far as defilement associated with foreign air, the Talmud (BT *Nazir* 54b) is uncertain whether the enactment was made specifically with respect to the air, perhaps to discourage people from emigrating from Israel, or whether it stems from the fact that the air overshadows the ground, which was considered *tamei* because of the previously cited reasons.[136]

That the decree regarding the impurity of foreign lands was in practice is evident from the following Mishnah:

> The story is told of Heleni ha-Malka whose son went to war, whereupon she said: "If my son returns intact from the war, I will be a Nazirite for seven years." And her son came back from the war and she became a Nazirite for seven years, and at the end of seven years she went up [immigrated] to the land [of Israel], and Beit Hillel instructed her to be a Nazirite another seven years (*Nazir* 3:6).

---

136. According to Rashi on *Nazir* 54b, if there is no enactment on the air, he is only *tamei* if he actually touches the land.

Explanation: Adiabene was an ancient kingdom in Assyria. Its king (Izates II), his wife, his brother and eventual successor Monbaz II, and his mother (known as Heleni ha-Malka) all converted to Judaism from Ashurism in the beginning of the first century. When Heleni's son Izates II went to war, she made the vow referred to in the above Mishnah, and eventually emigrated to Israel, showing her great piety. In Jerusalem, she built palaces for herself and her sons in the northern part of the City of David, south of the Temple Mount (See APPENDIX IV for more about Heleni). The reason she had to be a Nazirite another seven years is that the first seven years were not counted, since she was living out of Israel and hence impure the entire time.

This rabbinical extension can also be viewed as giving a physical dimension to spiritual impurity, Whether the decree was associated with the murder of innocents or the centrality of Israel to the realization of the Jewish mission, these are major tenets of the religion which are being concretized.

Appendix IV:

Heleni ha-Malka and Monbaz II

Both Heleni and Monbaz II were very generous. The Mishnah
states: "King Monbaz II made all of the handles of the vessels of
Yom Kippur of gold" (*Yoma* 3:10). The Talmud (BT *Yoma* 37b)
explains that since the vessels referred to are knives and axes,
whose blades could not be made of gold, he limited himself to
their handles and rims. Otherwise, he would have made them
completely of gold.

The Mishnah then says: "Heleni his mother made a chandelier
over the door of the Sanctuary," to which the Talmud adds: "When
the sun would shine, sparkling rays issued from it and everyone
would know that the time had arrived for the reading of the
[morning] *Shema*."

The Mishnah continues: "She also made a golden tablet on
which the portion of the adulteress woman [which was copied
to parchment and dipped in bitter water] was inscribed." Rashi
explains that doing so avoided the necessity of the priest bringing
in an entire Torah scroll to copy from. The text referred to is from

the following section describing the *sotah* (adulteress woman) in the book of Numbers, as detailed in the Mishnah (*Sotah* 2:3):

> 19. ... If no man has lain with you, and if you have not gone aside to uncleanness [to another] instead of your husband, you should be free from this bitter curse-causing water. 20. But if you have gone aside [to another] instead of your husband, and if you have become defiled, and a man has lain with you besides your husband 21. ... the Lord should make you a curse and an oath among your people, when the Lord makes your thigh descend and your belly swell. 22. And this curse-causing water should enter your bowels, and make your belly swell, and your thigh descend (Num. 5).

The Mishnah also cites the alternative view of R. Yehudah that only verses 21 and 22 are to be written on the parchment. Actually, the Talmud (BT *Yoma* 37b) explains that according to both views the verses are not written out in full (but rather the first letters of their words), since it is only permitted to write the *entire* Torah on parchment, not a fragment.

Appendix V:
Loving One's Neighbor

Loving one's neighbor can be implemented on three levels. The highest level is to experience feelings of love for one's fellow man. The second level is to actively help others in difficult situations. The minimal level is to merely refrain from hurting others physically, emotionally, or verbally.

Level 1 — True love:
Many have asked: how is it possible to legislate love, especially if one finds his neighbor to be repulsive? It has been suggested that in order to overcome an instinctive dislike, one should seek out at least one positive trait, focus on it, and ignore the neighbor's negative attributes.

From a legislative viewpoint, love can certainly not be measured, so that a law to love one's neighbor is not enforceable. However, the rabbis derived certain required acts from the overall obligation to love one's neighbor, and these can readily be described in detail. The situation is akin to that which R. J.B. Soloveitchik

(*Al ha-Teshuva*, p. 40) defined with respect to repentance. He explained that the true fulfillment of that mitzvah is in the heart of the sinner. But the associated act, which Rambam describes in his definition of *teshuvah* (repentance), is the command to verbally confess that one is guilty of having commited a sin. Rambam was apparently well aware of this distinction, because the behavioral aspects of loving one's neighbor are described in his laws of ethical behavior (*Hilchot De'ot*), while specific acts which manifest that love are formulated in his laws of mourning. These sources will now be examined:

With regard to a man's relationship to his fellow-man, Rambam states:

> Every person is commanded to love every Israelite as himself, for it says: "You should love your neighbor as yourself." Therefore, a person should (A) speak in praise of his neighbor and (B) be careful of his neighbor's property to the same extent that he is careful of his own property and (A) desirous of his own honor, and (C) he who glorifies himself in the dishonor of his friend has no portion in the world to come (*Hilchot De'ot* 6:3).

Of course, Rambam bases himself on the oral law. The mitzvah to love one's neighbor is elucidated in *Avot* (2:10), where the Mishnah states: "Let the honor of your friend be as dear to you as your own, and do not anger easily." Rabbeinu Yonah interprets the Mishnah to be saying that one should seek to honor his friend and desire that his friend attain it no less than if he himself were being feted. Clearly, Rambam's point A indicates that he understood the Mishnah similarly.

Rashi sees the second part of the Mishnah as a prerequisite for fulfilling the first part. *Magen Avot* (*Avot* 2:10) explains that one who allows himself to get angry with his friend may eventually embarrass him in public, thereby diminishing his honor.

Just as one should share in the enjoyment his friend experiences when being honored—as if it were his own honor, so he should be considerate of his friend's property as if it were his own. This is Rambam's point B, based on an (almost) adjacent Mishnah: "Let the property of your friend be as dear to you as your own" (*Avot* 2:12).

In the intervening Mishnah, R. Yehoshua b. Chananya says that one who is envious of his friend's social, professional, or financial achievements (which he calls "an evil eye") will meet an early death (*Magen Avot, Avot* 2:11), thereby delineating the consequence of not behaving in the positive manner advocated by the surrounding *Mishnayot*.

A similar idea was expressed by Rav when he said, upon visiting the cemetery: "Ninety-nine [have died] through an evil eye, and one through natural causes" (BT *Bava Metzia* 107b). Rav seems to have presciently predicted that happiness may have a positive effect on longevity and physiological health, implying that misery would have the opposite effect.[137] In the extreme case, when one's jealousy leads him to celebrate his neighbor's misfortune, the Jerusalem Talmud (*Chagigah* 2:1) states that he loses his portion in the next world, as cited by Rambam (point C).

---

137. Bruno S. Frey, "Happy People Live Longer," *Science* 331 (2011), pp. 542-543.

Level 2—Active help:

Rambam discusses the positive acts which are deemed to flow from the requirement to love one's neighbor in his Laws of Mourning, where he states:

> It is a rabbinical enactment (A) to visit the ill and to comfort mourners, and (B) to bring the dead [to burial], and (C) to accompany the bride to the bridal canopy, and (D) to escort guests [as they proceed with their journey], and (B) to be engaged in all aspects of burying [the dead]... and similarly (C) to delight the bride and groom and provide all of their needs, and (E) these are acts of kindness [*gemilut chasadim*] performed [physically] with his body [as opposed to financially] which are unlimited [in scope]. Even though all of these *mitzvot* are rabbinical [in origin], they are included in "Love your neighbor as you love yourself." Everything that you wish others to do for you, you should do for your brother in Torah and *mitzvot* (*Hilchot Evel* 14:1).

In listing these acts of benevolence and associating them with the mitzvah of loving one's neighbor, Rambam has drawn from numerous talmudic and Midrashic sources, such as:

a. "These are precepts that *have no prescribed limit*: ... acts of kindness [i.e., the deeds mentioned by Rambam]" (Mishnah Pe'ah 1:1). Rambam uses this Mishnah as his source for E.

b. "These are precepts whose fruits a person enjoys in this world, but whose principal remains intact for him in the world to come, and they are: honoring father and mother, acts of kindness... hospitality to guests, visiting the sick, accompanying the bride [to the bridal canopy], escorting the dead... bringing peace between man and his fellow man [and between a man and his wife—added in the daily prayer book]" (BT *Shabbat* 127a). This talmudic segment appears in abbreviated form in Mishnah *Pe'ah* 1:1 (source a), but the extended version was adopted for the daily prayer book, and is Rambam's source, with slight variations, for A-D.

c. "That which it says: 'It has been told to you, O man, what is good, and what the Lord requires of you: only to act justly, and to love mercy, and to walk humbly with your God' (Micah 6:8). 'To act justly' means [to act in accordance with] the law, 'to love mercy' refers to acts of kindness, and 'to walk humbly with your God' refers to bringing the dead [to burial] and accompanying the bride to the bridal canopy" (BT *Sukkah* 49b). This talmudic segment provides additional sources for B and C.

d. "The merit of attending a wedding lies in the words [of congratulation which bring joy to the young couple].... Whoever participates in the wedding meal of a groom and does not stimulate him to be joyful neglects 'the five voices' mentioned in the verse: 'The voice of joy and the voice of gladness, the voice of the groom and the voice of the bride, the voice of those who say, give thanks to the Lord of Hosts.' (Jer. 33:11). And if he does gladden him what is his reward? R. Joshua b. Levi said: He is privileged to acquire [knowledge of] the Torah (BT *Berachot* 6b). They said of R. Judah b. Ila'i that he used to take a twig of myrtle and dance before the bride and say 'beautiful and graceful bride.' R. Samuel the son of R. Isaac danced with three [twigs. Rashi: which he juggled]... R. Acha carried her [the bride] on his shoulder and danced" (BT *Ketubot* 17a). These texts supply further sources for C.

e. Jethro, in formulating the job description for Moses' function, stated: "And you will show them the way which they should walk in, and the actions which they should do" (Exod. 19:20). The Talmud annotated this verse as follows: "R. Joseph learned: 'And you will show them'—this is the basis of their life [Rashi: teach them a profession with which to support themselves]; 'the way'—[this means] acts of kindness; 'they should walk'— visiting the sick; 'in'—this is burial [of the dead]; 'and the actions'—this is the law; 'which they should do'—this refers to [acts] beyond the requirements of the law" (BT *Bava Metzia* 30b; *Bava Kamma* 99b).

f. In warning of the danger of seduction by false prophets, Moses states: "You should walk after the Lord your God" (Deut. 13:5), whereupon the Talmud (BT *Sotah* 14a) asks:

> Is it possible for a human being to walk after the *Shechinah*? Has it not already been said [by Moses in his exhortation against idol worship]: "For the Lord your God is a devouring fire" (Deut. 4:24)? But [the meaning is] to walk after the attributes of the Holy One, blessed be He. Just as He clothes the naked, for it is written: "And the Lord God made for Adam and for his wife coats of skin, and He clothed them" (Gen. 3:21), so should you also clothe the naked. The Holy One, blessed be He, visited the sick, for it is written: "And the Lord appeared to him by the oaks of Mamre [immediately after his circumcision]" (Gen. 18:1), so should you visit the sick. The Holy One, blessed be He, comforted mourners, for it is written: "And it came to pass [immediately] after the death of Abraham, and God blessed Isaac his son" (Gen. 25:11), so should

you comfort mourners. The Holy One, blessed be He, buried the dead, for it is written: "And He buried him [Moses] in the valley" (Deut. 34:6), so should you bury the dead.

Based on the exegeses of the verses from Genesis and Deuteronomy, *Baʾal Halachot Gedolot*[138] was of the opinion that these laws derive from the Torah itself, while Rambam (*Sefer ha-Mitzvot*, principle 1) felt that they were rabbinical, and the association with the biblical verses was no more than an *asmachta* (artificially relating a rabbinic enactment to the text of the Torah).

A simple act, which is also considered a means of fulfilling the requirement of performing acts of lovingkindness to one's fellow man, is to greet him upon seeing him (*Meromei Sadeh*, BT *Berachot* 14a, s.v. *amar Rav*).

Level 3—Refraining from hurting others:

The Talmud cites the following story, purportedly to show the great degree of tolerance exhibited by Hillel:

It happened that a certain heathen came before Shammai and said to him, "Convert me on condition that you teach me the entire Torah while I stand on one foot." He pushed him away with the builder's cubit [Rashi: a cubit to measure the amount of work done by a builder, in order to determine his salary] which was in his hand [Maharsha: he wished to imply that just as a building cannot stand on one leg, so the Torah is vast and cannot be summarized

---

138. Quoted by Ramban in *Sefer ha-Mitzvot*, principle 1, s.v. *ve-ha-teshuvah ha-shelishit*.

in a short period of time]. When he went before Hillel, he said to him: "What is hateful to you, do not do to your neighbor. That is the entire Torah, and the rest is commentary; go and learn it" (BT *Shabbat* 31a).

Maharsha asks why Hillel had to rephrase the biblical verse. Why didn't he merely quote it verbatim? He answers that the spoken language in Israel at the time was Aramaic, and it is unlikely that a non-Jew would know Hebrew. Nevertheless, why did he reformulate the maxim in a negative form, as opposed to the original positive command? I would suggest that since he was speaking to a potential convert, he did not want to overburden him with positive commands. He felt that initially it would suffice to warn him not to behave in an unwelcome or violent manner, just as the Talmud instructs one to teach a convert only "some of the minor and some of the major commandments" (BT *Yevamot* 47a; *Hilchot Issurei Bi'ah* 14:6). This then is the third and lowest level of the concept of loving one's neighbor.

The Gerrer Rebbe, R. Yitzchak Meir Alter, in *Chiddushei ha-Rim*,[139] takes this approach as well. He explains that as the convert was not yet Jewish, he could not appreciate loving one's neighbor in a positive sense, as manifested by joining together as a *minyan* (ten) or even a *mezuman* (three), so it was transmitted to him in a manner which he could readily understand at that stage.

Maharsha himself, however, believes that although the biblical verse (Lev. 19:18) is formulated in a positive manner, its true intention is to stress the importance of restraining oneself from behaving in a negative manner, basing his approach on the following points:

---

139. Quoted in Shaul Yosef Natanzon, *Divrei Shaul* on *Shemot, Terumah*, p. 49b.

a. Targum Yonatan and *Pesikta Zutrata* on the verse (with no connection to a convert) both use the negative formulation, with the latter even citing it in the name of Hillel.

b. Although the law is formulated as a positive one, it follows a series of negative commands (Lev. 19:11-18), such as not to steal, lie, swear falsely, oppress, rob, withhold wages, curse, trip, judge unjustly, gossip, allow bloodshed, hate, and take revenge or bear a grudge. The positive aspect of loving, according to the Jerusalem Talmud (*Nedarim* 9:4), is intended to dissuade one from performing evil actions by stimulating a feeling of unity among those involved in any particular incident. For example, suppose a person cut his left hand by mistake with a knife held in his right hand. It would be nonsensical for the left to cut the right in revenge, because in both cases the same person suffers. Similarly, when friends love each other, and each feels the other's pain, the same entity is affected if the quarrel persists.

c. Maharsha feels that loving your neighbor as yourself cannot be taken literally, based on the following talmudic segment (BT *Bava Metzia* 62a; Sifra *Behar, parshata* 5, ch. 6):

> Regarding two who were on a journey, and one has a pitcher of water, [and] if both drink, they will both die, but if only one drinks, he can reach a community — Ben Petura taught: It is better that both should drink and die, rather than that one should see the demise of his companion. [This view was accepted] until R. Akiva came and taught [with regard to the verse: "Do not take interest from him or increased money (beyond what you lent him), but fear your God] and let your brother live with you" (Lev. 25:36). Your life

takes precedence over his life [the verse requires you to forego extra income, but not your life. Your brother must be enabled to live with you, implying that your life takes first place, and only after your life is assured do you attempt to save his].

Malbim (Lev. 25:36) explains the disagreement as follows: Ben Petura says the words "live with you" show that the lives of both are equivalent. R. Akiva says if both are able to remain alive, there is an equivalence, but if only one can survive, he should be the possessor of the means to do so. According to R. Akiva, then, one must first save his own life, i.e. he does not love his neighbor to the same degree as he loves himself.

d. If it is not correct that one must love his neighbor as himself, then why was the verse formulated as a positive command? The answer is that in addition to the laws negating improper behavior, the Talmud also derived a positive ruling from the verse, namely that in cases of capital punishment, the death sentence should be implemented in a considerate manner. Accordingly, a woman who is to be stoned is not stripped of her clothing, since we do not wish to cause her additional humiliation (BT *Sanhedrin* 45a), and a person who is to be burnt to death is only burned internally, which is less painful than the alternative (BT *Sanhedrin* 52a). In both cases the Talmud states: "Love your neighbor as yourself; choose an easy death for him."

e. The Talmud (BT *Kiddushin* 41a) states:

> R. Judah said in the name of Rav: A man may not betroth a woman until he sees her, lest he [subsequently] see something repulsive in her, and

348

then she would become loathsome to him, and the All-Merciful said: "and you should love your neighbor as yourself" (Lev. 19:18).

One might say that a Jew is required to love the other even if he/she has a defect. The answer is that one may ignore the deficiencies and focus on the good qualities of a passing acquaintance, but this approach is not realistic with regard to a marital relationship, in which the couple spends much time together, and which involves a coalescing of their souls and not a mere exercise in mutual tolerance.

Nevertheless, once the decision to marry has been made, an appropriate strategy is to focus only on the virtues of one's spouse and not his/her shortcomings, since nobody is faultless, and no marriage could possibly be maintained if perfection were to be demanded.

The latter approach provides a basis for understanding the following talmudic marital reference:

> R. Hisda ruled: A man is forbidden to have marital relations during the day, for it says: "and you should love your neighbor as yourself." Why is this so? Abaye replied: He might see something repulsive in her, and then she would become loathsome to him (BT *Niddah* 17a).

In the intimacy of a marital relationship, even a physical blemish is capable of diminishing one's capacity to fully love one's neighbor (wife) as himself.

GENTILES

A. Respecting righteous Gentiles:

The Talmud states:

> R. Meir says: Where do we know that even a heathen who studies the Torah is like a high priest? For it says: "[And you should keep my statutes, and my judgments] which, if man does, he will live by them" (Lev. 18:5). Priests, Levites, and Israelites are not specified, but man: hence you learn that even a heathen who studies Torah is like a high priest! [What is meant by a heathen studying Torah?] That refers to their own seven laws [i.e. the Noahide laws] (BT *Sanhedrin* 59a).

This segment actually appears three times in the Talmud (also in BT *Bava Kamma* 38a and BT *Avodah Zarah* 3a), so it apparently reflects the normative Jewish view. The Tosefta (*Sanhedrin* 13:1) quotes R. Yehoshua as saying: "There are righteous people among the heathens who will have a portion in the world to come," while in the Talmud R. Yehoshua widens the scope of this approach even more by saying: "Balaam will not enter [the future world], but other [Gentiles] will enter" (BT *Sanhedrin* 105a), a view supported by the anonymous (*stam*) opinion quoted in the Mishnah (BT *Sanhedrin* 90a). Rambam accepts this approach when he succinctly states:

> Whoever accepts the seven [Noahide] commands and observes them – behold, he is numbered among the righteous Gentiles, and he has a portion in the world to come (*Hilchot Melachim* 8:11).

What does this imply with regard to everyday relations with Gentiles? Rambam states: "One interacts with non-Jewish residents [of Israel who accept the Noahide laws] with courtesy and lovingkindness, as with Israelites" (*Hilchot Melachim* 10:12).

B. Providing for the needs of Gentiles:

The Talmud teaches:

> We support the poor of the heathen along with the poor of Israel, and visit the sick of the heathen along with the sick of Israel, and bury the poor of the heathen along with the dead of Israel [but not in the same cemetery] in the interests of peace (BT *Gittin* 61a).

Rambam (*Hilchot Melachim* 10:12) notes that this segment refers to all non-Jews, even those who do not observe the Noahide laws, based on the following biblical verses: "The Lord is good to all, and His mercy extends to all of His works" (Ps. 145:9); "her ways are ways of pleasantness, and all her paths are peace" (Prov. 3:17). It is important to note that when Rambam says "in the interests of peace" he is not taking a utilitarian approach, as if to say that in principle one does not care about non-Jews, but self-interest dictates that one be nice to them. On the contrary, the verse quoted from Proverbs is the one which Rambam uses to define the purpose of the entire Torah (*Hilchot Megillah ve-Chanukkah* 4:14), and which R. Yehuda Unterman (*Shevet mi-Yehudah*, ch. 70) stresses as its primary approach.

LOVING NON-OBSERVANT JEWS

The Talmud states:

Our rabbis taught: "You should not hate your brother in your heart" (Lev. 19:17). You might think one may [only] not smite him, slap him, curse him. [Therefore,] the text states "in your heart." Scripture speaks of hatred in the heart [which is also prohibited]. How do we know that if a man sees something indecent in his neighbor, he is obliged to reprove him? For it says "you should surely rebuke" (Lev. 19:17). If he rebuked him and he did not accept it, how do we know that he must rebuke him again? The text states "surely rebuke," in all possible ways. You might think [this is obligatory,] even though his face blanched [from embarrassment]. The text continues: "You should not bear sin because of him [by publicly shaming him]" (BT *Arachin* 16b).

The import of this segment is that one should not hate another Jew. Since one might have bad feelings toward someone he sees misbehaving, the Talmud explains that it is preferable to rebuke him and allow your ill feelings to dissipate when he changes his ways. But what happens if he persists in his evil ways? Another talmudic segment discusses that situation:

Three the Holy One, blessed be He, hates: he who speaks one thing with his mouth and [thinks] another thing in his heart; and he who knows evidence concerning his neighbour and does not testify for him; and he who sees something indecent in his neighbour and testifies against him alone [as a single witness, whose testimony is not decisive]. [This is] like what happened to Tobias, [who had] sinned, and Zigud came alone and testified against him before R. Papa. He [R. Papa] had Zigud punished. He [Zigud] said to him: "Tobias sinned and Zigud is punished?" He answered him: "Yes, for it is written: 'One witness should not testify against a man' (Deut. 19:15), and you testified against him alone; you merely bring him into ill repute [Rashi: since your lone testimony will not be accepted, and you thereby transgress the prohibition: 'You must not circulate as a tale-bearer among your people' (Lev. 19:16)]." R. Samuel son of R. Isaac said in Rav's name: He is permitted to hate him [as a sinner], for it says: "If you see the ass of your hated [enemy] lying under its burden, [should you refrain from helping him? You, together with its owner, should surely help it free itself]" (Exod. 23:5). Which enemy [is meant]? If we say a Gentile enemy—but it was taught [in a *baraita*]: The enemy of whom they spoke is an Israelite enemy, not a Gentile enemy. Hence, it obviously means an Israelite enemy. And is it permitted to hate him? But it is written: "You should not hate your brother in your heart" (Lev. 19:17). Perhaps there are witnesses that he had transgressed a prohibition—then everybody hates him, so why single out this person? Hence, it must apply to a case where he had seen something indecent in him. R. Nahman b. Isaac said: [In this case] it is a duty to hate him, as it is said: "One fears the Lord by hating evil" (Prov. 8:13). R. Aha son of Raba asked R. Ashi: What about telling his teacher to hate him? He said to him: If he knows that his teacher regards him as trustworthy as two [witnesses], he should tell him; but if not, he must not tell him (BT *Pesachim* 113b).

353

The implication of this talmudic segment is that one may in fact hate a person who chooses to sin and disobey important Torah laws. Is this the case even if he was never rebuked and told to change his ways? Regarding that there is a rabbinic dispute:

1. *She'iltot de-Rav Achai* (*Vayeshev, she'ilta* 27): The prohibition to hate (discussed in *Arachin*) only relates to non-sinners. Sinners may be hated even if they were never rebuked, for as long as they continue to sin.

2. Rashi (BT *Arachin* 16b, s.v. *yachol*) says that rather than hating him, he should rebuke him even to the extent of slapping him. Only if he refuses to listen may he be hated, and even so he must help him load and unload his beast, which is the case referred to in *Pesachim*. Rambam and R. Yosef Karo agree with Rashi (*Hilchot Rotzei'ach* 13:14; *Choshen Mishpat* 272:11).

3. Tosafot (BT *Pesachim* 113b, s.v. *she-ra'ah*) says that the prohibition to hate in *Arachin* refers to intensive hatred, which is prohibited, while the hatred referred to in *Pesachim* with respect to transgressors is low-level hatred. This distinction is elucidated by R. Shneur Zalman of Liadi (the first Lubavitcher Rebbe):

> Even with regard to those who are close to him, and whom he has rebuked, yet they have not repented of their sins, in which case he is enjoined to hate them, there still remains the duty to love them also, and both are right: hatred, because of the wickedness in them; and love on account of the aspect of the hidden good in them, which is the Divine spark in them, which animates their Divine soul (*Tanya*, ch. 32).

Rashi could theoretically agree with this viewpoint, because the verse in Exodus, although calling him a "hated enemy," still requires an Israelite to help him with his load, so he obviously is not hated in the extreme.

4. Chafetz Chaim is of the opinion that today people do not know how to properly administer rebuke, and as a result it is forbidden to hate any Jew.[140]

---

140. Yisrael Meir ha-Kohen, at the end of *Ahavat Chesed* in *Marganita Tava* 17.

APPENDIX VI:

SOME BASICS OF JEWISH HISTORY

THE TEMPLES

The Bible itself does not provide dates for the occurrence of seminal events, such as the exodus or the destruction of the Temples, but it does on occasion record the duration of certain events. Some of the important traditional sources are listed below:

1. The time elapsed from the exodus until the construction of the First Temple:

    > And it came to pass in the four hundred and eightieth year after the Children of Israel came out of the land of Egypt, in the fourth year of Solomon's reign over Israel, in the month Ziv, which is the second month, that he began to build the house of the Lord (1 Kings 6:1).

2. The length of the Babylonian exile from the destruction of the First Temple to the construction of the Second Temple: "For thus said the Lord: After seventy years are filled in Babylon, I

will remember you and perform My good word regarding you, to return you to this place" (Jer. 29:10).

3. The number of years that the Temples stood:

> Rabbah b. Bar Hana said: What is the meaning of the passage: "The fear of the Lord prolongs days, but the years of the wicked will be shortened" (Prov. 10:27)? "The fear of the Lord prolongs days" refers to the First Temple, which remained standing for four hundred and ten years and in which there served only eighteen high priests. "But the years of the wicked will be shortened" refers to the Second Temple, which stood for four hundred and twenty years and in which more than three hundred [high] priests served (BT *Yoma* 9a, based on *Seder Olam*, composed by R. Yossi b. Chalafta, 2nd century CE).

Rabbinical sources attribute a considerably shorter number of years to the Persian period during the Second Temple than archaeological and historical evidence available today indicates. Source 3 gives the number of years which the Temples stood as 410 and 420 respectively, while more recent research has shown that the Temples existed for 380 and 586 years respectively.[141] The table below presents dates according to the scientific approach and the rabbinic approach:

---

141. Based on Mitchell First, "The Date of the Exodus: A Guide to the Orthodox Perplexed," Seforim Blog (April 3, 2011). This information is not part of the oral law, and hence R. First felt it was acceptable to update it based on the latest findings.

Event	Rabbinic Theory	Modern Theory
Exodus	1310 BCE	1446 BCE
First Temple constructed	830 BCE	966 BCE
Ten tribes exiled	556 BCE	722 BCE
First Temple destroyed	420 BCE	586 BCE
Second Temple constructed	350 BCE	516 BCE
Second Temple destroyed	70 CE	70 CE

Reigns Until the Destruction of the Temple (Modern Theory)		
King	**Reign Began**	**Descripion**
Ahaz	739 BCE	Wicked. Passed his son through fire (2 Kings 16).
Hezekiah	720 BCE	Righteous. Destroyed high places and copper serpent (2 Kings 18).
Manasseh	692 BCE	Wicked. Idols, witchcraft. Spilled innocent blood (2 Kings 21:1-20).
Amon	638 BCE	Wicked. Was assassinated (2 Kings 21:19-26).
Josiah	637 BCE	Righteous. High priest Hilkiah found Torah scroll (2 Kings 22:8).
Jehoahaz	607 BCE	Wicked. Second son of Josiah. Pro-Assyrian. Deposed by Pharaoh (2 Kings 23:31-33).
Jehoiakim	607 BCE	Wicked. Older son of Josiah. Pro-Egyptian. Deposed by Nebuchadnezzar, exiled to Babylon (2 Chron. 36:5-8).[1]
Jehoiachin	597 BCE	Wicked. Son of Jehoiakim. Exiled to Babylon by Nebuchadnezzar. Reigned only 3 months (2 Kings 24:8-16).
Zedekiah	597 BCE	Wicked. Son of Josiah. Chosen by Nebuchadnezzar (2 Kings 24:17).

1. However, 2 Kings 24:6 says he was buried with his fathers, implying he died in Judea, perhaps at the hands of Nebuchadnezzar.

Reasons for the
Destruction of the Temples

The Talmud suggests the following reasons for the destruction of the two Temples:

> Why was the First Temple destroyed? Because of three [evil] things which were present there: idolatry, immorality, and bloodshed... But regarding the Second Temple, when they occupied themselves with Torah, [observance of] precepts, and acts of lovingkindness, why was it destroyed? Because there prevailed [in those days] groundless hatred. This teaches you that groundless hatred is considered to be of equal weight as all three of the [following] sins: idolatry, immorality, and bloodshed together (BT *Yoma* 9b).

Groundless hatred (*sin'at chinam*) is said to be equal in weight to the three cardinal sins. A parallel text in the Jerusalem Talmud (*Yoma* 1:1) cites an Amora who says that *sin'at chinam* is considered to be even worse than those sins, a proof being the fact that after the destruction of the First Temple, another one was built, which did not happen after the destruction of the Second Temple. A second indication cited by the Jerusalem Talmud is that only the roof of the First Temple was destroyed, while even the walls of the Second Temple were razed, implying a greater degree of culpability.

But why is *sin'at chinam* considered to be worse? R. Eliezer (quoted in both BT and JT) explains:

The earlier ones [in the time of the First Temple], whose sins were revealed [Rashi: they did not hide their sins], had their end revealed [Rashi quotes the verse from JT 29:10, indicating that the exile would only last seventy years]. [Regarding] the later ones [in the time of the Second Temple], whose sins were not revealed [Rashi: they were secret sinners], their end [the end of the second exile] was not revealed (BT *Yoma* 9b).

Maharsha explicates that just as a thief, who steals in secret, is more deplorable than a robber, who physically confronts his victim, similarly sinning in private is more severe than doing so openly. In the former case, the villain manifests a greater fear of his fellow man, who can be fooled into thinking he is righteous, than of God, Who is aware of the fact that he is transgressing His laws. A robber, on the other hand, is disrespectful toward everyone, and thus does not single out God as the object of his indifference.

The Talmud proceeds to define exactly what is meant by groundless hatred when it says: "This refers to people who eat and drink together and then thrust each other through with the daggers of their tongue" (BT *Yoma* 9b).

One might ask what enabled the people who lived during the Second Temple period to overcome their tendency to perform the three cardinal sins? The simplest answer would be that the trials and tribulations which they experienced in exile, and the exposure to the wickedness of their Gentile neighbors, influenced them positively. However, the following excerpt from the Talmud implies that the improvement was a Divine gift: "He [Ezra] prayed for mercy [from God] to neutralize the drive to worship idols, and He removed it" (BT *Arachin* 32b).

Since the talmudic text only mentions idol worship, perhaps the other improvements did in fact result from the difficulty of the exile. However, if Torah is meant to refine one's personality, the more troubling question is why, when the people were both more learned and more observant, was their degree of righteousness inferior?

One might answer that if, God forbid, a person is ill with cancer, he may be given chemotherapy. He suffers greatly as a result of this treatment, but the hope is that eventually he will feel much better, and also that he will survive. Similarly with regard to man's progress toward salvation. Initially, he acts instinctively, thinking only of pleasuring himself. When he starts obeying the laws of the Torah, he monitors his outward behavior, but has difficulty making a total catharsis, and as mentioned, his personality traits may even degenerate. Only by passing through this stage, however, will he eventually be able to perfect his character to the point that his intimate feelings, reflected by his behavior in private, are as immaculate as his public behavior.

R. J.B. Soloveitchik (*Al ha-Teshuvah*, p. 40) has distinguished between *ma'aseh mitzvah* (the act associated with a Torah command) and *kiyum mitzvah* (fulfilling the command). Consider the law not to commit murder. The command is clear-cut and easily implemented in the initial stages of religiosity. But true fulfillment of the law—which would include not harming one's fellow man physically or even verbally, not developing prejudicial feelings toward unfamiliar groups, and proactively helping the wretched—is considerably more difficult, and will only occur after making concerted attempts at self- improvement and self-abnegation.

An intriguing talmudic maxim is: "He who is greater than his friend, has a greater evil inclination" (BT *Sukkah* 52a). In light of the present discussion, one might interpret this slogan as indicating that as a person grows in Torah learning, he soon reaches a point where he understands the intricacies of talmudic knowledge, but has not yet assimilated the true message of the commands. At this point he is able to use the tools of the Talmud to arrive at conclusions which are inimical to the true intentions of the Creator, thus enabling his evil inclination (*yetzer ha-ra*) to be more successful in its malicious endeavors than that of his less informed colleagues.

DIFFERENCES BETWEEN THE TWO TEMPLES

The Talmud states:

> In five things the first Sanctuary differed from the second: in [1] the Ark, the Ark-cover, the Cherubim, [2] the fire, [3] the *Shechinah*, [4] the holy spirit, and [5] the *urim ve-tumim* (BT *Yoma* 21b).

The Ark, Ark-cover, and Cherubim were either hidden towards the end of the tenure of the First Temple, or captured at the time of its destruction.[142] The Talmud *in situ* explains that fire miraculously descended from heaven in both Temples, just that in the first it also consumed the sacrifices, while in the second it appeared, but was impotent. The exact meaning of *Shechinah* is not provided by Rashi, but is supplied by Tosafot (BT *Arachin* 6a, s.v. *ke-gon*), where it is stated that in the First Temple the holiness permeating the atmosphere was actually felt by the entire congregation and indeed by all creatures, to the extent that birds refrained from flying over it. In the Second Temple the holiness was not palpable, and it was necessary to set up an image to frighten away the birds. The holy

---

142. Abba Engelberg, *The Ethics of Exodus*, pp. 379-381.

spirit refers to prophecy. The last prophets (Haggai, Zechariah, and Malachi) all served in the first years of the Second Temple. *Urim ve-tumim* refers to the parchment on which the sacred name of God was written. It was inserted between the folds in the material which formed the high priest's breastplate, and enabled the letters on the precious stones embedded in it to light up, thus enabling the high priest to read God's answers to questions which he posed.

The Talmud explains that when King Josiah realized that the Temple would soon be destroyed and the nation exiled, based on a verse in the newly rediscovered book of Deuteronomy (see 2 Kings 22:8), he immediately hid the Ark and a number of additional items (BT *Horayot* 12a):

At the time when the Holy Ark was hidden there were also hidden the oil for anointing kings, the jar of manna, Aaron's rod with its almonds and blossoms, and the box which the Philistines had sent to Israel as a gift and concerning which it is said: "And the vessels of gold, which you returned to Him as a guilt offering, place them in a box by the side of it [the Ark], and send it away that it may go" (1 Sam. 6:8). And who hid them? It was Josiah, King of Judah, who hid them; because, having observed that it was written in the Torah: "The Lord will bring you and your king [who you will appoint over you, to a nation that you do not know]" (Deut. 28:36), he gave orders that they should be hidden, as it says: "And he [King Josiah] said to the Levites that taught all of Israel, who were holy to the Lord, 'Put the Holy Ark into the house which Solomon the son of David, King of Israel, built; it will no more be a burden upon your shoulders'" (2 Chron. 35:3).

When God supplied the Children of Israel with manna, Moses had requested of Aaron to preserve a sample in a jar to be placed near the Ark (Rashi, Exod. 16:33). At the time of Korah's rebellion, each of the princes had deposited a rod with Moses, as did Aaron. The next morning, only Aaron's had blossomed, bearing ripe almonds, and God requested of Moses to place Aaron's rod near the Ark (Num. 17:16-26). Finally, after the Philistines had captured the Ark and been stricken by the Lord, they returned it together with various golden objects placed at its side, which remained in place until Josiah had them hidden.

In summary, the Talmud apparently attributes more grandeur to the First Temple than to the Second. But this would seem to be contradicted by the verse: "The glory of this latter house will be greater than that of the former, said the Lord of hosts; and in this place will I give peace, said the Lord of hosts" (Hag. 2:9).

Radak *in situ* explains the latter part of the verse by noting that even though there were many battles during the Second Temple period (from the time of the Hasmoneans until its destruction), the majority of the time (from 515 BCE until 165 BCE) peace reigned.

The Talmud (BT *Bava Batra* 3a) suggests three ways in which the Second Temple was greater than the first: in the number of years which it stood (as previously noted, 420 rather than 410), in size, and in beauty. The Talmud states:

> He who did not see the Temple of Herod has never seen a beautiful building. Of what did he build it? Rabbah said: of yellow and white marble. Some say, of blue, yellow, and white marble... He originally intended to cover it with gold, but the rabbis advised him not to, since it was more beautiful as it was, looking like the waves of the sea (BT *Bava Batra* 4a).

Interestingly, remnants of Herod's colorful tiles were discovered recently.[143] At any rate, on the most basic level, the contradictory statements from the Talmud may be reconciled by noting that the text from *Yoma* refers to the greater spirituality associated with the First Temple, while the segment form *Bava Batra* refers to the superiority of the Second Temple with respect to various physical aspects. A number of additional answers have been suggested:

1. Ibn Ezra *in situ* says that the verse in Haggai was stated not factually but conditionally, if the nation would have been righteous during the Second Temple period. Since it was not, the miraculous occurrences which graced the First Temple were never realized in the Second Temple.

2. Malbim (*in situ, Peirush ha-Milim*) says that even though the Second Temple was destroyed because of groundless hatred, the associated holiness remains in place until the Third Temple will be built. Accordingly, the verse is not saying that the Second Temple itself was greater in any way than the first, but rather that the glory (which is what the word "greater" modifies) associated with it, which will remain and will be amplified when the Third Temple comes into existence, will be greater than that associated with the First Temple.

3. R. Kook (*Me'orot ha-Ra'ayah*, p. 237) explains the greatness of the Second Temple in terms of its contribution to *tikun olam* (improving the world). He explains that had Israel overcome their inter-personal weaknesses that led to baseless hatred, the Second Temple would have been the final Temple, and the Messiah would have arrived. Since they did not succeed in that task, their ranks would have to be reinforced by non-

---

143. Daniel Eisenbud, "Archeologists Restore Ancient Tiles from Second Temple in Jerusalem," *Jerusalem Post*, Sept. 6, 2016.

Jews who are influenced by the positive traits of the Jewish nation. He even felt that Ahasuerus was positively influenced by Queen Esther, and later fathered King Cyrus with her. Cyrus eventually allowed the building of the Second Temple, which led to much interaction between the Jewish and Gentile worlds, enabling more progress in the area of *tikun olam*. Or ha-Chayim (Deut. 21:11) goes even further and says that it is beneficial to the eventual salvation of the Jewish nation for outstanding Gentiles to convert and thus raise the level of righteousness, as did such illustrious converts as Ruth the Moabite, Shemaya and Abtalion, and Onkelos.

The talmudic texts are thus reconciled. The narrative from *Yoma* which speaks of the miracles that occurred during the First Temple period demonstrates that in those years God's presence was explicitly manifested. With the destruction of the First Temple, the period of miracles ended, the task of the Jewish nation was universalized, and the nation's mission became to influence by example and to develop empathy among non-Jews, to the extent that they occasionally even convert and swell the ranks of the Jewish people.

Source Material

Al ha-Teshuvah. Compilation by Pinchas Peli of lectures on repentance given by R. Joseph B. Soloveitchik, published in 1989.

Akedat Yitzchak. Classical work of ritual matters and moralizing legends by R. Yitzchak Arama.

Avot de-Rabbi Natan. Tannaitic work by R. Natan, parallels *Avot* (Ethics of the Fathers).

Be'er Mayim Chayim. Explanatory notes by the Chafetz Chayim on the eponymous book about *lashon hara* (slander).

Da'at Zekenim mi-Ba'alei Tosafot. Commentary on Torah written by the Tosafists in the twelfth and thirteenth centuries, mostly from the school of Rashi in Germany and France, but some from England and Italy.

Divrei David. Commentary of the *Taz* on the Torah, by David ha-Levi Segal.

Divrei Eliyahu. Commentary on Torah and Talmud by R. Eliyahu of Vilna (the Gaon).

Divrei Yatziv. Responsa of Yekusiel Yehuda Halberstam, Sanz-Klosenberger Rebbe.

Ein Ayah. Commentary of R. Abraham Isaac Kook on the aggadic sections of BT *Berachot*, BT *Shabbat*, and selected Mishnayot from the order of *Zera'im*.

Emunot ve-De'ot. First systematic attempt to integrate Jewish theology with components of Greek philosophy. Written by Saadiah Gaon.

God, Man, and History. Modern Jewish philosophy by Dr. Eliezer Berkovits.

Guide for the Perplexed. Basic Jewish philosophy by Rambam.

Haggadah. Manual with prayers and customs for conducting the Passover Seder.

Igrot Moshe. Seven-volume responsa of R. Moshe Feinstein.

Kuzari. Basic Jewish philosophy by Yehuda Halevi.

Likkutei Moharan. Chasidic interpretations of biblical and Midrashic stories by R. Nachman of Breslav, published and disseminated after his death by his disciple, Reb Nosson. *Moharan* stands for *Moreinu ha-Rav Nachman*.

Ma'or va-Shemesh. Collected writings of Kalonymus Kalman Epstein, replete with kabbalistic references. Considered the *Shulchan Aruch* of *chasidut*. Stresses obligation of a *chasid* to attach himself to a *tzaddik* as a model for emulation, and preaches against asceticism.

Matnot Kehunah. Simple, well-documented commentary on Midrash Rabbah by R. Yissocher Ber ha-Kohen Katz.

Mechilta de-Rabbi Yishmael. Halachic Midrash on Exodus. Based on the teachings of R. Yishmael b. Elisha, R. Akiva's contemporary, and redacted by Rav.

Mechilta de-Rashbi (R. Shimon b. Yochai). Halachic Midrash on Exodus. Based on the teachings of R. Akiva. Compiled in 5th century.

Midrash ha-Gadol. Comprehensive Midrash on the entire Torah based on talmudic, Geonic, and classical Midrashim, edited by the Yemenite leader, R. David b. Amram Adani, in the 14th century and considered the magnum opus of Yemenite Jewry.

Midrash Lekach Tov. See *Pesikta Zutrata*.

Midrash Rabbah. Name given to ten sets of Midrashim on Torah and the five Megillot. Compiled and edited between 6th–10th centuries.

Mishneh Torah. See *Yad ha-Chazakah*.

Mizrachi. Super-commentary on Rashi, written by R. Eliyahu Mizrachi.

Mul Etgarei ha-Tekufah. Essays on the Jewish approach to modern issues by Professor Yehuda Levi.

Netivot Shalom. Series of books by the Slonimer Rebbe, R. Shalom Noach Berezovsky, on the Torah, holidays, chasidism, and Talmud.

Orchot Chaim. Expanded version of the *Kol Bo*, a guide to customs and halacha, by Aharon b. Jacob ha-Kohen of Narbonne. *Tur* used same order and superseded it, being more practical. Cited hundreds of times by R. Yosef Karo. *Kol Bo* may be earlier version or summary.

Or ha-Chaim. Commentary on the Torah by R. Chaim Ben Attar.

Oznayim la-Torah. Commentary on the Torah by R. Zalman Sorotzkin.

Pesikta Rabbati. Composed in 845, containing 51 homilies. Called Rabbati to distinguish it from earlier *Pesikta de-Rav Kehana*. Many have the exordium "Yelamdeinu Rabbeinu" and "Patach R. Tanchuma."

Pesikta Zutrata. Also called *Lekach Tov*. Each homily starts with "*tov*." Written by Tuvia b. Eliezer, Rashi's contemporary. Explains weekly portions and Megillot.

Pirkei de-Rabbi Eliezer. 54-chapter Midrash aggadah. Retells biblical stories. Traditionally ascribed to R. Eliezer b. Hyrcanus, but Zunz claims it was written in the 8th century in an Islamic country.

Seder Olam Rabbah. Chronological record from Adam to Bar Kochba, attributed to the Tanna Yosi b. Chalafta (ca. 160). Quoted in Talmud, Mishnah, Mechilta, Sifra, Sifrei.

Sefer ha-Chinnuch. Systematic discussion of the 613 *mitzvot*, published anonymously in 13th-century Spain, variously attributed to Aharon ha-Levi or his brother Pinchas. Based on Rambam's count, ordered according to the weekly portion. Gives biblical source, philosophical underpinnings, basic laws. *Minchat Chinnuch* by Yosef b. Moshe Babad, (1800–1874) provides legal commentary.

Sefer ha-Ikkarim. Written by R. Yosef Albo. Proposes three principles of faith: existence of God, revelation, and Divine justice (i.e., reward and punishment).

Sha'arei Teshuvah. Moral and ascetic work by Rabbeinu Yonah, allegedly written to atone for earlier attacks on Rambam. It preaches simple piety, modesty, and sincerity in the worship of God as means of reaching a higher religious level.

She'iltot de-Rav Achai. Collection of homilies on Jewish law and ethics. Based on the order of the weekly portions, written by Rav Acha, an 8th-century Talmudist of high renown.

Shevet ha-Levi. Responsa of R. Shmuel ha-Levi Wosner.

Sifra (Torat Kohanim). *Midrash halachah* (legal biblical exegesis) on Leviticus. Rambam attributes it to Rav, and Malbim to R. Chiya. From school of R. Akiva. Quoted frequently in Talmud.

Sifrei. Midrash halachah (legal biblical exegesis) on the books of Numbers and Deuteronomy, preceded and followed by aggadic sections. Final redaction in the time of the Amora'im.

Siftei Chachamim. Supercommentary on Rashi's commentary on the Pentateuch, gathered from earlier exegeses on Rashi. Written by Shabtai ben Yosef Bass. Considered so essential that there exists a concise summary, *Ikkar Siftei Chachamim*, which appears with Rashi.

Siftei Kohen. Allegoric commentary on the Torah, by renowned Kabbalist R. Mordechai ha-Kohen of Safed, with kabbalistic explanations and *gematriot*.

Tanna de-Vei Eliyahu. Midrash taught to 3rd-century Amora, Anan, by Elijah (BT *Ketubot* 106a). Consists of *Seder Eliyahu Rabbah* (larger) and *Seder Eliyahu Zuta* (smaller). Final redaction at end of 10th century. Describes evolution of the world, Jewish history.

Tanchuma. Aggadic interpretations of the weekly portions, attributed to R. Tanchuma. Edited in 5th century, before Midrash Rabbah and Talmud, which quotes it.

Targum Onkelos. Official translation for reading the Torah in talmudic times (and today for Yemenites). Tradition: conveyed to Moshe at Sinai, but forgotten and re-recorded by Onkelos the convert. "Reading the weekly portion twice and targum once" refers to Targum Onkelos.

Targum Yonatan. Official translation of prophets, ascribed to Yonatan b. Uziel. Targum Yonatan on the Torah (pseudo-Yonatan) composed in 7th or 8th century.

Tiferet Yisrael. Commentary on Mishnah, composed by R. Yisrael Lifshitz, in two parts (after the two Temple pillars): Yachin - basic explanation; Boaz - new ideas, more analytical.

Torah Or. Chasidic explanations of the weekly Torah portions and holidays, written by *Ba'al ha-Tanya.*

Torah Sheleimah. Encyclopedia of oral teachings on the Torah, edited by R. M.M. Kasher.

Torah Temimah. Collection of talmudic and Midrashic teachings related to the verses of the Torah, with commentary. Prepared by R. Baruch ha-Levi Epstein.

Yad ha-Chazakah. Code of law containing 14 books (the Hebrew numerical value of *yad* is 14), written by Rambam. Also called *Mishneh Torah*—the repetition of the Torah.

Yefeh To'ar. Commentary by Shmuel Yafeh on Midrash Rabbah on the Torah. A summarized version appears in the Vilna edition of Midrash Rabbah.

Zohar. Literally, "splendor." Foundational work of Jewish mystical thought known as Kabbalah. Discusses the nature of God, structure of the universe, nature of the soul. Traditionally attributed to R. Shimon b. Yochai. Academic scholars believe it was redacted (or possibly even composed) by Moses de León (1240-1305).

COMMENTATORS

Abarbanel, Isaac (1437-1508) — Born to a wealthy family in Lisbon, Portugal. Wrote three types of works: exegesis of Bible and Haggadah, philosophy, and apologetics.

Acha, R. (700-770) — Also known as Achai Gaon. Leading scholar in the period of the Geonim. First known rabbinical author after the close of the Talmud. Moved from Babylonia to Eretz Yisrael.

Aharon b. Ya'akov ha-Kohen of Narbonne (1250?-1330?) — Expelled from Narbonne, Provence in 1306, reached Majorca. Great-grandfather was student of Ra'avad. Contemporary of Rosh. Wrote *Kol Bo and Orchot Chayim.*

Albo, Joseph (1380-1444) — Born in Monreal, Aragon. Student of Hasdai Crescas. Had medical knowledge. Versed in Aristotle. Wrote *Sefer ha-Ikkarim.*

Alshich, Moshe (1508-1593) — Student of R. Joseph Karo, from whom he received ordination (true *semicha*) with Sanhedrin, and teacher of R. Yitzchak Luria (Arizal). Wrote *Torat Moshe* on Torah.

Arama, Yitzchak (1420-1494) — Born in Spain. Talmudist, philosopher. Wrote *Akedat Yitzchak* (Binding of Isaac) - philosophical, homiletic commentary on Torah.

Asevilli, Yom Tov b. Avraham (1250-1330) — Born in Seville, Spain (Asevilli - from Seville). Student of Ra'ah and Rashba. Became rabbi of Saragossa. Famous for his commentary on the Talmud. Known as the Ritva (Hebrew acronym of his name).

Asher b. Yechiel (Rosh, Rabbeinu Asher) (1250-1328) — Born in Germany. Great-grandson of Ra'avan (Tosafist). Student of Meir of Rothenburg. Worked in money-lending, wealthy. Fled to Toledo, became rabbi after being recommended by Rashba. Magnum opus is an abstract of talmudic law at the end of each tractate. Father of *Tur*.

Ashkenazi, Issachar Baerman — See Katz, Yissocher Ber ha-Kohen.

Ba'al ha-Tanya — See Borukhovich, Shneur Zalman.

Bass, Shabtai ben Yosef (1641–1718) — Born in Kalisz, Poland. Wrote Siftei Chachamim. Studied Talmud, singing. Appointed bass singer at Prague Altneuschule (where he got his name).

Ben Attar, Chaim (1696-1743) — Born in Meknes, Morocco. Talmudist, Kabbalist. Wrote *Or ha-Chaim* commentary on Torah. One of four called holy (*kadosh*), in addition to Ari, Alshich, Shlah. Teacher of Chidah. Buried on Mount of Olives.

Berezovsky, Shalom Noach (1911-2000) — Born in Baranovitch, Belarus. Moved to Israel in 1936. Re-established Slonimer *chasidut* after WWII, became rebbe in 1981. Magnum opus is *Netivot Shalom*.

Berkovits, Eliezer (1908-1992) — Born in Hungary. Ordination from R. Akiva Glasner (*Dor Revi'i*) and R. Yechiel Weinberg at Hildesheimer. Ph.D. in Philosophy, U. of Berlin. Wrote *T'nai be-Nissu'im u-ve-Get*; *God, Man, and History*.

Borukhovich, Shneur Zalman (Shneur Zalman of Liadi, the Alter Rebbe, 1745-1812) — Born in Poland. Great-grandson of Maharal. Wrote *Shulchan Aruch ha-Rav*, *Tanya* (exposition of chassidic philosophy), *Torah Or*, and *Likkutei Torah* on weekly portion. Founder of Chabad dynasty.

Botschko, Moshe (1917-2010) — Modern Orthodox Rosh Yeshiva in Montreaux, Switzerland. In 1986 established the hesder yeshiva Heichal Eliyahu in Jerusalem, later in Kochav Ya'akov. Author of *Hegyonei Moshe*.

Chanoch Zundel b. Yosef (1780?-1859) — Lived in Bialystok, where he taught and composed commentaries on Midrash (*Tanchuma, Midrash Rabbah, Pesikta de-Rav Kehanah*), *Ein Ya'akov, Seder Olam Rabbah*, the *Siddur*, and the Haggadah (*Meishiv Nefesh*). Commentaries are in two parts and named after his father: short explantions (*Etz Yosef*), longer explanations (*Anaf Yosef*).

Chizkuni (Chizkiya b. Mano'ach, 1250-1310) — Born in France. Wrote Chizkuni, based on Rashi, but used twenty other commentaries. Wandered the world to find proper explanations. Quotes by name only Rashi, Dunash ben Labrat, *Yosippon*, and *Physica*.

Eidels, Shmuel Eliezer ha-Levi (Maharsha, 1555-1631) — Born in Poland to Maharal and Klonymus families. Mother-in-law, Eidel, supported him. Wrote commentary on Tosafot and aggadic parts of Talmud. Knew Kabbalah. Believed in reincarnation.

Einhorn, Ze'ev Wolf (Maharzo, 1790?-1862) — Born in Grodno, Lithuania. Wrote commentary on *Midrash Rabbah*, which he extended in *Netiv Chadash*. Showed that Midrashic interpretation follows from a detailed analysis of the Hebrew text of biblical verses.

Epstein, Baruch ha-Levi (Torah Temimah, 1860-1941) — Lithuanian rabbi, son of author of *Aruch ha-Shulchan*. Learned in Volozhin under his uncle the Netziv. Wrote *Torah Temimah* commentary on Torah and Megillot, citing Talmud and Midrash on each verse, with explanations.

Epstein, Kalonymus Kalman ha-Levi (*Ma'or va-Shemesh ha-Kadosh*, 1754-1823) — born in Prudnik, Poland. Was student of R. Elimelech of Lizhensk and later of the Seer of Lublin and Levi Yitzchak of Barditshev. Introduced *chasidut* in Krakow. Became one of the greatest chassidic masters but did not initiate, nor was he part of, a dynasty. Known for his Torah commentary, *Ma'or va-Shemesh*. Asked to be buried without a tombstone.

Feinstein, Moshe (1895-1986) — Born in Uzda, Belarus on 7 Adar, was great-great-grandson of brother of Vilna Gaon. Studied under R. Isser Zalman Meltzer. Moved to New York in 1936, headed Mesivta Tiferet Yerushalayim and Mo'etzet Gedolei ha-Torah. Considered foremost posek in US. Wrote *Igrot Moshe* (responsa), *Dibrot Moshe* (talmudic novella), *Darash Moshe* (weekly portion). Died in 5746, and 5746th verse in the Torah states: "Moshe had finished writing down the words of this Torah." (Deut. 31:24).

Frand, Yissocher — Born in Seattle. Educated at Ner Yisroel in Baltimore, where he became a senior lecturer. Skilled orator. Author of numerous books on Jewish topics, especially the weekly portion.

Gerondi, Yonah b. Avraham (Rabbeinu Yonah, 1180-1263) — born in Gerona, Spain (birthplace of R. Zerachiah ha-Levi, Ran, and Ramban). Student of R. Shlomo Min Hahar and teacher of Rashba. Talmudic works: commentary on Rif (only Berachot preserved) and *Aliyot de-Rabbeinu Yonah* novella on Bava Batra. Ethical works: commentary on *Avot* called *Sha'arei Teshuva*.

Ha-Kohen, Mordechai (1523-1598) — Born in Safed. Student of Moshe di Trani (Mabit) and R. Joseph Karo, contemporary of R. Yosef di Trani (Maharit, son of Mabit). Wrote *Siftei Kohen* on Torah. Left Safed for financial reasons, became rabbi in Aleppo in 1570.

Ha-Kohen, Shabtai ben Meir (1621-1662) — Born in Vilna, married the daughter of the wealthy Shimon Wolf, a great-grandson of the Rama. His magnum opus is *Siftei Kohen* (*Shach*), a commentary on *Yoreh De'ah*. In *Nekuddot ha-Kesef* he responded to criticisms by the *Taz*.

Halberstam, Yekusiel Yehudah (1905-1994) — Born in Rudnik, Poland, great-grandson of R. Chaim Halberstam (*Divrei Chaim*, founder of Sanzer dynasty), first Sanz-Klausenberg Rebbe. Lost wife and eleven children in WW II, remarried and had seven children, re-established community in Israel (Kiryat Sanz) and Brooklyn, founded *Mifal ha-Shas*, predicted Mumbai attack, wrote *Divrei Yatziv* (Torah novellae), *Shefa Chayim*. Student was Menashe Klein (*Mishneh Halachot*).

Halevi, Judah (1075-1141) — Born in Spain. Student of Moses Ibn Ezra and Rif. Educated in Jewish scholarship, philosophy, medicine. Knew Avraham Ibn Ezra. Wrote poetry, *Kuzari*. Legend is that he was killed by Arab horseman on arrival in Jerusalem.

Hertz, Joseph (1872-1946) — Born in Hungary, left for New York in 1884. Ordained at JTS in 1894, was a rabbi in the U.S. and South Africa before becoming chief rabbi of England in 1914. Wrote commentary on Torah and the *Siddur*.

Hirsch, Samson Raphael (1808-1888) — Born in Hamburg. Student of R. Jacob Ettlinger. Rabbi in Frankfurt. Father of Torah with *derech eretz*. Wrote *Nineteen Letters of Ben Uziel* —defense of tradition; *Horeb* — explanation of *mitzvot*; commentary on the Torah.

Hoffman, David Zvi (1843-1921) — born in Verbo, Hungary. Rabbincial training under Maharam Schick and R. Azriel Hildesheimer, and doctorate from U. of Tubingen. Taught for R. S.R. Hirsch in Frankfurt, then at Rabbinical Seminary in Berlin, which he headed after the death of R. Hildesheimer. Wrote Bible commentaries negating biblical criticism and halachic responsa (*Melamed le-Ho'il*).

Ibn Ezra, Avraham (1089-1167) — Born in Tudela. Excelled in philosophy, astronomy/astrology, mathematics, poetry, linguistics, and biblical exegesis. In Granada, met his friend (and perhaps father-in-law) Judah Halevi. Wrote biblical commentary.

Isserles, Moshe (1520-1572) — Known as the Rama. Received questions from R. Joseph Karo. Wrote *Ha-Mappah* on R. Karo's code and Darchei Moshe on the *Tur*. Inscribed on his tombstone is: "From Moshe [ben Maimon] until Moshe [Isserles] there was none like Moshe."

Karo, Joseph (1488-1575) — Born in Toledo. After Spanish expulsion, spent time in Turkey prior to his arrival in Safed in 1535, where he was ordained by R. Ya'akov Beirav, and taught R. Moshe Alshich and R. Moshe Cordovero. For 32 years wrote and proofread his *Beit Yosef* commentary on the Tur, which he then summarized in his classic Code of Law, based on majority decisions of Rambam, Rosh, and Rif.

Katz, Yissocher Ber ha-Kohen (1500s)— Born in Poland. Wrote *Matnot Kehunah* on *Midrash Rabbah*, *Mar'eh Kohen* on *Zohar* and Jewish theology. Student of Rama. Knew medicine, astronomy. False rumor: emigrated to Israel, became student of R. Moshe Cordovero.

Kimchi, David (Radak, 1160-1235) — Born in Provence. Wrote commentaries on Prophets, Genesis (seeks historical, ethical underpinnings), Psalms, Chronicles. Influenced by Ibn Ezra and Rambam; favored the latter in controversy regarding his works. Delved into philosophy, science.

Kook, Avraham Yitzchak (1865-1935) — Born in Latvia, student of Netziv, son-in-law of Aderet. Became rabbi of Yaffo (1904); first Israeli chief rabbi (1921); founded Mercaz HaRav (1924). Close with secular, religious, Zionist, and charedi communities. Wrote on Talmud, Jewish thought.

Kramer, Eliyahu (Vilna Gaon, 1720-1797) — Born in Grodno. Teacher: Moshe Margalit, author of *Pnei Moshe*. Talmudist, halachist, Kabbalist. Encouraged study of secular sciences. Main students: Chaim of Volozhin, Yisroel of Shklov, and Hillel Rivlin (descendants founded neighborhoods in Jerusalem).

Lifshitz, Yisrael (1782-1861) — Grandson of rabbi who aranged Cleves get. Born in Danzig, became head of local *bet din*. Wrote *Tiferet Yisrael* on Mishnah, *Shvilei de-Rakiya* on rabbinical astronomy, and *Derush Or ha-Chaim* on the age of the universe.

Luria, David (Radal, 1798-1855) — Born in Belarus, child prodigy, scion of wealthy family (Maharshal). Knew science, medicine, foreign languages. Wrote responsa and commentaries on Mishnah, Talmud, *Midrash Rabbah* (*Chiddushei ha-Radal*), *Zohar*.

Maharsha — See Eidels, Shmuel Eliezer.

Maimonides — See Rambam.

Malbim (Meir Leibush b. Yechiel Michel, 1809-1879) — Born in Ukraine. Became chief rabbi of Bucharest (1859). Argued with upper class, who wanted changes. Imprisoned, then liberated by Montefiore on condition that he leave Romania. Magnum opus is a commentary on the Bible.

Mizrachi, Eliyahu (Re'em, 1435-1526) — Born in Turkey. Knew Arabic, Greek. Discovered how to extract square roots. Became chief rabbi of Turkey (1495). Sensitive to *agunot*, Karaites. Wrote commentary on Rashi, math book, responsa used by R. Joseph Karo.

Nachman of Breslav (1772-1810) — Born in Medzhybizh, Ukraine, great-grandson of Ba'al Shem Tov. Founder of Breslav chasidism. Believed in closeness to God, speaking to God as with a best friend, and *hitbodedut* - unstructured, spontaneous prayer.

Nachmanides — See Ramban.

Onkelos (1st century) — Nephew of Hadrian. Converted between 35-120, translated Torah into Aramaic. Contemporary of R. Akiva and R. Yishmael.

Ovadiah mi-Bartenura (1445-1515) — Student of Maharik (Yosef Colon). Born in Bertinoro, where he became rabbi. In 1486 he moved to Eretz Yisrael. Best known for his popular commentary on the Mishnah, based mainly on Rashi and Rambam.

Ra'avad (1120-1199) — R. Avraham ben David (also called Third Ra'avad). Became rabbi and rosh yeshiva in Posquières. Wrote critiques on Rif and Rambam, as well as *Ba'alei ha-Nefesh*, and studied Kabbalah.

Radak — See Kimchi, David.

Radal — See Luria, David.

Rama — See Isserles, Moshe.

Rambam (Maimonides, 1138-1205) — Born in Cordoba. Wrote commentary on Mishnah, *Sefer ha-Mitzvot*, *Yad ha-Chazakah*, *The Guide for the Perplexed*. Court physician. Buried in Tiberias. Epitaph: From Moshe (Rabbeinu) to Moshe (Maimonides) there was none like Moshe.

Ramban (Nachmanides, 1194-1270) — Born and became rabbi in Gerona. Medical doctor. Wrote *Chiddushei ha-Ramban* on Talmud, *Iggeret ha-Kodesh* on marriage, Torah commentary. Students: Rashba, Ra'ah (*Chinnuch*). Won debate with Pablo Christiani (1263), but had to relocate to Israel .

Rapoport, Menachem ha-Kohen (1520-1596) — Born in Porto, descendant of Rapa family. Changed name to Rapoport (i.e. Rapa of Porto). Learned Talmud, medicine. Witnessed burning of Talmud in Venice. Rabbi in Verona and Cologne. Wrote *Minchah Belulah*, edited *Yalkut Shimoni*.

Rashbam (Shmuel b. Meir, 1085-1158) — Born in Ramerupt, Northern France. Mother was Yocheved, Rashi's daughter. Shepherd, vintner. Rashi's student, elder brother of Rabbeinu Tam. Earliest Tosafist. Wrote basic commentary on Bible. Completed Rashi on *Bava Batra, Pesachim*.

Rashi (Shlomo Yitzchaki, 1040-1105) — Born in Troyes. Student of Ya'akov b. Yakar (Worms), who was student of Rabbeinu Gershom. Wrote commentary on Talmud and Tanach (supercommentaries on Rashi include *Gur Aryeh* by Maharal, *ha-Mizrachi* by Re'em, *Yeri'ot Shlomo* by Maharshal).

Rif. Hebrew acronym for R. Yoshiyahu Pinto, the author of the eponymous commentary on *Ein Ya'akov*. The same acronym is used for the earliest codifier of halacha, Yitzchak Alfasi.

Ritva — See Asevilli, Yom Tov b. Avraham.

Rosh — Acronym for Rabbeinu Asher. See Asher b. Yechiel.

Saadiah b. Yosef Gaon (882-942) — Prominent rabbi, Jewish philosopher, and exegete of the Gaonic period. Active in opposition to Karaism and defense of rabbinic Judaism. Founder of Judeo-Arabic literature. Magnum opus is *Emunot ve-De'ot* (Jewish philosophy).

Segel, David ha- Levi — See *Taz*.

Sforno, Ovadia b. Ya'akov (1475-1550) — Born in Cesena, Italy. Studied math, philosophy, medicine. Contacts included Reuchlin, Meir Katzenellenbogen, Maharik. Wrote commentary on Torah and Megillot, selecting from Rashi, Ibn Ezra, Rashbam, Ramban, and adding his own interpretations.

Shach — see ha-Kohen, Shabtai ben Meir.

Shneur Zalman of Liadi — See Borukhovich, Shneur Zalman.

Soloveitchik, Joseph B. [Yosef Dov ha-Levi] (1903-1993) — Born in Russia, descendant of R. Chaim of Volozhin and Tosfot Yom Tov. Mother was cousin of R. Moshe Feinstein. Wrote *Lonely Man of Faith*, *Halachic Man*. Advocated compatibility of Torah and academic scholarship.

Sorotzkin, Zalman (1880-1966) — Born in Lithuania, studied in Slabodka, Volozhin, and Telz. Rabbi of Luzk, Ukraine. Escaped Holocaust to Israel in 1940. Wrote *Oznayim la-Torah*, *Ha-De'ah ve-ha-Dibbur*. Headed Israeli Council of Sages.

Taz (**David ha- Levi Segel,** 1586-1667) — Student and son-in-law of *Bach* (Yoel Sirkus). Wrote a commentary on *Shulchan Aruch*, called *Turei Zahav* ("Golden Columns"), known by the acronym

Taz. Fled to Moravia from the pogroms of 1648. In 1654 chosen rabbi of Lvov.

Tur — See Ya'akov b. Asher.

Unterman, Isser Yehuda (1886-1976) — Ordained at Kollel Volozhin. In 1923 R. Chaim Ozer told him to go to Liverpool, where he served as a rabbi. In 1946-64 he was chief rabbi of Tel Aviv, and in 1964-72 chief rabbi of Israel. Wrote responsa *Shevet mi-Yehudah.*

Vilna Gaon — See Kramer, Eliyahu.

Ya'akov b. Asher (*Tur, Ba'al ha-Turim*, 1269-1343) — Son of Rosh, born in Cologne. Moved to Castile with his father. Wrote *Arba'ah Turim* code of law; *Rimzei Ba'al ha-Turim* is a concise Torah commentary; *Perush al ha-Torah*, which quotes Ramban, Saadiah Gaon, Rashi, and Ibn Ezra.

Wosner, Shmuel ha-Levi (1913-2015) — Born in Vienna, studied at Yeshivat Chachmei Lublin under R. Meir Shapiro. Emigrated to Jerusalem in 1939, studied under R. Yosef Zvi Dushinsky, who appointed him as a *dayan* (judge). *Chazon Ish* and R. Dov Berish Widenfeld suggested he move to Bnei Brak, where he re-established Yeshivat Chachmei Lublin. Wrote responsa *Shevet ha-Levi.*

Yafeh, Shmuel b. Yitzchak Ashkenazi (1525-1595) — Born in Turkey, studied in Constantinople, where he became rabbi of the Ashkenazic community in 1564, and in Adrianople, under Shlomo Alkabetz. May have been related to Mordechai Yafeh (author of *Levush*) and Shmuel Yafeh (father of *Bach*). Wrote commentary on *Midrash Rabbah* (on Torah – *Yefeh To'ar*, on Megillot – *Yefeh Kol, Yefeh Anaf*) and on *aggadot* of the Jerusalem Talmud (*Yefeh Mar'eh*).

www.ingramcontent.com/pod-product-compliance
Lightning Source LLC
Chambersburg PA
CBHW021351090426
42742CB00009B/814